FONDATION VINCENT VAN GOGH ARLES

Sjraar van Heugten

Van Gogh in Provence: Modernizing Tradition

ACTES SUD

Maja Hoffmann, Founder of the LUMA Foundation,
President of the Fondation Vincent van Gogh Arles

Bice Curiger, Artistic director of the Fondation Vincent Van Gogh Arles

With *Van Gogh in Provence: Modernizing Tradition*, the Fondation Vincent van Gogh Arles now presents the third part of a trilogy that was initiated with the inauguration of the institution in April 2014 and has been curated throughout by the distinguished Van Gogh expert Sjraar van Heugten. The first exhibition, *Colours of the North, Colours of the South*, looked at the influences of Courbet, Pissarro, Monet, Monticelli and others upon Van Gogh's art and traced the evolution of Vincent's palette from sombre hues to the clear and explosive colours of his late work. The second exhibition, *Van Gogh Drawings: Influences and Innovations*, focused on Van Gogh's single-minded pursuit of drawing as a crucial facet of his rich artistic production. Some fifty drawings by the Dutch master demonstrated the breath-taking development of his graphic oeuvre over the barely ten years of his career, and thereby testified to Van Gogh's far-reaching renewal of the medium of drawing, too.

The current exhibition now brings together thirty-one paintings which illustrate, with regard to the classic genres of portraiture, the still life and landscape, the continuity that goes hand in hand in Vincent's work with energetic new departures and innovations. Right from the start, the simple life, people and landscapes stand at the centre of Vincent's artistic vision and his inimitable expressive will. And here, in Arles and Saint-Rémy-de-Provence between 1888 and 1890, he finds the light, the motifs and the inspiration that spur him on to his most important works.

Sjraar van Heugten has accompanied the adventure of the foundation of our new institution in Arles, and we are greatly indebted to him for his knowledgeable, painstaking and inspiring work and for his commitment to the projects that, over the past two years, have successfully attracted and delighted a large public.

We are deeply grateful to the Vincent van Gogh Foundation in Amsterdam, the Van Gogh Museum and the Kröller-Müller Museum for continuing to show their confidence in us through loans of works from their prestigious collections.

Thanks to the patron and founder of the Fondation Luc Hoffmann, paintings by Vincent have been regularly on show in Arles since 2014. That Van Gogh is always presented in a dynamic dialogue with contemporary art is inscribed within the history of the Fondation. In the light of our work, however, it has become obvious how powerfully and inexhaustibly Van Gogh's work continues to invite rediscovery today.

Note to the reader

F numbers refer to J.-B. de la Faille, *The Works of Vincent van Gogh. His Paintings and Drawings*, Amsterdam 1970.

JH numbers refer to Jan Hulsker, *The New Complete Van Gogh. Paintings, Drawings, Sketches. Revised and enlarged edition of the catalogue raisonné of the works of Vincent van Gogh*, Amsterdam and Philadelphia 1996.

The letter numbers refer to Leo Jansen, Hans Luijten and Nienke Bakker, *Vincent van Gogh—The Letters. The Complete Illustrated and Annotated Edition*, Amsterdam etc. 2009. See also the online edition, with more extensive annotation: vangoghletters.org.

FOR JEAN-PAUL TARIS

Jean-Paul Taris (1955–2015) was founding member and treasurer of the Fondation Vincent van Gogh Arles. He was instrumental in the realization of the three exhibitions on Van Gogh mounted by the Fondation in 2014, 2015 and 2016. His warmth, generosity, intelligence and humour are greatly missed.

Sjraar van Heugten

Van Gogh in Provence: Modernizing Tradition

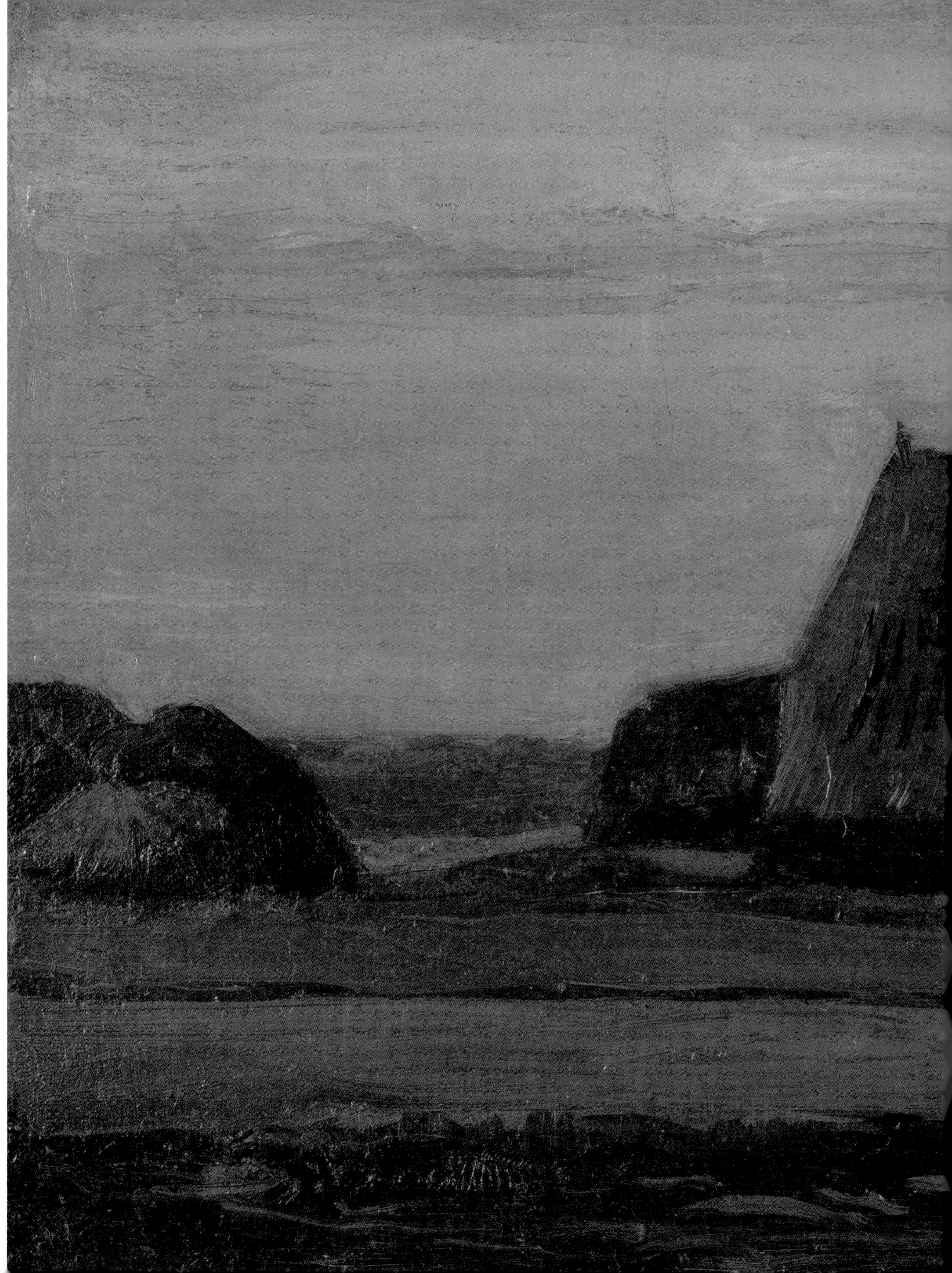

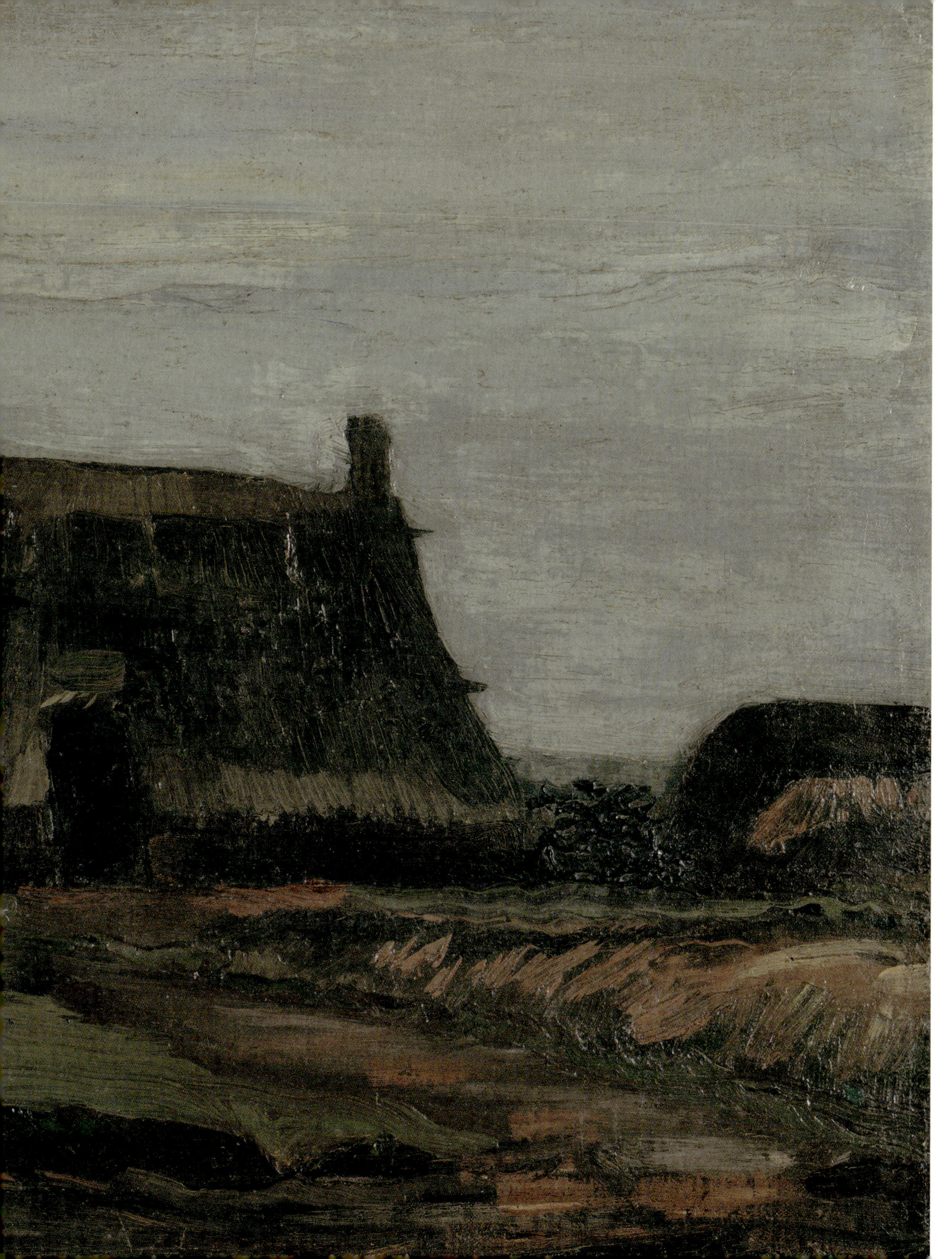

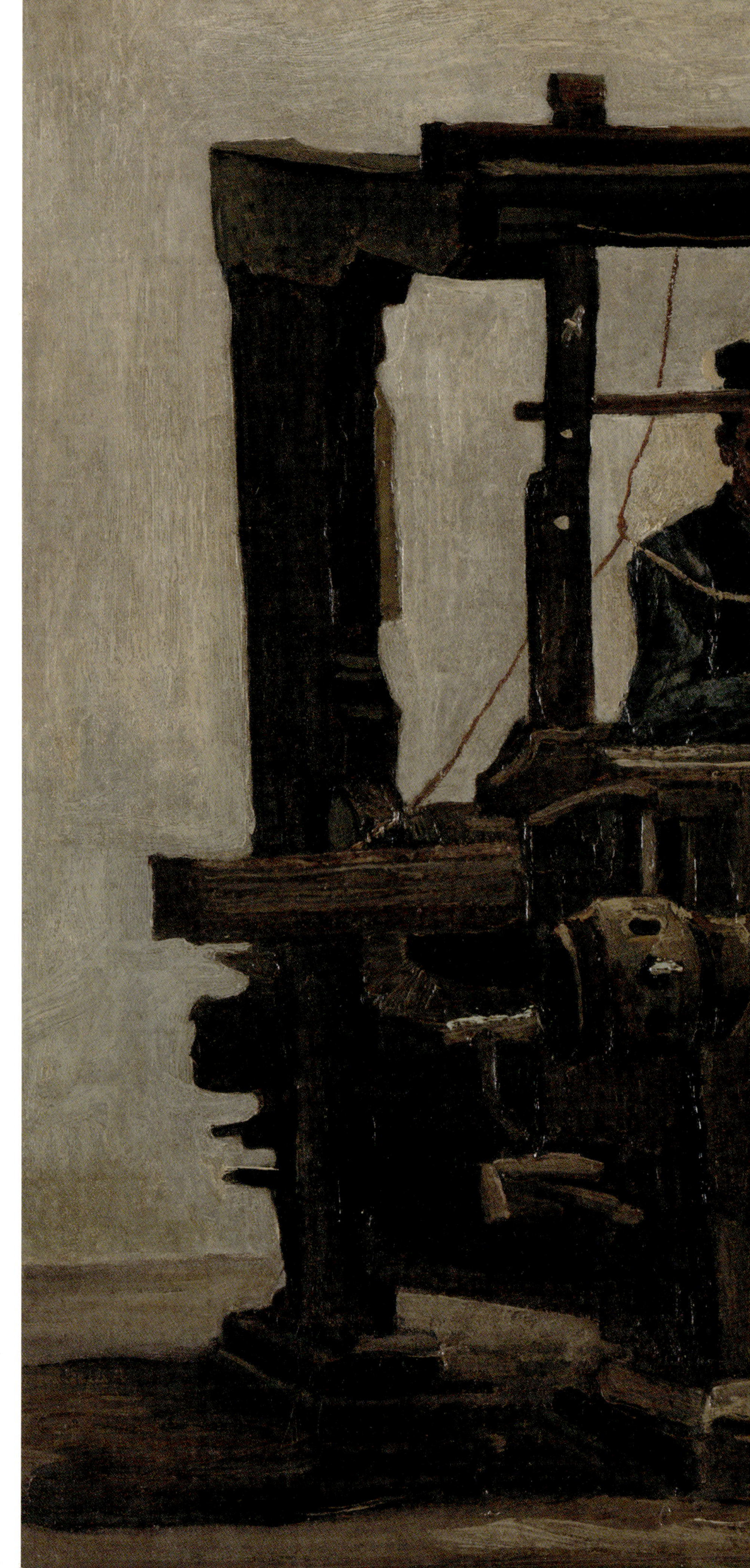

←
Cat. 1
Vincent van Gogh, *Farm with Stacks of Peat,* Nieuw-Amsterdam, October 1883
Oil on canvas, 37.5 × 55.0 cm

Cat. 2
Vincent van Gogh, *Loom and Weaver,* Nuenen, April–May 1884
Oil on canvas, 68.3 × 84.2 cm

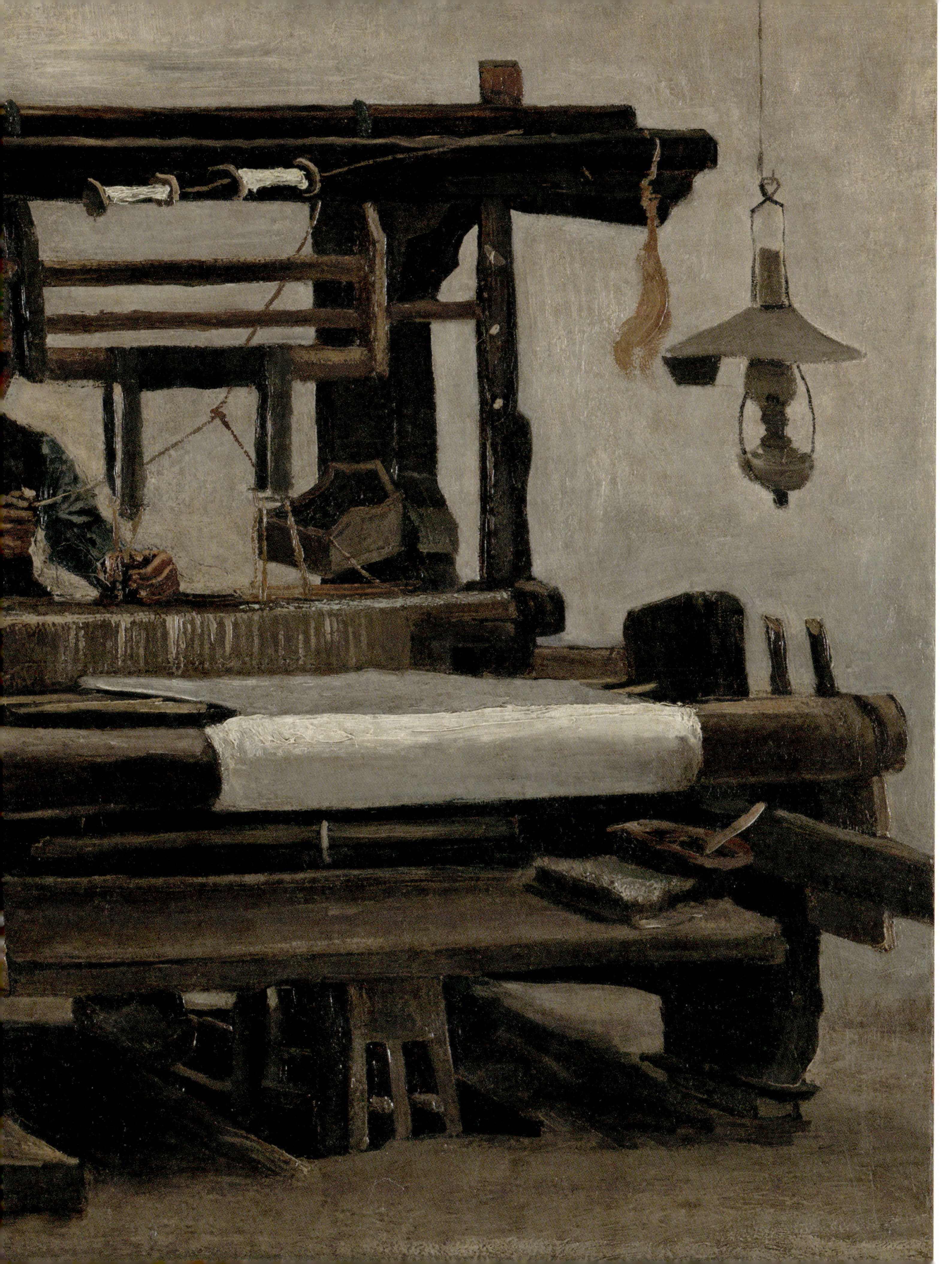

Cat. 3
Vincent van Gogh, *Avenue of Poplars in Autumn,* Nuenen, October 1884
Oil on canvas on panel, 99 × 65.7 cm

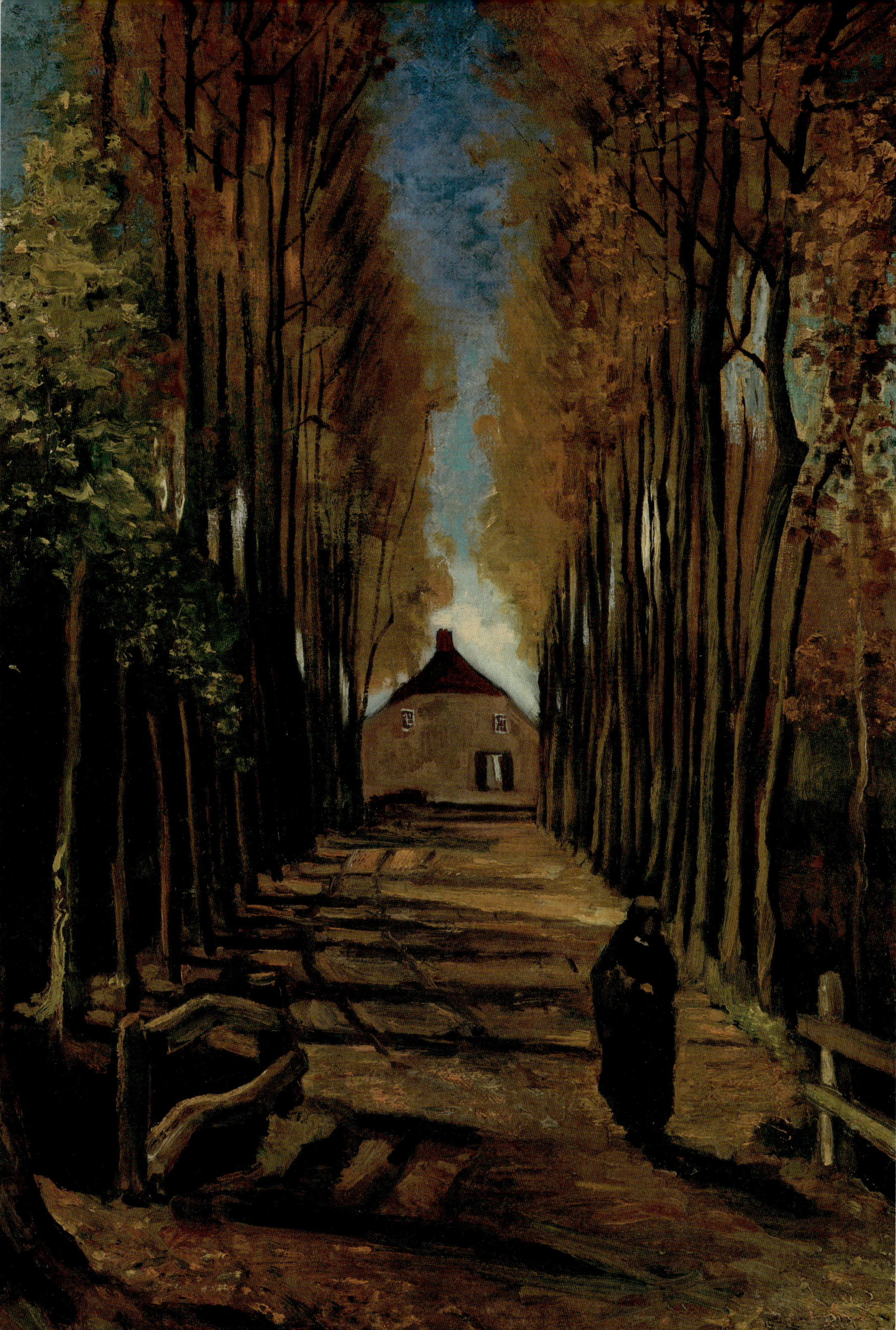

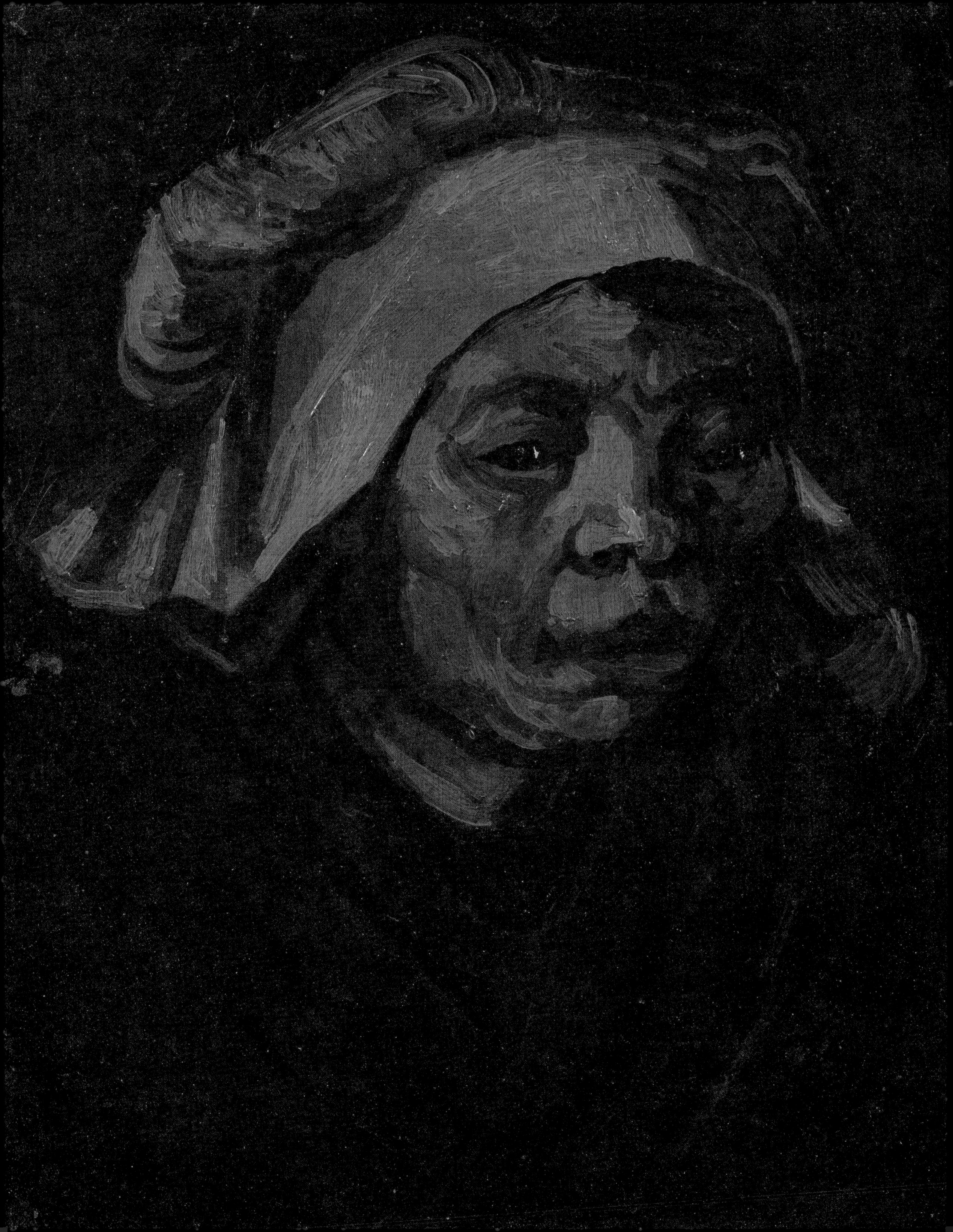

Cat. 4
Vincent van Gogh, *Head of a Woman,*
Nuenen, March 1885
Oil on canvas on triplex, 42.2 × 34.8 cm

Cat. 5
Vincent van Gogh, *Woman Winding Yarn,*
Nuenen, March 1885
Oil on canvas. 40.5 × 31.7 cm

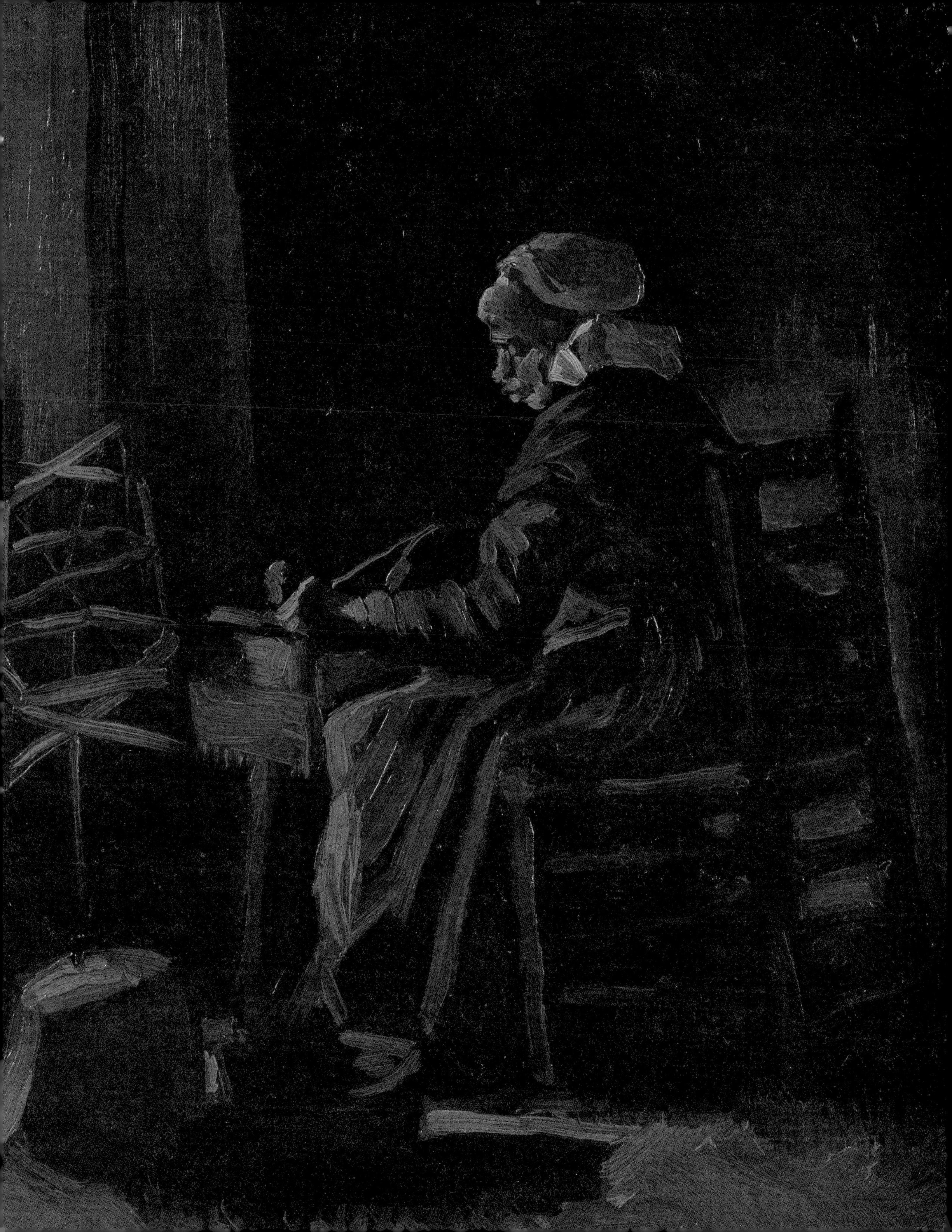

Cat. 6
Vincent van Gogh, *Man at a Table,* Nuenen, March–April 1885
Oil on canvas, 44.3 × 32.5 cm

→
Cat. 7
Vincent van Gogh, *Still Life with Apples and Pumpkins,* Nuenen, September 1885
Oil on canvas, 59 × 84.5 cm

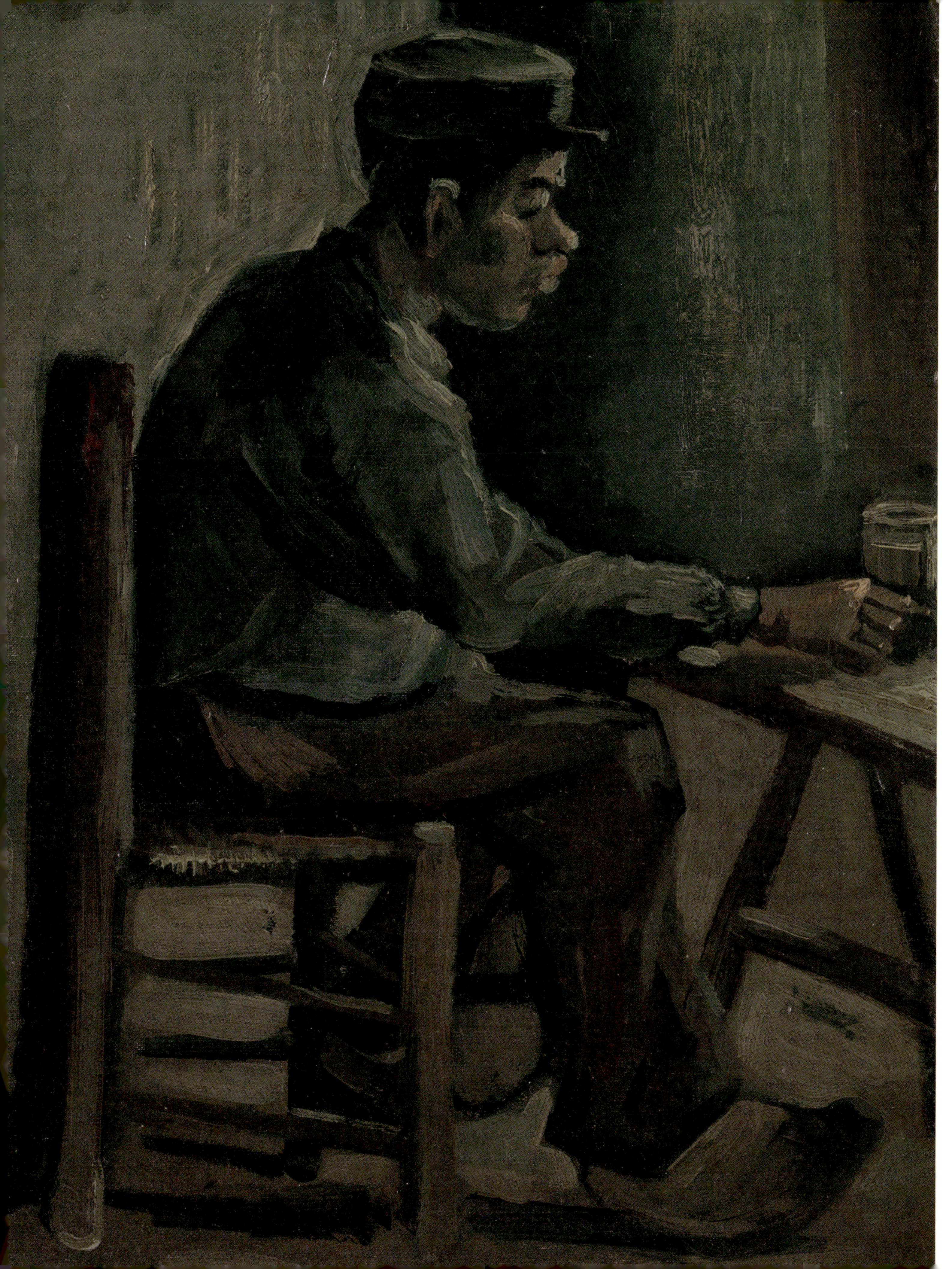

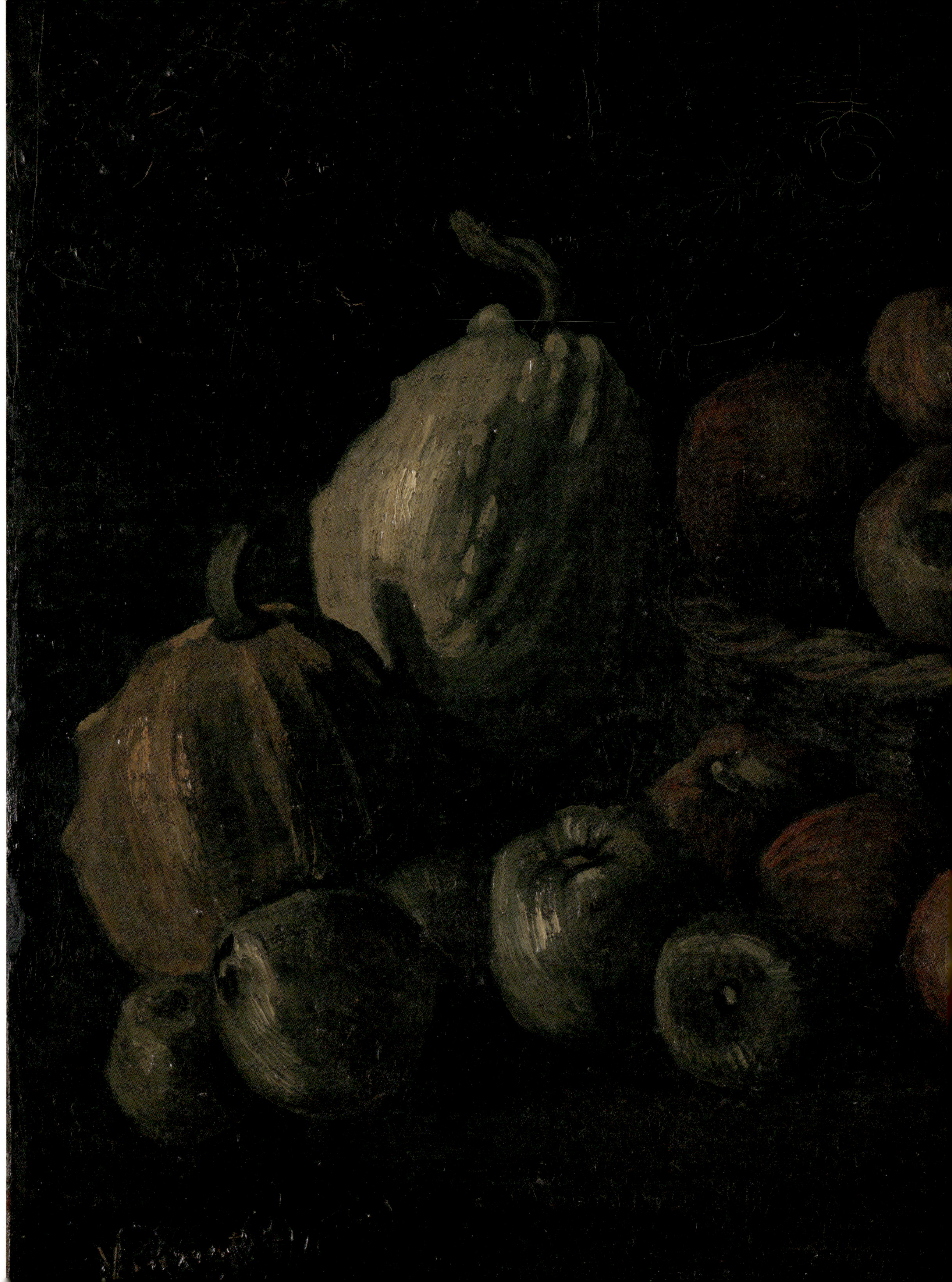

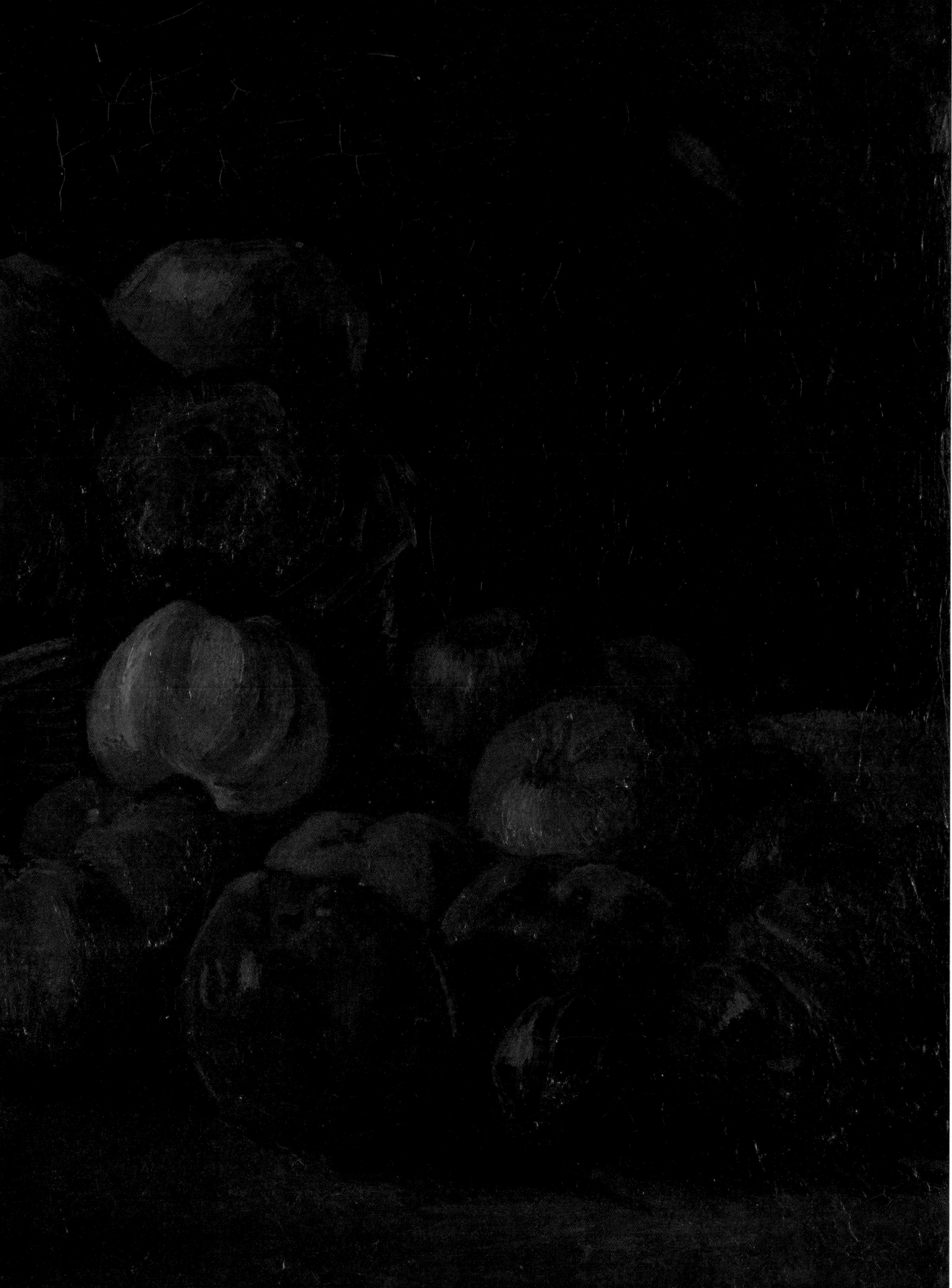

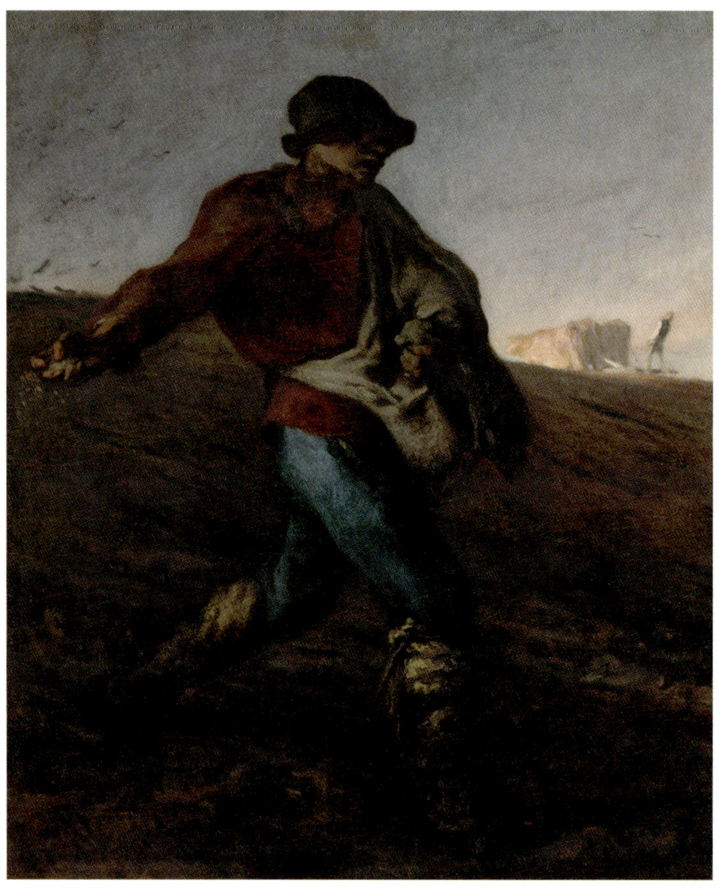

fig. 1

1 Jean-François Millet, *The Sower*, 1850
Oil on canvas, 101.6 × 82.6 cm
Museum of Fine Arts, Boston
Gift of Quincy Adams Shaw through Quincy Adams Shaw, Jr., and Mrs. Marian Shaw Haughton

2 Jules Breton, *Calling in the Gleaners*, 1859
Oil on canvas, 90 × 176 cm
Musée d'Orsay, Paris

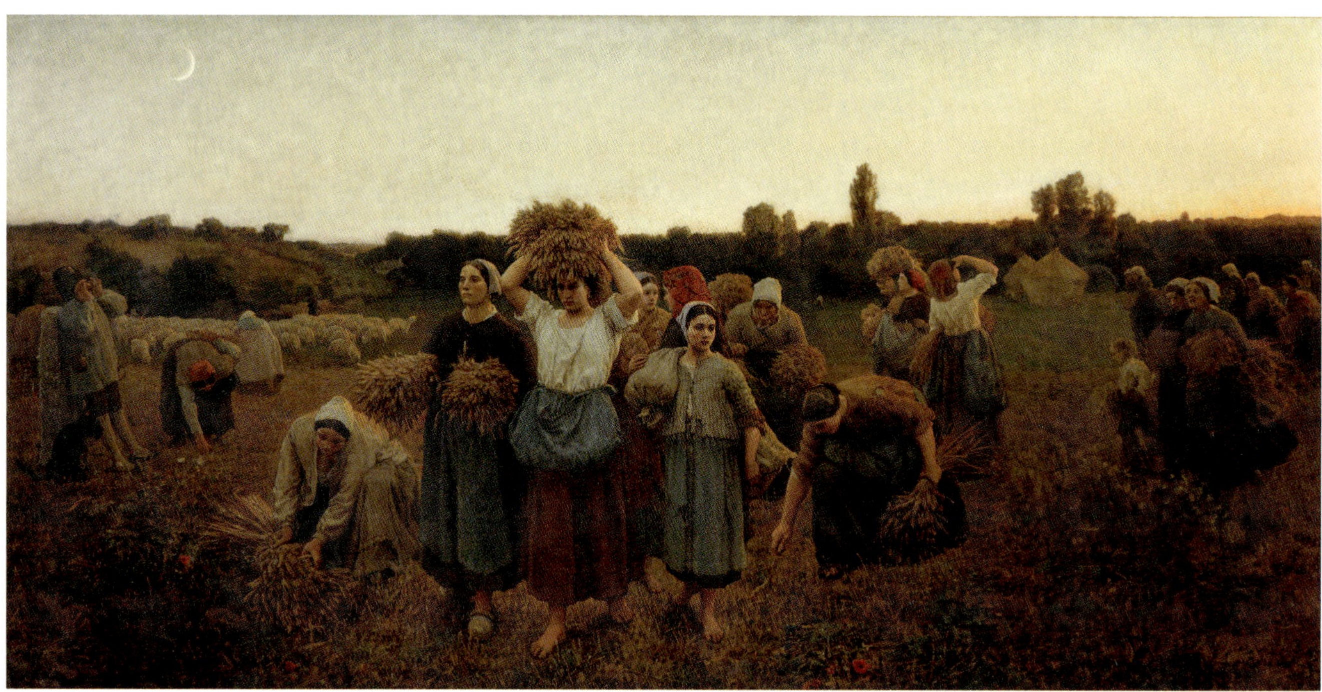

fig. 2

In a career spanning a mere ten years, Van Gogh evolved from an old-fashioned artist into one of the most revolutionary painters of his time. Remarkably, the development of his very modern style did not come at the expense of certain traditions that had been defining elements of his art from the outset. As he grew and matured over the course of a decade, he never changed course completely; instead, he remained loyal to many artistic principles—some with traditions extending back several decades—with which he had deliberately engaged when he resolved to become an artist in August 1880.

Since the mid-nineteenth century, Western art had seen sweeping modernization. The traditional hierarchy of genres—crowned by history painting, whose narratives derive from history, mythology, the Bible and the classics—had been toppled. Realism had gained a firm foothold in many European countries and had attracted modern followers, such as the Impressionists. Figural scenes of everyday life, landscapes and still lifes had become increasingly popular among a broad public. They were now fully fledged genres with their own young traditions, such as the nature scenes painted in the open air by the artists of the Barbizon School, and the scenes of peasant life produced by the realists, foremost among them the French and the English.

As a young artist, Van Gogh was unaware of the most modern art of his day, but he did know the work of its forerunners. He had been employed for a considerable time in the art trade, where he had become thoroughly acquainted with the masters of the School of Barbizon, the Hague School and other exponents of realism. They were his role models, and helped him to consolidate a body of artistic ideas that not only defined his early endeavours, but also provided in many respects the foundation for his modernist French work.

Van Gogh was, after all, not one to betray old artistic loves. This held true for the work of the painters he admired, as well as for his own ambitious undertakings of the past. At the end of April 1890, he wrote to his brother Theo from the asylum at Saint-Rémy: "Please send me what you can find of *figures* among my old drawings, I'm thinking of redoing the painting of the peasants eating supper, lamplight effect" [863]. The work in question was *The Potato Eaters*, which he had painted five years earlier in the village of Nuenen in rural Brabant. Despite its old-fashioned character, it occupied a special place in Van Gogh's œuvre. This must have been clear to Theo too, since it hung above the fireplace in the dining room of his apartment, which was otherwise decorated mainly with Vincent's avant-garde work.[1] The plan, conceived at Saint-Rémy, to make a modern version of his Dutch masterpiece illustrates Van Gogh's allegiance to his personal preferences. Several weeks later he settled in Auvers-sur-Oise, where he had high hopes of making modern portraits—a variant figure piece—and actually put this plan into action.

Van Gogh's loyalty to the choices he made early on enabled him, in a certain sense, to be highly innovative, because he could focus on the search for colour, technique and style without having to reinvent the content. Instead of letting go of trusted traditions, he cast them in a modern mould. This specific aspect of his development is discussed here with reference to three genres that make up an important part of his œuvre: figure pieces / portraits, landscapes and still lifes.

When Van Gogh embarked on his artistic career, he already knew which path he would take and whose example he would follow. His love of art was broad, but he admired, above all, the artists who portrayed everyday life in figure pieces, chief among them Jean-François Millet (fig. 1). Such painters as Jozef Israëls and Jules Breton (fig. 2), as well as seventeenth-century masters like Rembrandt and Frans Hals, also featured in his pantheon.

At the outset, therefore, Van Gogh devoted himself passionately to the study of the human figure, though he also depicted landscapes with some regularity: time and again he proved to have an intuitive talent for portraying nature in appealing and original compositions. Throughout 1884 he struggled to make convincing portrayals of peasant figures, yet in the spring of that year he was already making landscape drawings of very high quality (fig. 3). From a young age, Van Gogh had had a great love of nature and a high regard for painted landscapes by such masters of the Barbizon School as Jules Dupré and Théodore Rousseau, and by seventeenth-century painters like Ruisdael and Van Goyen. His letters repeatedly show that he often saw nature through their eyes. Although his greatest ambition was to master the depiction of the human figure, he excelled as a painter of landscape, in which he proved to be one of the great innovators of his time.

Still lifes also came to occupy a very important place within Van Gogh's œuvre, despite their initially scant presence. Although the first paintings he made under the brief mentorship of Anton Mauve, a leading representative of the Hague School, were still lifes, his next attempts in this genre were long in coming. Mauve let him practise with oil paints, and the five still lifes he painted in The Hague in 1881 (three of which are still known) were therefore intended as exercises in the rendering of various materials. Van Gogh soon decided, however, to focus for the time being on drawing—in particular the human figure. This decision was based on his belief that good drawing skills were essential to the mastery of painting, but another factor was his reluctance at this point to tackle problems of colour. It was not until later, in Nuenen, that still lifes assumed a serious place in his work, but even then, they continued to serve primarily as exercises in colour and brushwork. Some of these were more ambitious works, however, such as the *Still Life with a Bible*. In fact, Van Gogh continued until the end of his life to explore the still life as a means of mastering colour and technique, as evidenced, for example, by the many flower still lifes he painted in Paris. Yet in Arles in particular (and to a lesser extent in Saint-Rémy and Auvers-sur-Oise), the still life took on an importance for him that went far beyond purposes of study.

THE FIGURE PIECE: THE IMITATION OF REVERED MASTERS

"There was a sale here of drawings by Millet, I don't know whether I've already written to you about it. When I entered the room in Hôtel Drouot where they were exhibited, I felt something akin to: Put off thy shoes from off thy feet, for the place whereon thou standest is holy ground," in the words of twenty-two-year-old Vincent, writing from Paris to his brother Theo on 29 July 1875 [36]. Jean-François Millet, who had died earlier that year, was, like Gustave Courbet, among the pioneering artists who had embraced realism in the 1840s. At that time, Millet had begun to paint scenes of peasant life by portraying figures realistically in large format. These depictions received mixed reactions at first, but the grandeur of his paintings brought him ample recognition even in his lifetime. Millet's generation included the peasant painters Jules Breton and Jules Dupré, also much admired by Van Gogh, who admitted the young Frenchman Léon Lhermitte to this company a couple of years later.

Van Gogh's decision to follow such artists must be seen in the context of the utter failure of previous career choices. In mid-1878 he had gone to Brussels, hoping to become a Protestant minister. He was unsuccessful in this endeavour, but was none the less given the chance to work as an evangelist on a trial basis for six months. He chose to go to the Borinage, a mining district in Belgium, where he hoped to bring religion and comfort to the deprived working classes. This plan also came to nothing: Van Gogh appeared to have little talent for preaching, but this did not mean that he was not well-intentioned. After all, he had grown up in a clergyman's

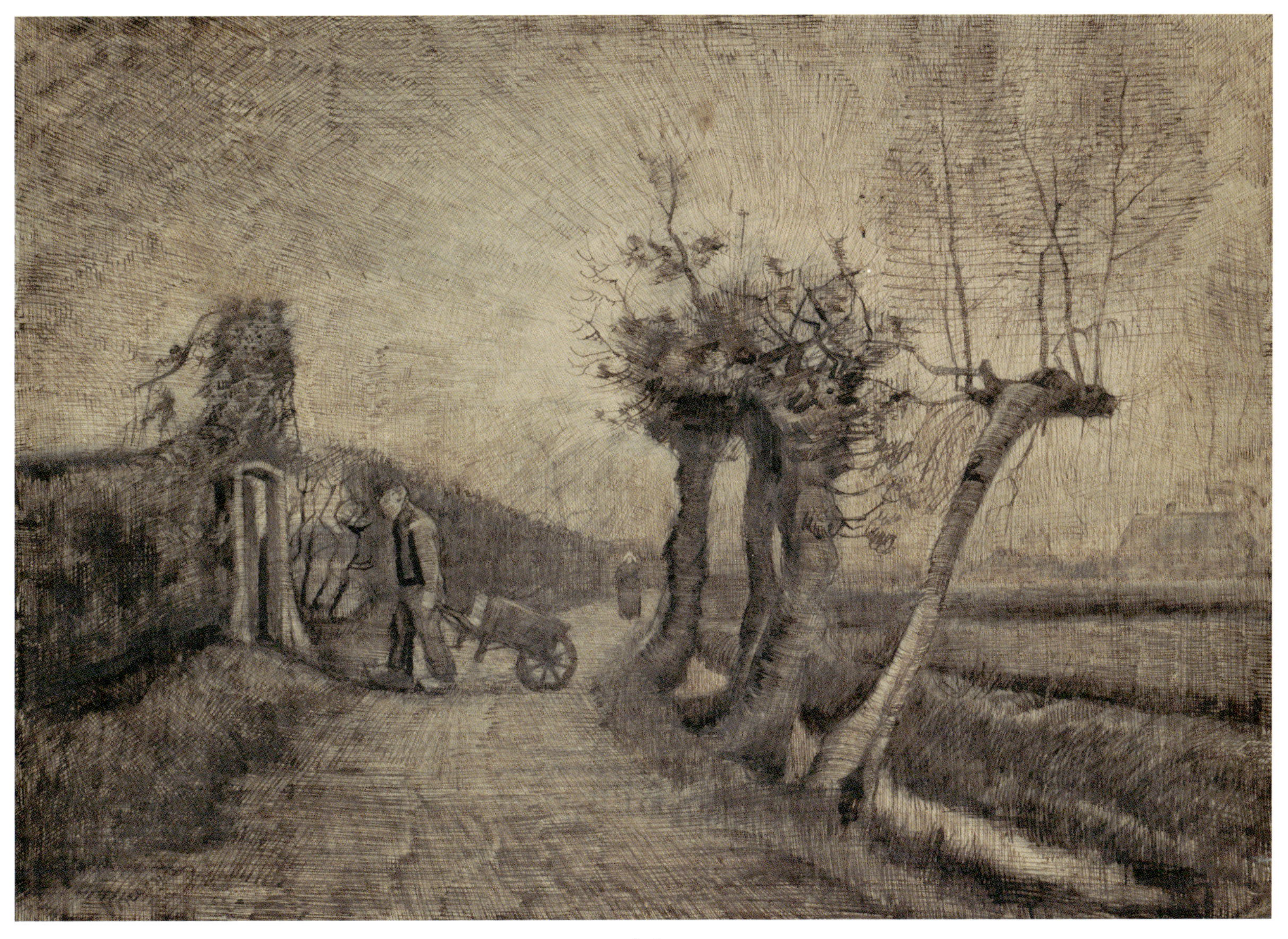

fig. 3

3 Vincent van Gogh, *Road behind the Parsonage Garden in Nuenen ('Behind the Hedges')*, March 1884
Pencil, pen and brush and brown ink on paper, 39.3 × 53.8 cm
Rijksmuseum, Amsterdam

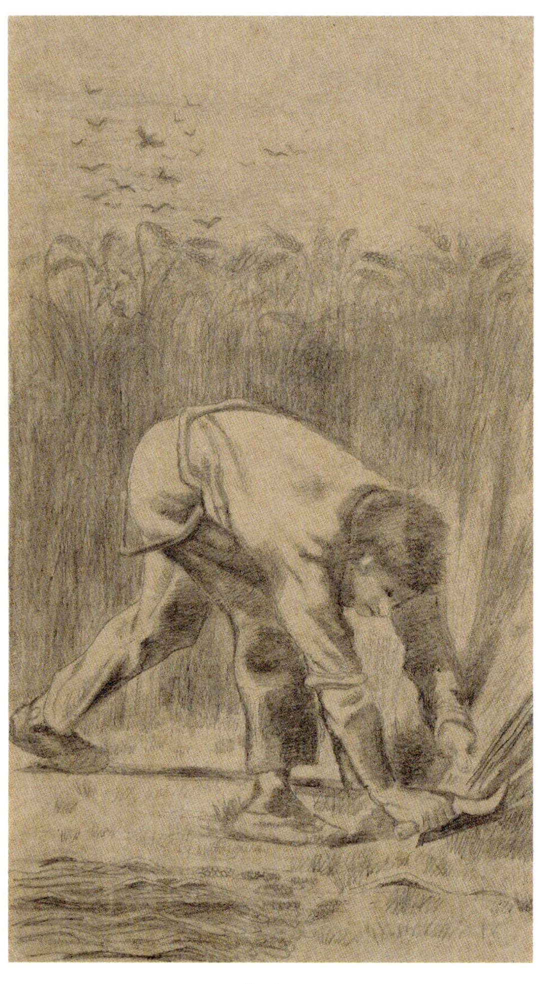

fig. 4

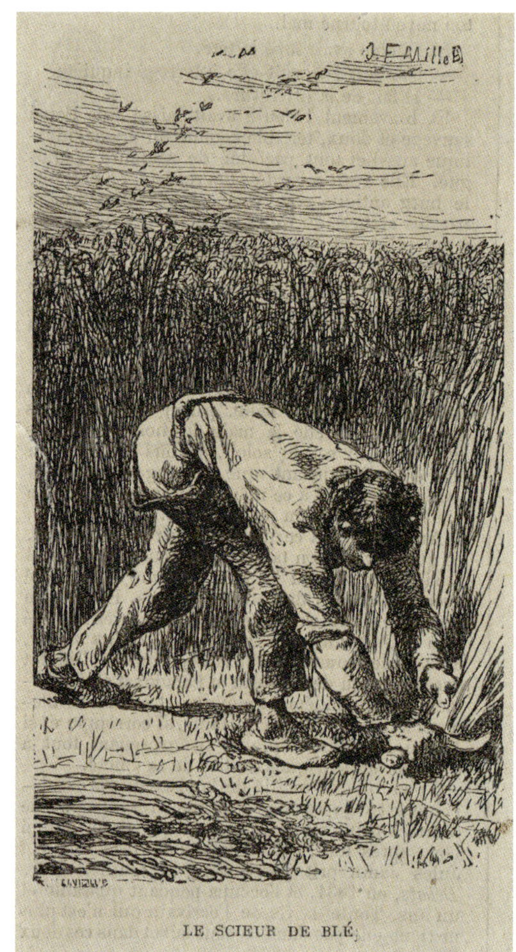

fig. 5

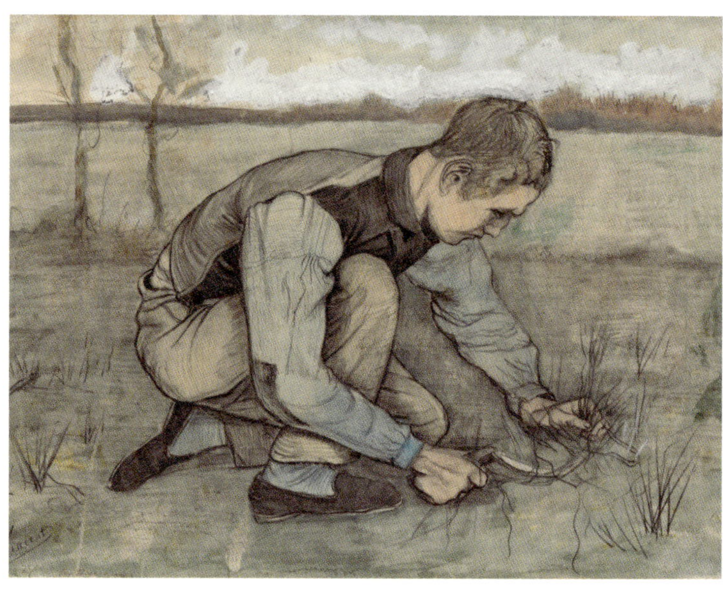

fig. 6

4 Vincent van Gogh, *Reaper with Sickle (after Jean-François Millet)*, September 1880
Pencil, ink on paper, 55.5×30.5 cm
Uehara Museum of Modern Art, Shimoda, Japan

5 Jacques Adrien Lavieille, *The Mower (after Jean-François Millet)*, 1853
Wood engraving, 13.5×7.5 cm
Van Gogh Museum, Amsterdam (Vincent van Gogh Foundation)

6 Vincent van Gogh, *Boy with a Sickle*, November 1881
Black chalk, charcoal, grey wash, opaque watercolour on laid paper, 46.6×60.4 cm
Kröller-Müller Museum, Otterlo

family, where the importance of Christian charity was emphasized daily. Indeed, Van Gogh had a deep-seated desire to do something meaningful for his fellow human beings. His failure as an evangelist was just one more let-down on a rocky career path pitted with obstacles, and it brought him to the brink of despair. At the end of June 1880, after months of sober reflection that would soon culminate in his decision to become an artist, he wrote the following to Theo: "In the springtime a bird in a cage knows very well that there's something he'd be good for; he feels very clearly that there's something to be done but he can't do it; what it is he can't clearly remember, and he has vague ideas and says to himself, 'the others are building their nests and making their little ones and raising the brood', and he bangs his head against the bars of his cage. And then the cage stays there and the bird is mad with suffering" [155]. Van Gogh's desire to do something meaningful with his life also became a guiding principle of his artistic career. His art was meant to give people something, and he chose his subjects from the lives of those for whom his work was intended.

To achieve proficiency as an artist, Van Gogh drew up, while still in the Borinage, a programme of his own devising, but based on the practice of art academies, where the copying of existing compositions was an important part of the training. He copied prints and sample drawings by various artists, but the inventions of Millet were predominant, as evidenced by the many copies Van Gogh made of Millet's *Sower* and his ten-print series of the *Labours of the Fields* (*Travaux des champs*). Later he destroyed almost all of these works; only one copy from the Borinage survives (fig. 4, 5). After going to live with his parents in the village of Etten in Brabant in April 1881, Van Gogh still made the occasional copy, but rural life now tempted him to create his own compositions, a stage of the artistic process in which he had little previous experience. Millet's example continued to influence him, however, because much of his output in Etten consisted of his own variants of *The Sower* and sundry prints from the *Labours of the Fields* series (fig. 6). As he wrote to Theo in mid-September, his studies were beginning to bear fruit: "I've learned to measure and to see and to attempt the broad outlines &c. So that what used to seem to me to be desperately impossible is now gradually becoming possible, thank God. I've drawn a peasant with a spade no fewer than 5 times, 'a digger' in fact, in all kinds of poses, twice a sower, twice a girl with a broom. Also a woman with a white cap who's peeling potatoes, and a shepherd leaning on his crook, and finally an old, sick peasant sitting on a chair by the fireplace with his head in his hands and his elbows on his knees. And it won't stop there, of course, once a couple of sheep have crossed the bridge the whole flock follows. Diggers, sowers, ploughers, men and women I must now draw constantly. Examine and draw everything that's part of a peasant's life. Just as many others have done and are doing" [172].

The work on the land, as well as indoor chores such as preparing meals, acquired a permanent place in Van Gogh's œuvre. Many such compositions originated in Etten, but in The Hague, too, where he lived from late December 1881 to mid-September 1883, he depicted rural labourers, including various sowers. In Nuenen in the summer of 1885, while drawing dozens of peasants—men and women alike—engaged in reaping wheat and other rural labours, he never lost sight of Millet's example. And in Arles in the summer of 1888, when he resolved to make a truly modern figure painting, he chose the motif of the sower, which he worked out that year in a number of variations.

In The Hague, Van Gogh's passion for portraying folk types was given an additional impulse by reading a book on Millet's life and work—Alfred Sensier's *La Vie et l'Œuvre de Jean-François Millet* (Paris 1881)—which he had borrowed from Théophile de Bock, a fellow artist. Sensier was a personal friend of Millet, and Van Gogh raved about his book: "It interests me so much that I wake up at night and light the lamp and go

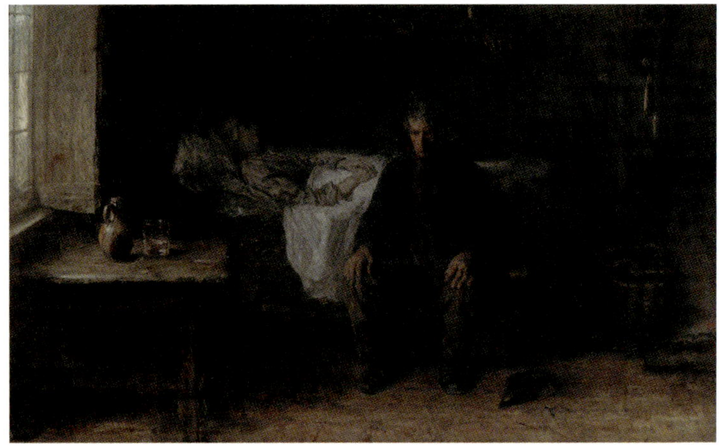

fig. 7

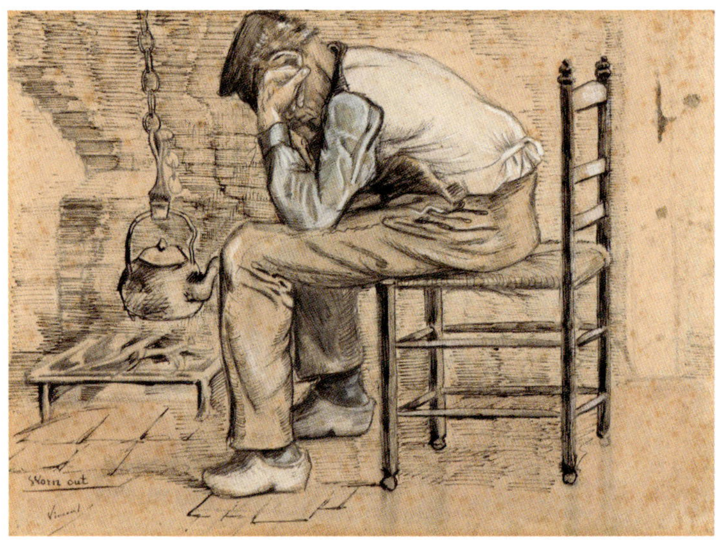

fig. 8

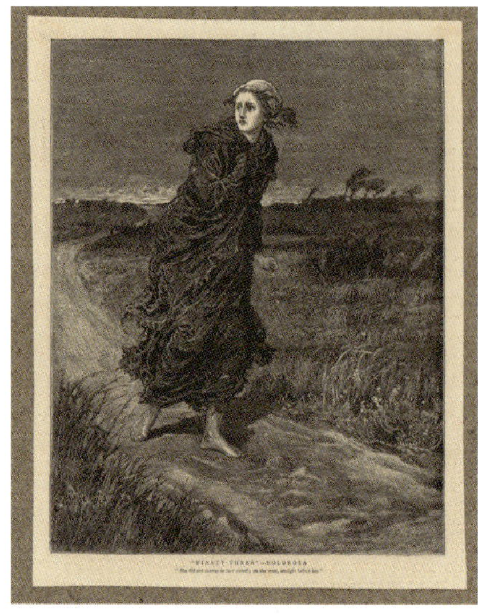

fig. 9

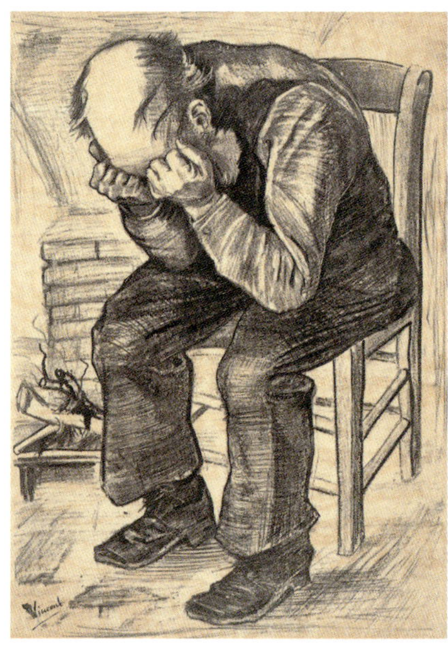

fig. 10

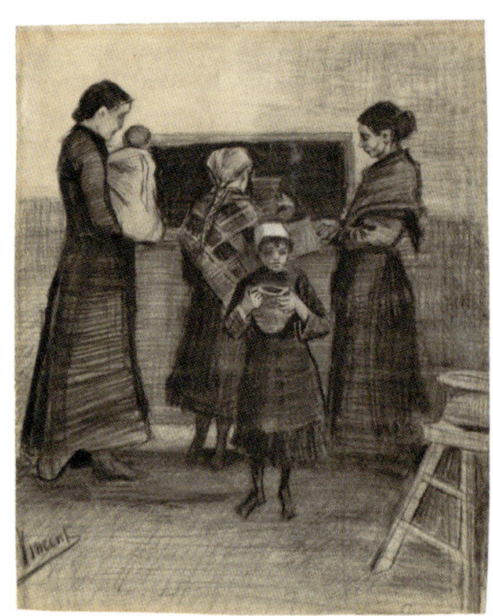

fig. 11

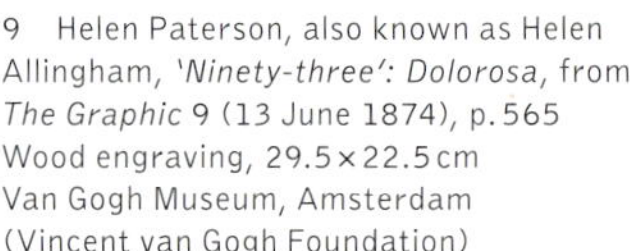

7 Jozef Israëls, *Alone*, c. 1880–1881
Oil on canvas, 125 × 200 cm
The Mesdag Collection, The Hague

8 Vincent van Gogh, *Worn Out*, September 1881
Pencil, pen and ink, watercolour on paper, 23.4 × 31.2 cm
Collection P. & N. de Boer Foundation, Amsterdam

9 Helen Paterson, also known as Helen Allingham, *'Ninety-three': Dolorosa*, from *The Graphic* 9 (13 June 1874), p. 565
Wood engraving, 29.5 × 22.5 cm
Van Gogh Museum, Amsterdam
(Vincent van Gogh Foundation)

10 Vincent van Gogh, *At Eternity's Gate*, The Hague, November 1882
Lithography, 50 × 34.2 cm
Van Gogh Museum, Amsterdam
(Vincent van Gogh Foundation)

11 Vincent van Gogh, *Soup Distribution in a Public Soup Kitchen*, The Hague, March 1883
Chalk, brush and paint, watercolour, on paper, 56.5 × 44.4 cm
Van Gogh Museum, Amsterdam
(Vincent van Gogh Foundation)

on reading" [210]. More than ever before, Millet became his artistic and spiritual guide, and the working class became his artistic terrain.

Many of the motifs inspired by Millet that Van Gogh depicted in 1882–83 are fairly straightforward portrayals of simple tasks, unencumbered with layers of meaning. He also made a number of more ambitious works, however, which he endowed with astute anecdotal content. The inspiration for these had come from English and French realists, whose work was represented in his collection of prints from illustrated magazines—artists such as Hubert von Herkomer, Luke Fildes, Charles Paul Renouard and Paul Gavarni.[2] Of paramount importance was Jozef Israëls, a painter of the Hague School, whose work portrayed in a subdued way the wretched living conditions of workers and fishermen (fig. 7). Van Gogh, deeply impressed by subjects of this kind, followed in the footsteps of these masters. In Etten he had already drawn a sorrowful old man by the fireplace and given it the revealing English title *Worn Out* (fig. 8). In The Hague he gave this man a kind of female pendant, a downcast woman, naked and pregnant, with an equally telling English title, *Sorrow*. The model was Sien Hoornik, his companion at that time. A prostitute who had had a hard life, Sien was actually pregnant when Van Gogh portrayed her. In one of his favourite books, Jules Michelet's *La Femme* (Paris 1863), Van Gogh had read about the difficult and distressing lives of such women, and he must have been shocked by the similarities between them and Sien. Another possible source of inspiration was a print from *The Graphic* in his collection of magazine illustrations (fig. 9). This print depicts a desperate woman looking for her children in the turbulent aftermath of the French Revolution. The title reads *'Ninety-three': Dolorosa*, which means "sorrowful".[3]

In the autumn of 1882, Van Gogh made a sequel to *Worn Out* with the same title, again a man with his head in his heads, sitting by a dying fire. In November of that year, he had experimented with lithography and made a series of six prints after his figure drawings; *Sorrow* and *Worn Out* were among them, though the latter was spruced up for the occasion with an even more doleful English title: *At Eternity's Gate* (fig. 10). Here Van Gogh added his own personal variant to the many examples of sorrowful figures in the work of other nineteenth-century painters and illustrators.

Van Gogh's study of figures—his models' heads in particular—was guided in part by a book he had read in 1880, Alexandre Ysabeau's *Lavater et Gall. Physiognomonie et phrénologie rendues intelligibles pour tout le monde* (*Lavater and Gall: Physiognomy and Phrenology Rendered Comprehensible for Everyone*), published in Paris in 1862. According to the theories of Johann Kaspar Lavater and Franz Joseph Gall, a person's character is expressed in the face (Lavater's theory of physiognomy) and the shape of the skull (Gall's phrenology). Lavater and Gall compared certain human figure types with animals; Van Gogh did this too on several occasions, as in December 1882, when he described a sower as "a sort of cockerel type" [291].

Van Gogh hoped that one day he would be able to depict complex scenes with numerous figures, such as he had seen in paintings and in the popular prints in magazines, which he cut out and kept in portfolios. In The Hague, he made several attempts to portray figures in both drawings and paintings (fig. 11). In most of those compositions, however, they tend to stand on their own and fail to form a convincing group. One would be justified in saying that Van Gogh never became adept at grouping figures in a coherent way. Even so, in The Hague he became much more skilled in the depiction of striking single figures. His earliest figure drawings had shown no innate, intuitive talent for the medium, but his incessant drawing from a model and experimentation with numerous materials eventually enabled him to discover his potential and to make expressive drawings in a powerful—almost rugged—style.

THE LANDSCAPE

In 1877, Van Gogh lived for a time in Dordrecht, where he worked in a bookshop. In a letter written to Theo in February, he reminisces about his native village of Zundert: "Memories of times past came back to me, including how often we walked with Pa to Rijsbergen and so on in the last days of February and heard the lark above the black fields with young green wheat, the shimmering blue sky with white clouds above—and then the paved road with the beech trees—O Jerusalem Jerusalem! or rather O Zundert O Zundert!" [102]. Many years later, in January 1889 in Arles, where he had recently suffered the first attack of his illness, he thought back nostalgically to that provincial backwater: "During my illness I again saw each room in the house at Zundert, each path, each plant in the garden, the views round about, the fields, the neighbours, the cemetery, the church, our kitchen garden behind—right up to the magpies' nest in a tall acacia in the cemetery" [741]. The Zundert where Van Gogh grew up was a rural village surrounded by heath and marshland, and it was here that his lifelong love of nature was born. Indeed, the importance of living with nature was a focal point in the life of his family, who took an hour-long walk together every day. As a youngster, Van Gogh also went for long walks on his own, and became strongly attached to the surrounding countryside. His mother kept a large garden behind the parsonage, and gardens continued to play an important role in his life, as places where one could find solace, peace and natural beauty.

In the religious sense, too, the importance of nature was impressed upon Van Gogh from a very young age. His father, the Protestant minister Theodorus Van Gogh, was a follower of the enlightened Groningen School, in which nature and religion were closely connected: nature was a creation of God, and God was expressed in nature.

It stands to reason that Van Gogh's reverence for nature led to his predilection for the painted landscape. His work in the art trade and his visits to museums—including those in The Hague, London and Paris—had familiarized him with a great many landscape painters, including the previously mentioned masters of the School of Barbizon (such as Daubigny, Dupré, Millet and Rousseau), and the somewhat older Michel and Corot. In a letter to Theo of July 1883, Vincent describes a work by Théodore Rousseau: "An edge of a wood in the autumn after rain, with a vista of meadows stretching away endlessly, marshy, with cows in them, the foreground rich in tone... The dramatic effect of these paintings is something that helps us to understand 'a corner of nature seen through a temperament'" [361].[4] These artists had added their own layer of interpretation to nature, which in turn led Van Gogh to see nature through their paintings.

It is hardly surprising that Van Gogh, equipped with all this baggage, was highly receptive to nature motifs in his own work. But because he was determined to pursue, above all, his ambition to become a figure painter, it was rather late in his career before he attempted to portray landscapes on a larger scale. In Etten, he had made a few evocative landscape drawings, and a number of landscapes also originated in The Hague. A large drawing of a tree with gnarled branches and enormous roots, to which Van Gogh gave the obvious title *Les Racines (Tree Roots)* (fig. 12), displays an aspect that became typical of many of his landscape compositions, an aspect that he himself mentioned explicitly. In a letter written on 1 May 1882, he told Theo that he had made a drawing of a sorrowful naked woman, the now famous *Sorrow*, and that he had also drawn *Les Racines,* which he had attempted to imbue with the same feeling of melancholy as the mournful female figure: "Frantically and fervently rooting itself, as it were, in the earth, and yet being half torn up by the storm. I wanted to express something of life's struggle, both in that white, slender female figure and in those gnarled black roots with their knots. Or rather, because I tried without any philosophizing to be true to nature, which

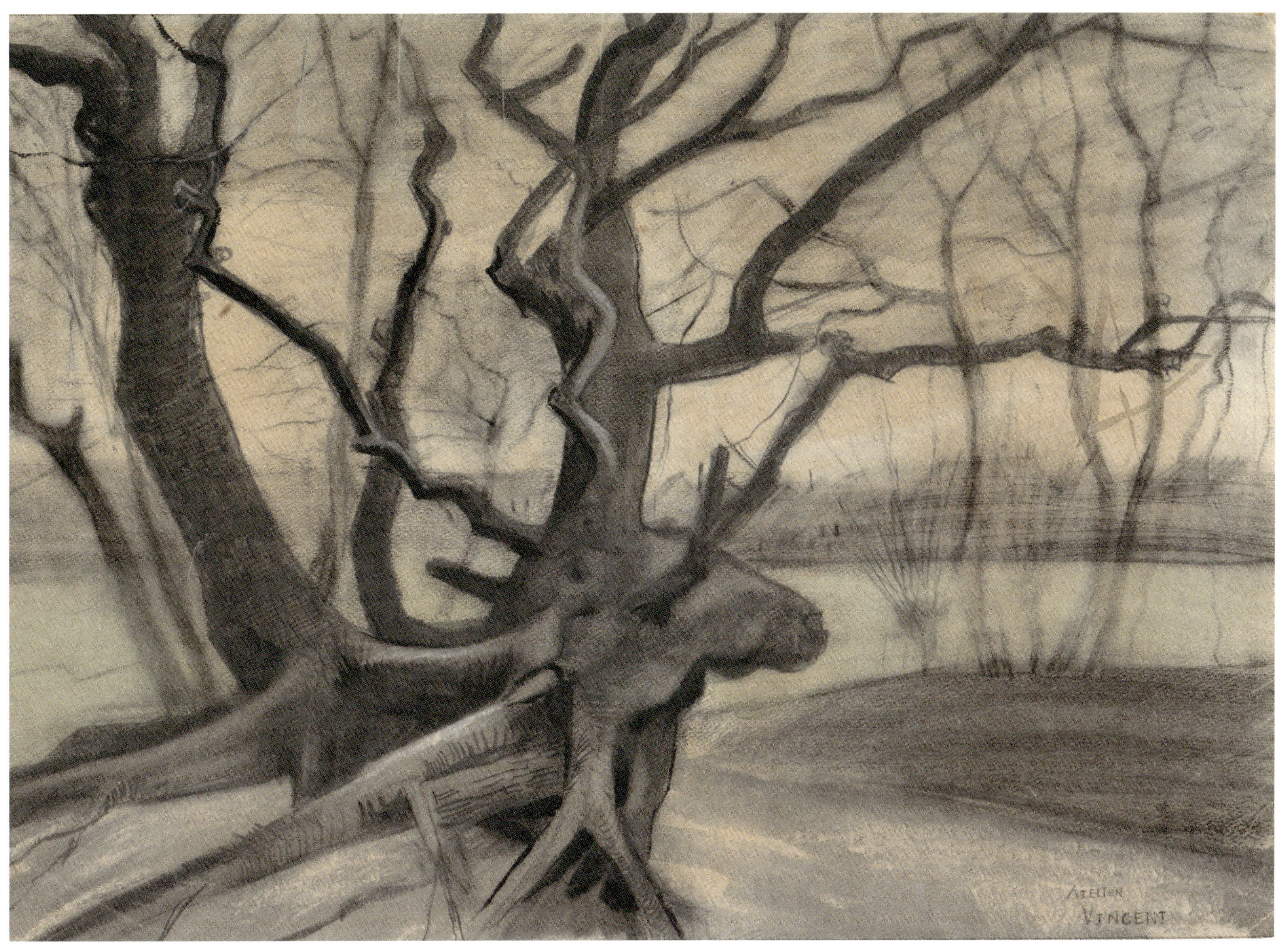

fig. 12

12 Vincent van Gogh, *Tree Roots in Sandy Ground ('Les Racines')*, April–May 1882
Pencil, black chalk, brush and ink, brown and grey wash, opaque watercolour, on watercolour paper, 51.5 × 70.7 cm
Kröller-Müller Museum, Otterlo

I had before me, something of that great struggle has come into both of them almost inadvertently. At least it seemed to me that there was some sentiment in it, though I may be mistaken, anyway, you'll have to see for yourself" [222]. Such anthropomorphizing of trees and natural elements is typical of the way Van Gogh treated nature in his drawings and paintings. Although he did not make such clear statements about the meaning of later works, they presumably contain similar sentiments. In this respect he is closely related to the painter Rousseau, for example, who often endowed nature with distinctly animate features.

In the summer of 1882, Van Gogh worked extensively with oil paint for the first time, and this presented the tempting possibility of painting landscapes. He worked on the beach at Scheveningen and also painted wooded views. The latter plainly show, once again, his affinity with the Barbizon masters (fig. 13). After this excursion into painting, however, he focused on figure drawing for the rest of his stay in The Hague.

On 11 September 1883, Van Gogh left for Drenthe. During his three-month stay, he was plagued by a lack of materials and was therefore not very productive. Among the few paintings he made there is *Farm with Stacks of Peat* (cat. 1), a view of the Drenthe heathland with a picturesque farmhouse that he was pleased to encounter, since it reminded him of the work of Jules Dupré.[5] Though Van Gogh produced little in this period, the descriptions in his letters clearly reveal his thoughts and feelings. He was not particularly struck by the outstretched heath in the midday heat, but at dusk it was as sublime as a canvas by Dupré, while the folk types there made him think of Millet.[6]

The extent to which Van Gogh saw nature and people through the eyes of his favourite painters is apparent from a particularly fine passage in a letter to Theo of 3 October: "I see no way of describing the countryside to you as it should be done, because words fail me. But imagine the banks of the canal as miles and miles of Michels or T. Rousseaus, say, Van Goyens or P. de Koninck. Flat planes or strips differing in colour, which grow narrower and narrower as they approach the horizon. Accentuated here and there by a sod hut or small farm or a few scrawny birches, poplars, oaks. Stacks of peat everywhere, and always barges sailing past with peat or bulrushes from the marshes. Here and there thin cows of a delicate colour, often sheep—pigs. The figures that now and then appear on the plain usually have great character, sometimes they're really charming. I drew, among others, a woman in the barge with crepe around her cap brooches because she was in mourning, and later a mother with a small child—this one had a purple scarf around her head. There are a lot of Ostade types among them, physiognomies that remind one of pigs or crows, but every so often there's a little figure that's like a lily among the thorns. In short, I'm very pleased about this trip, for I'm full of what I've seen. The heath was extraordinarily beautiful this evening. There's a Daubigny... that expresses that effect precisely. The sky was an inexpressibly delicate lilac white—not fleecy clouds, because they were more joined together and covered the whole sky, but tufts in tints more or less of lilac—grey—white—a single small rent through which the blue gleamed. Then on the horizon a sparkling red streak—beneath it the surprisingly dark expanse of brown heath, and a multitude of low roofs of small huts standing out against the glowing red streak" [392].

In the following letter, Van Gogh invokes Ruisdael, Dupré and Van Goyen to give his brother some idea of what he had encountered in Drenthe. Corot and Millet similarly figure in a somewhat later letter, which is likewise filled with beautiful characterizations of the landscape.[7] The artists of the Barbizon School are presented both individually and jointly, for as a group they also embodied an ideal, in Van Gogh's view.[8] He thought their close collaboration and friendship exemplary, and in his letters from Drenthe he used this as an argument to persuade Theo to give up his job

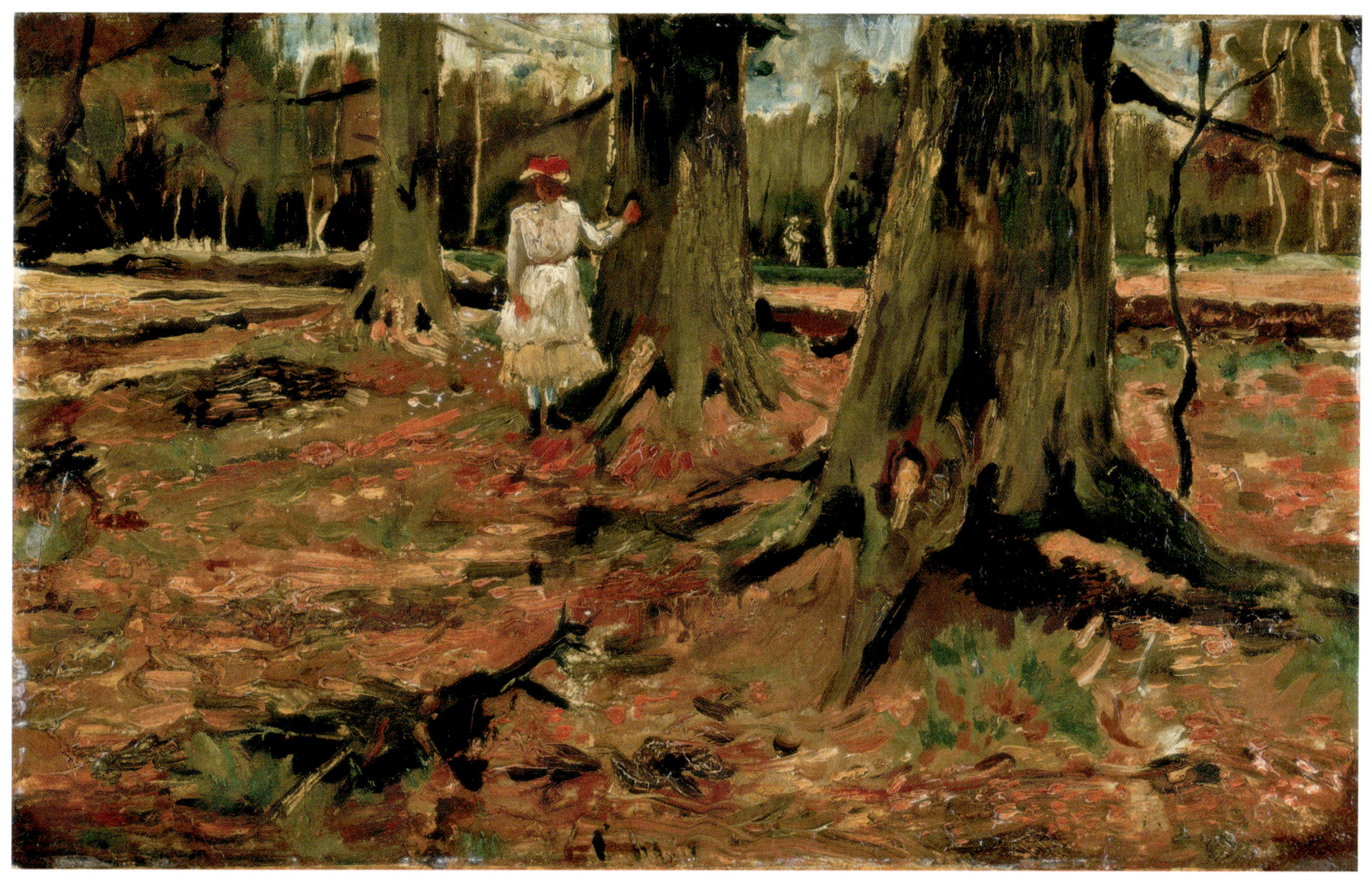

fig. 13

13 Vincent van Gogh, *Girl in a Wood*,
August 1882
Oil on paper mounted on canvas,
37×58.8 cm
Kröller-Müller Museum, Otterlo

→
Cat. 8
Vincent van Gogh, *Self-Portrait with Pipe*,
Paris, September–November 1886
Oil on canvas, 46×38 cm

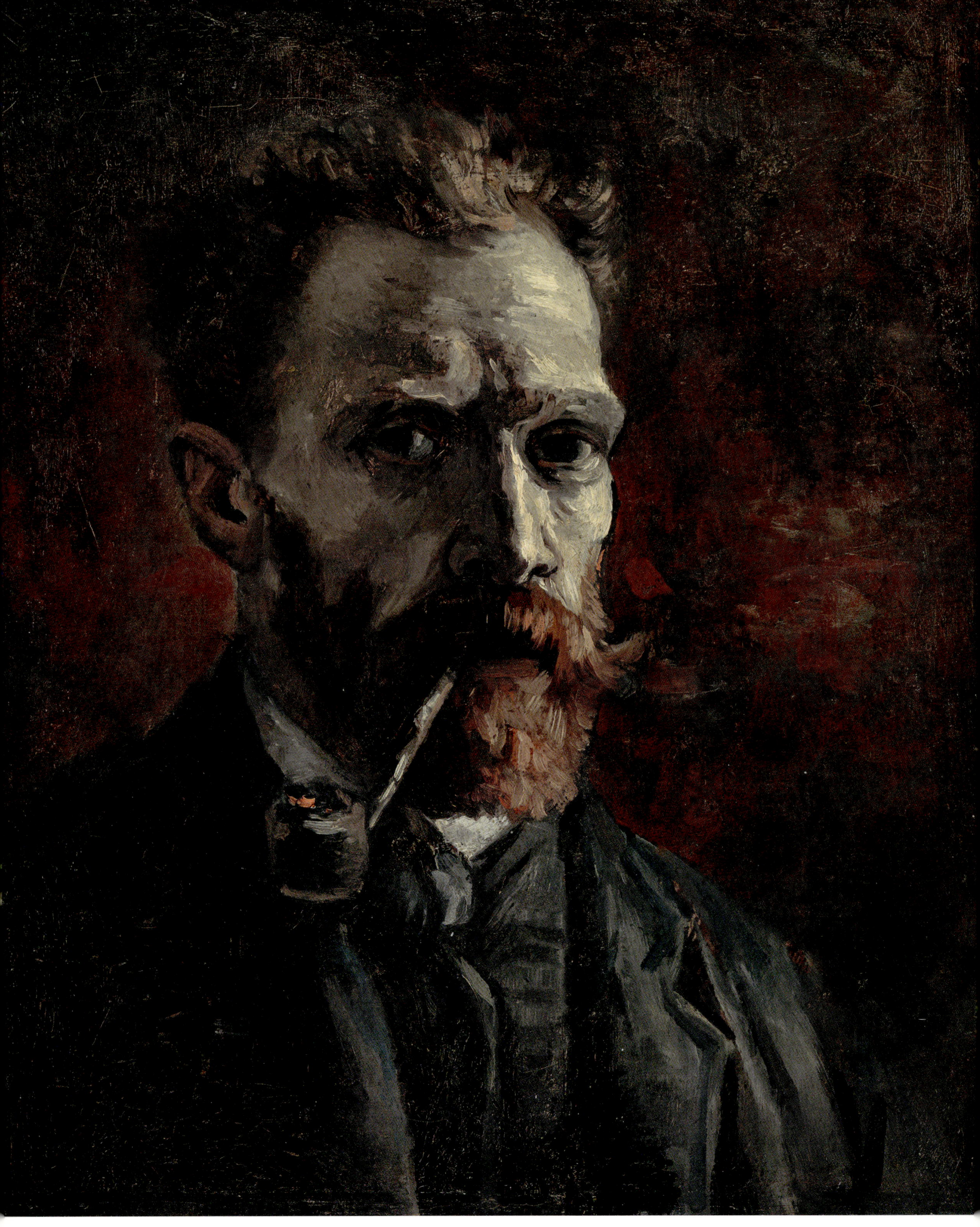

as an art dealer in Paris in order to become an artist and join him in Drenthe. Theo was, of course, unwilling to go along with this unfeasible plan.

On 5 December 1883, Van Gogh left Drenthe and travelled to Nuenen, where he settled in with his parents. This parsonage also had an impressive garden at the back, and it fascinated Van Gogh: "This garden set me so to dreaming," he wrote in mid-March 1884 to his friend Anthon van Rappard, after making two drawings there, both of which he named *Winter Garden* [437]. These sheets belong to a group of stunning landscape drawings that originated at this time (fig. 3).[9] Van Gogh hoped that these works would enjoy some commercial success, but in this he was disappointed. In April he also made drawings—the medium in which he had meanwhile become highly skilled, in contrast to painting—of the surrounding countryside, but his priorities began to shift to figure drawing, because the rural village of Nuenen provided opportunities to work from a model.

NUENEN FIGURE PIECES

In Nuenen, Van Gogh found that the lives of peasants and craftsmen contained an abundance of subjects, which he now tackled with zeal. The large number of weavers he encountered there was the fulfilment of an old dream. He had admired these artisans even before becoming an artist, having seen them on his journey from the Borinage to Pas-de-Calais in 1880.[10] At that time he had expressed the hope that one day he would have an opportunity to draw them. He described the weavers as serene in character—"a dreamy, almost pensive, almost a sleep-walker's air"—and, as far as he knew, they were seldom portrayed [158]. In the summer of 1882, his sister Willemien (Wil) wrote to him about the weavers in Nuenen, and they immediately aroused his interest.[11] Soon after arriving in December 1883, he made his first compositions of the subject, and the weavers continued to inspire him until well into the summer of the following year (cat. 2). These endeavours were no doubt influenced by the thought, formulated already in the Borinage, that depictions of weavers were rare: this time, too, he hoped to find a commercial outlet for his work. It soon began to dawn on him, however, that weavers were not a simple subject: "So far I've made 3 watercolours of them. These folk are difficult to draw because in the small rooms one can't get far enough away to draw the loom. I think this is why attempts to do it usually fail. However, I've found a room here where there are two looms and where it can be done. Rappard painted a study of it in Drenthe, which I found beautiful" [419]. Van Gogh was eventually forced to revise his romantic view of these artisans, "for these weavers are very poor people".

Van Gogh soon realized that it would take a great deal of effort to depict the complicated looms in a convincing way. The scenes of weavers were intended as figure pieces, but he found the machines themselves equally fascinating, if not more so, as he told Van Rappard in a letter of March 1884, written in response to the latter's remarks about a drawing of a weaver: "As far as the loom is concerned, that really is a study of the machine made from start to finish in the place itself and was difficult—because one had to sit *so* close that it was very tricky to take measurements. I drew the figure in after all—but I don't want to say anything with it except: 'when that black monster of begrimed oak with all its slats somehow shows up like this against the greyness in which it stands, then *there*, in the centre of it, sits a black ape or goblin or apparition, and clatters with those slats from early till late'. And indicated the spot by setting down a sort of a shape of a weaver with a few scratches and blotches at the place where I saw him. Consequently, I didn't give the slightest thought to the proportions of arms or legs at the time" [437]. Now, however, he was becoming increasingly eager to portray characteristic figures. Depictions of seasonal labours and traditional artisans' work had been popular for hundreds of years, but the rise of realism in the nineteenth century had turned them into serious and saleable subjects. Van Gogh was determined to make his own contribution to the genre. After sending several drawings of weavers to Theo (also in March), Vincent was prompted to remark: "It would disappoint me a bit to get these little weavers back. And if nobody else you know wants to take them on, I'd think this is an article that perhaps you could take for yourself, in order to bring together a number of pen drawings of Brabant artisans, with this as the start. Which I'd be happy to undertake and—on the assumption that I'll be in Brabant quite a lot now—would be very keen to do" [434]. Van Gogh also depicted figures preparing for the actual weaving: men and women at spinning wheels or bobbin winders. We know a number of such drawings, but he also worked them up into paintings. In June he mentions a large study (now lost) of a woman spinning, which was very likely the image reproduced on one of the calling cards he later had printed (fig. 14). He made a smaller variation of that composition, probably the spinner visible in an X-radiograph of a winter scene of 1884–85 (fig. 15).[12] There exists another depiction of a woman spinning that was also overpainted later.[13]

Thanks to his years in the art trade, Van Gogh knew that there were buyers for such work. He had photographs taken in Eindhoven of various figure pieces, and had a number of them made into the above-mentioned *cartes de visite* in the early autumn of 1884. Among these were scenes of peasants planting potatoes, a shepherd with his flock, a sower, the large canvas of a woman at the spinning wheel, and two weavers. A man at his loom, seen against an illuminated wall, also appears on one of these calling cards (cat. 2, fig. 16). Van Gogh must have had great faith in those paintings, but around this time the weaver motif began to lose its appeal and eventually made way for new subjects.

PEASANT LIFE

The scenes of peasants planting potatoes and a shepherd with his flock that Van Gogh had had printed as calling cards were photographs of two large paintings from a series of six. This series, commissioned by the Eindhoven goldsmith and amateur painter Antoon Hermans to decorate his dining room, was carried out by Van Gogh in August and September 1884. What Hermans had in mind were episodes from the lives of the saints, but Van Gogh persuaded him to choose instead scenes of peasant life in rural Brabant, which could double as portrayals of the four seasons. Van Gogh would make the designs, and Hermans himself would execute the paintings. It was agreed that Hermans would pay for the models and materials, then borrow the finished works from Van Gogh and give them back after completing his decoration.

Van Gogh set to work enthusiastically. He worked out his first ideas in small sketches, changed his mind somewhat, and finally completed designs for six subjects: "Planting potatoes, Ox-plough, Wheat harvest, Sower, Shepherd, storm effect, Wood gatherers, snow effect" [459]. Hermans's dining room must have been rectangular, with the first two canvases (representing spring) on one long side, opposite the sower and the shepherd (autumn), and the wheat harvest (summer) and the peasants in the snow (winter) on the short walls.

This series meant the realization of a theme that was close to Van Gogh's heart, namely the seasons. He had previously portrayed them in separate compositions, and had depicted them in The Hague in four small watercolours. These new, large, painted figure studies were an important step for Van Gogh.The subject of the shepherd with his flock fascinated him: he worked it out in three other compositions, which

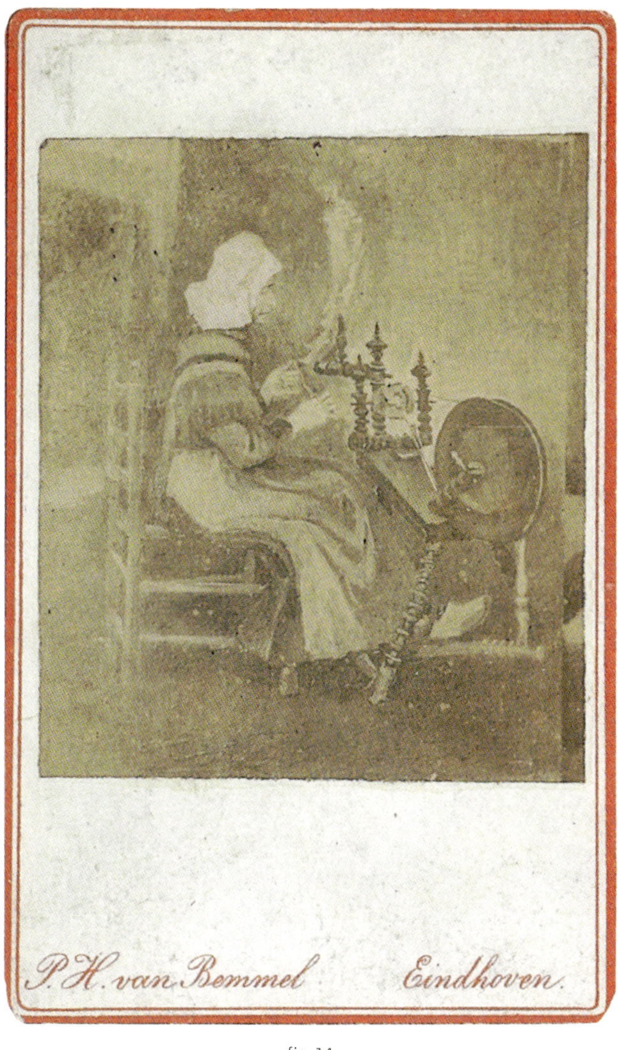

fig. 14

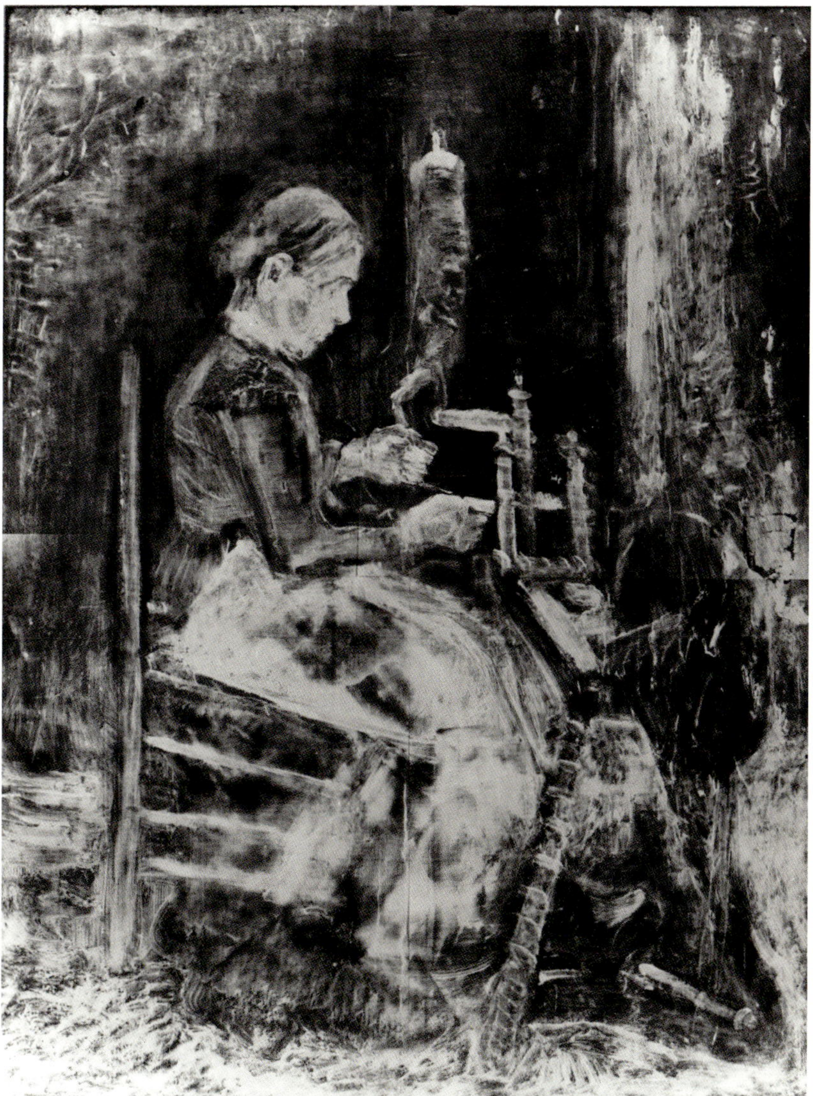

fig. 15

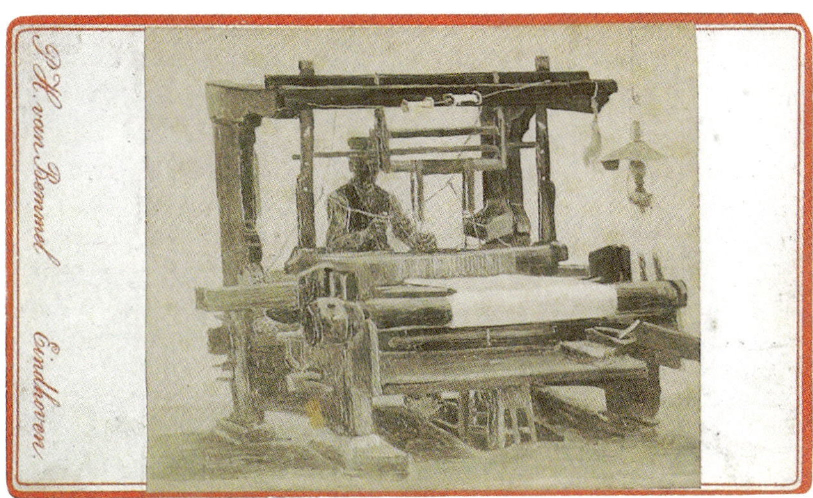

fig. 16

14 Pieter Henricus van Bemmel
Vincent van Gogh, *A Woman Spinning*, September 1884
Photograph of a lost painting on a *carte de visite*, 10.6×6.3 cm
Van Gogh Museum, Amsterdam
(Vincent van Gogh Foundation)

15 X-radiograph of *Winter (The Vicarage Garden under Snow)*, 1885
showing *A Woman Spinning*, 1884
Oil on canvas on panel, 51×77 cm
Norton Simon Art Foundation

16 Pieter Henricus van Bemmel
Vincent van Gogh, *Loom and Weaver*, September 1884 (cat. 2)
Carte de visite with a photograph of Vincent van Gogh, F30 (Kröller-Müller Museum), 6.3×10.6 cm
Van Gogh Museum, Amsterdam

cannot be given precise dates. Evidently he thought they were not good enough, however, because he later overpainted them. One of them, in very large format, is now covered by *The Cottage* of May 1885.[14]

In the summer of 1884, another event fuelled Van Gogh's passion for the peasant life even more—inasmuch as that was possible. Sensier's biography of Millet—the borrowed book that had kept Van Gogh awake at night in The Hague—was given to him as a present in August or early September, presumably by Hermans, though possibly by Theo.[15] Van Gogh read the book about his artistic mentor with great enthusiasm and later referred to it many times in his letters. It contained, in addition to Sensier's text and illustrations, letters written by Millet himself, which brought the man he had long admired very close to him. Millet presented himself as a true peasant painter who lived among his subjects, which was exactly what Van Gogh wanted to do. He would soon be completely immersed in peasant life, but first he became caught up in two intermezzos.

AUTUMN LANDSCAPES AND STILL LIFES

Van Gogh always greeted autumn with enthusiasm. He liked all the seasons, but he was particularly fond of autumn: "How beautiful it is outside—I sometimes yearn for a country where it would always be autumn, but then we'd have no snow and no apple blossom and no corn and stubble fields," he wrote to Van Rappard from The Hague in 1882 [273]. Seasonal effects were also popular motifs among the Barbizon painters, and once again Van Gogh followed in their footsteps. He painted three autumn landscapes, the largest of which is *Avenue of Poplars in Autumn* (cat. 3). On the lower right he added a woman wearing a hooded mourning cape, a reference to a recent sorrowful event in her life that was in keeping with the melancholy landscape.[16] Around this time he also made a few paintings of watermills.

The still life was a genre Van Gogh had not tackled since working with Mauve in 1881. With their emphasis on the rendering of materials, still lifes are more suited to painting than to drawing, which Van Gogh had focused on for so long. Besides, he had been more interested in other subjects. In Nuenen—or rather, nearby Eindhoven—an opportunity presented itself, in November 1884, for Van Gogh to assume the role of teacher: he was asked to give lessons in painting, using objects from Antoon Hermans's collection to compose still-life subjects. In addition to the goldsmith, he had three other pupils—Anton Kerssemakers, Willem van de Wakker and Dimmen Gestel—who grouped and regrouped the "many beautiful objects—like old jars and other antiques" from Hermans's collection into ever-changing compositions [471]. Van Gogh also painted these things himself: compared with the still lifes he would make the following year, these works are indeed distinguished by the presence of unusual objects, such as a *baardmanskruik*, a jug featuring a bearded head in relief (fig. 17). Hermans also allowed him to take some of these objects home with him, so that he could paint still lifes in his Nuenen studio; in the letter quoted above, Van Gogh suggested painting a somewhat more impressive composition (with "Gothic things, for instance") for Theo's apartment.

While Van Gogh was teaching his pupils about the rendering of materials, the effects of light and shade and colour theory, the still lifes also provided him with the ideal means of studying the last of these aspects. Earlier that year, he had read a lot about colour theories, particularly as applied by Eugène Delacroix, and since then they had been central to his thought.[17] Two books by Charles Blanc, *Grammaire des arts du dessin* and *Les Artistes de mon temps*, with a chapter on Delacroix, had completely overwhelmed him, and books by other authors further piqued his interest in colour. This new constant in his career eventually became a defining aspect of his

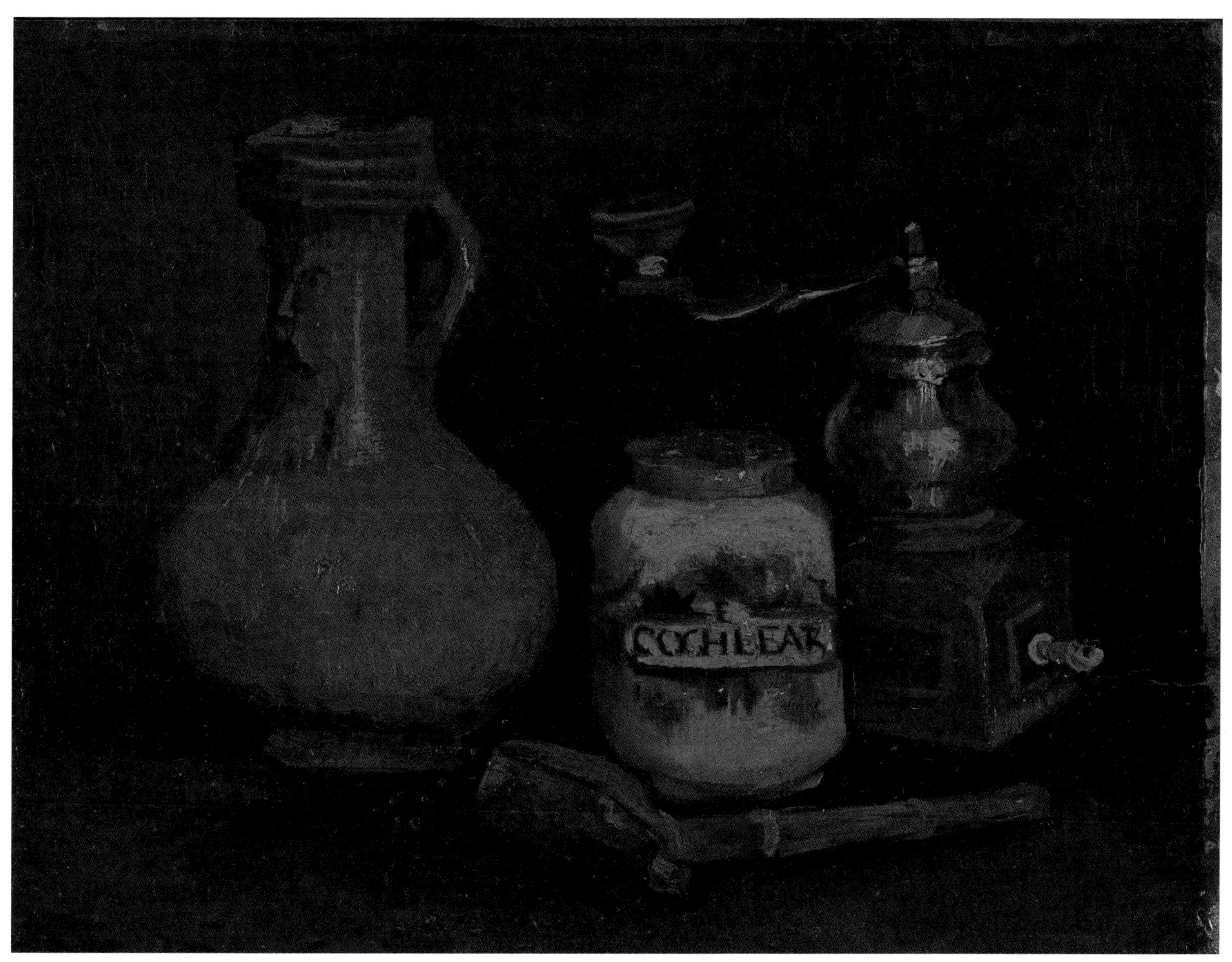

fig. 17

17 Vincent van Gogh, *Still Life with a bearded-man jug*,
November 1884–April 1885
Oil on cardboard mounted on panel,
33.7 × 42.7 cm
Kröller-Müller Museum, Otterlo

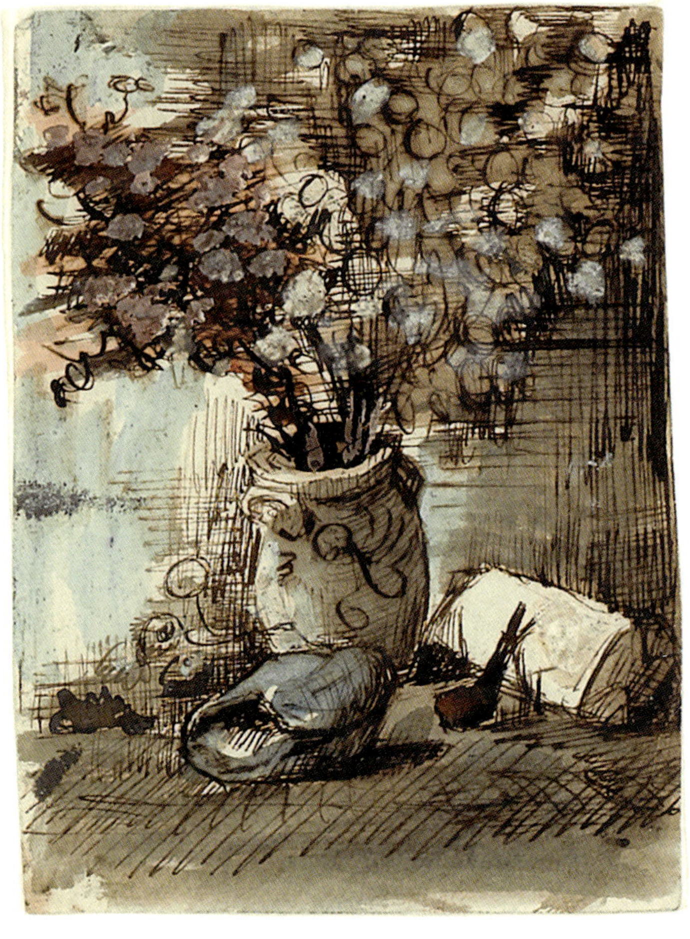

fig. 18

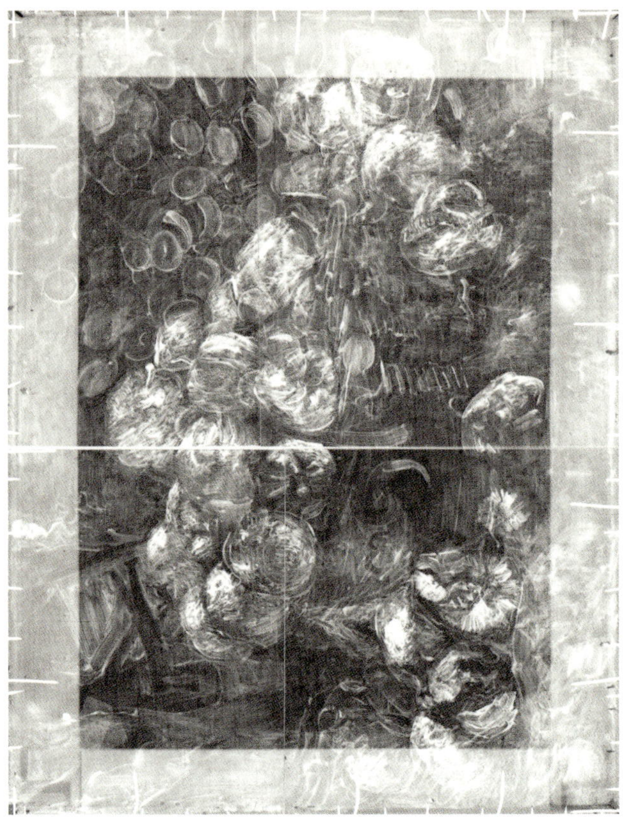

fig. 19

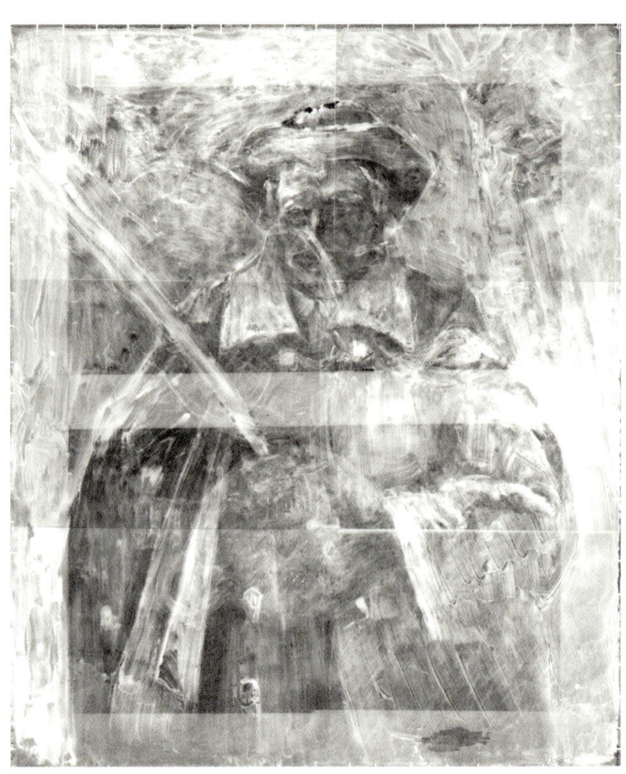

fig. 20

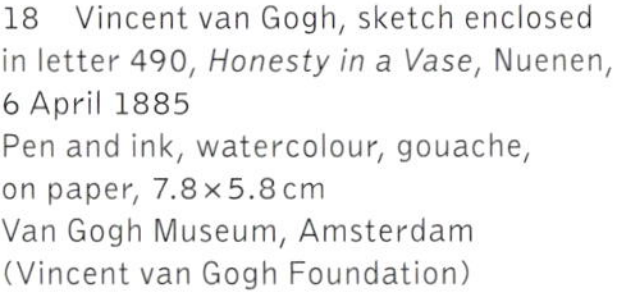

18 Vincent van Gogh, sketch enclosed in letter 490, *Honesty in a Vase*, Nuenen, 6 April 1885
Pen and ink, watercolour, gouache, on paper, 7.8 × 5.8 cm
Van Gogh Museum, Amsterdam
(Vincent van Gogh Foundation)

19 X-radiograph of *Basket of Apples*, Nuenen, September 1885, showing *Honesty in a Vase*, April 1885
Oil on canvas, 45 × 60.4 cm
Van Gogh Museum, Amsterdam
(Vincent van Gogh Foundation)

20 X-radiograph of *Still Life with Brass Cauldron and Jug*, Nuenen, September 1885, showing a shepherd
Oil on canvas, 65.5 × 80.5 cm
Van Gogh Museum, Amsterdam
(Vincent van Gogh Foundation)

modern work, as the colour theories he had read about in 1884 and the thinking of Delacroix came to form a lasting basis for his art.[18]

Van Gogh continued to produce the occasional still life until sometime in April 1885. Among them were two flower still lifes (quite rare in his Dutch œuvre), both featuring the translucent seed pods of white-flowered honesty (*lunaria annua*). One of these paintings carried a special meaning: the Reverend Theodorus Van Gogh had died on 26 March, and shortly afterwards Vincent painted a large still life of honesty in a Cologne ware pot, with his father's pipe and tobacco pouch in front of it. He wrote about this painting to Theo and enclosed a small drawing of it (fig. 18). This drawing is rather detailed and even done in colour, which is highly unusual for his letter sketches and a clear indication of the importance of the canvas. The painting, long assumed to be lost, had been overpainted with a still life of apples,[19] but was finally revealed by an X-radiograph (fig. 19). This shows—as the letter sketch does not—how Van Gogh later added flowers to the foreground, presumably doing more harm than good, at least in his eyes, for in the autumn this unusual composition disappeared underneath the subsequent still life.

By this time, however, Van Gogh's top priority was to portray peasant life in a full-blown figure painting. He still had no idea what the composition should look like, but he was well aware of the thorough preparation necessary to execute it. In late October 1884, he devoted himself almost wholly to studying the peasant type.

AMONG PEASANTS AGAIN

Anthon van Rappard, with whom Van Gogh had become acquainted in Belgium in 1880 and who remained his most important painter friend during his Dutch years, spent the second half of October 1884 with Van Gogh in Nuenen, and the two men worked together from models. Vincent wrote to Theo that he was working "on a figure of a shepherd wearing a greatcoat... If I have some luck with the shepherd, it will be a figure that will have something of the *very old Brabant* in it. Anyway, it isn't finished yet, and we'll see how it turns out" [466]. In the end, the figure proved not to have the power he had been hoping for, and he reused the canvas for the *Still Life with Brass Cauldron and Jug* (fig. 20, 26).[20]

Van Rappard made studies of heads and stressed the importance of such work to Van Gogh, who followed his friend's advice with alacrity. He resolved to paint a series of thirty *tronies* (studies of heads), a number he later raised to fifty.[21] Up to now, Van Gogh had always demonstrated great self-discipline and had usually done exactly what he set out to do (such as copying sample drawings in Belgium and his ceaseless study from a model in The Hague). He did not deviate from his plan this time either, as evidenced by the forty-seven surviving studies of peasant heads, painted between November 1884 and May 1885. In addition, he made quite a few drawings, including a series of small pen drawings after the painted studies.

Such studies were not intended as portraits of his fellow villagers, but rather as portrayals of the peasant type; indeed, the names of those who posed are, with one exception, unknown.[22] In The Hague, Van Gogh, inspired in part by English examples, had drawn the heads of ordinary people and had strongly favoured models who bore clear signs of a hard, poverty-stricken life. His friend Van de Wakker recalled how Van Gogh always chose the ugliest models, in Nuenen too.[23] Reading Sensier, he had learned that Millet also preferred physiognomies marked by toil and misery, so that his work would exude the atmosphere of the hard peasant life. Van Gogh, adopting the same approach, went in search of models with striking, even coarsened, features (cat. 4).

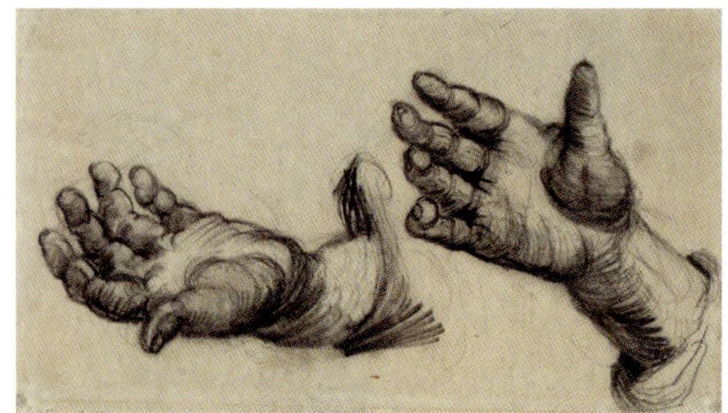

fig. 21

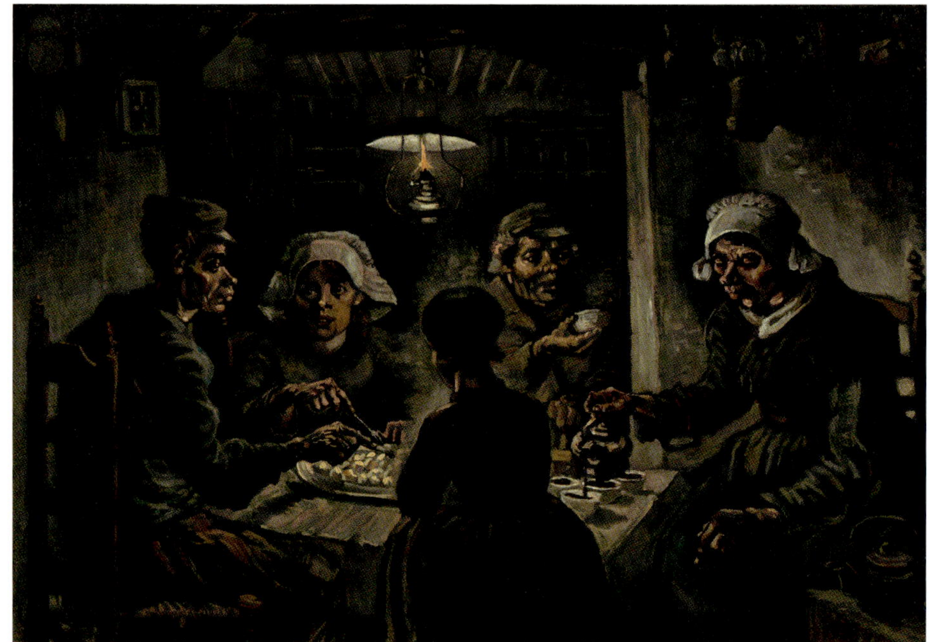

fig. 22

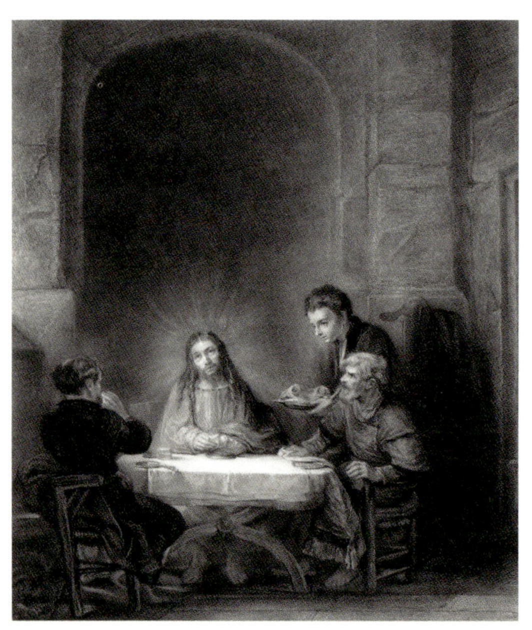

fig. 23

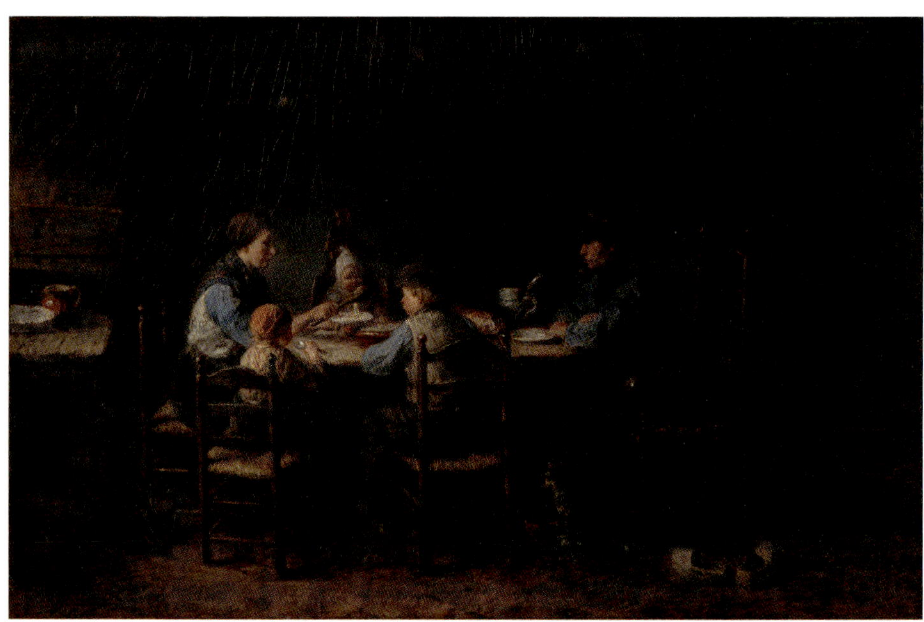

fig. 24

21 Vincent van Gogh, *Two Hands*, December 1884–May 1885
Chalk on paper, 21.1×34.6 cm
Van Gogh Museum, Amsterdam (Vincent van Gogh Foundation)

22 Vincent van Gogh, *The Potato Eaters*, Nuenen, April–May 1885
Oil on canvas, 82×114 cm
Van Gogh Museum, Amsterdam (Vincent van Gogh Foundation)

23 Amadée and Eugène Varin after Rembrandt, *The Pilgrims of Emmaus*, 1875
Engraving
Collection Musée Goupil, Bordeaux

24 Jozef Israëls, *Peasant Family at the Table*, 1882
Oil on canvas, 71×105 cm
Van Gogh Museum, Amsterdam (Vincent van Gogh Foundation)

He soon expanded his study to include hands, making more or less anatomically correct drawings as well as expressive renderings of coarse peasant hands (fig. 21). From February to April 1885, he enlarged his repertoire further, and began to experiment with figures drawn or painted indoors (cat. 5) and figures seen against the light. A man seated at a table (cat. 6), also stemming from March–April, anticipates the large painting that was beginning to take shape in Van Gogh's mind. Gradually, he conceived the idea of a group of peasants eating a meal in a simple cottage, and this eventually crystallized into *The Potato Eaters* (fig. 22).

The motif of a group of people seated at a table, eating and drinking, had been in use for centuries. A famous example is the Last Supper of Christ and his disciples; Van Gogh knew Leonardo da Vinci's version from a reproductive print. In 1875 he had seen in the Louvre a painting by Rembrandt that he was fond of, *The Supper at Emmaus*; that same year his employer, Goupil, had published a print after it, with which Van Gogh was also familiar (fig. 23). This mealtime motif was popular in the nineteenth century, and Van Gogh was aware of other examples too. Charles de Groux had made a monumental painting of a father saying grace with his family, which Van Gogh mentioned in October 1882 in the same breath as Da Vinci's *Last Supper*.[24] And in March of that year he had also seen a painting by Jozef Israëls of a worker's family at a table, though it is not clear which work that was, because Israëls painted a number of very similar versions (fig. 24).[25]

Van Gogh, who was blessed with an excellent visual memory, no doubt remembered these and other variations on the theme. When he embarked on his own version, he did not necessarily have a specific example in mind, but he took his place in a rich tradition with illustrious predecessors. Not only do Van Gogh's thorough preparations underline the importance of the undertaking, but his choice of subject matter also shows that this was a conscious attempt on his part to prove himself as an artist by producing a "master piece", that is to say, a true test of his workmanship.

At first he was in doubt about whether to depict a daytime or a nocturnal scene, and he experimented in March 1885 with compositional drawings and detail sketches. Van Gogh actually worked in the cottage of the De Groot family, which meant a lot to him, for in his eyes such cottages were symbols of their inhabitants, the nests which gave them a sense of security. He first made a study, painted on the spot, with four people, then a larger one with five.[26] Of the latter study, he immediately made a lithograph, an impression of which he sent to Van Rappard, who severely criticized it, especially the rendering of the figures.[27]

Initially, Van Gogh dismissed Van Rappard's criticism, though he must have realized that it contained a kernel of truth, because he spent the rest of the spring and summer immersed, for the most part, in figure studies. After the fiasco of his intended masterpiece, Van Gogh did not attempt another large figure painting in the Netherlands, and it was years before he again dared to test his ambitions on that high a level. Still, thc importance of *The Potato Eaters* in his œuvre cannot be overestimated. Not without reason did he quote, while working on the painting, a pronouncement on Millet made by Théophile Gautier (also quoted by Sensier): "*His peasants seem to have been painted with the soil they sow*" [499].[28] The problem of colour had been one of Van Gogh's greatest difficulties when painting *The Potato Eaters*, and for the flesh tones of the peasants' heads he had chosen, completely in the manner of Millet, an earth colour, "*something like the colour of a really dusty potato, unpeeled of course*". He had already explained to his brother in an earlier letter that it was good if "a peasant painting smells of bacon, smoke, potato steam", thus emphasizing its earthy character [497].

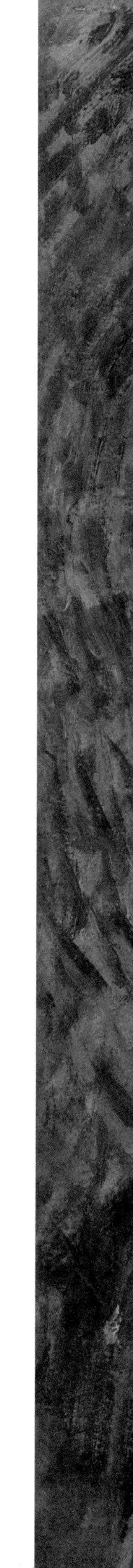

Cat. 9
Vincent van Gogh, *Self-Portrait with Grey Felt Hat,* Paris, September–October 1887
Oil on canvas, 44.5 × 37.2 cm

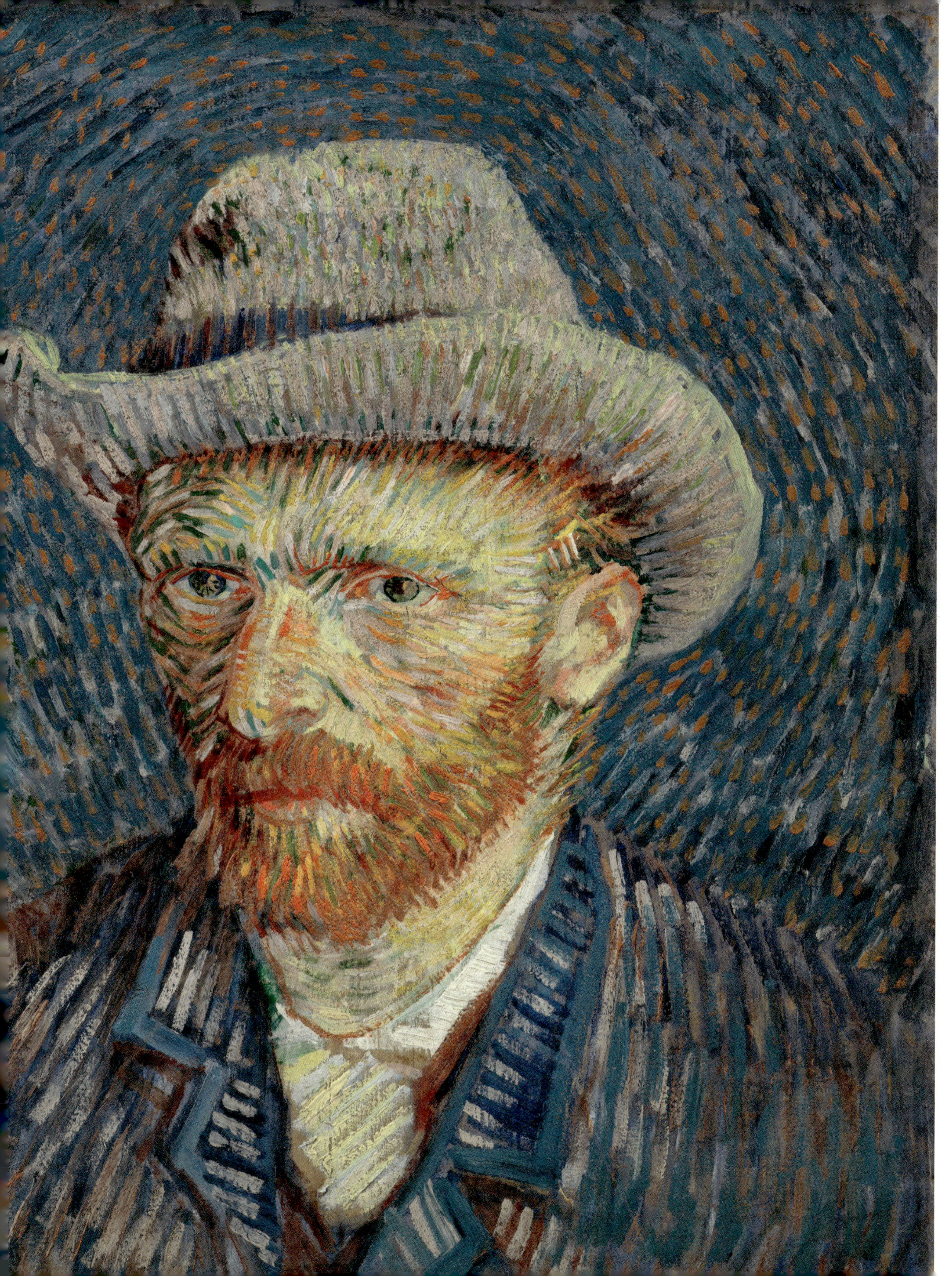

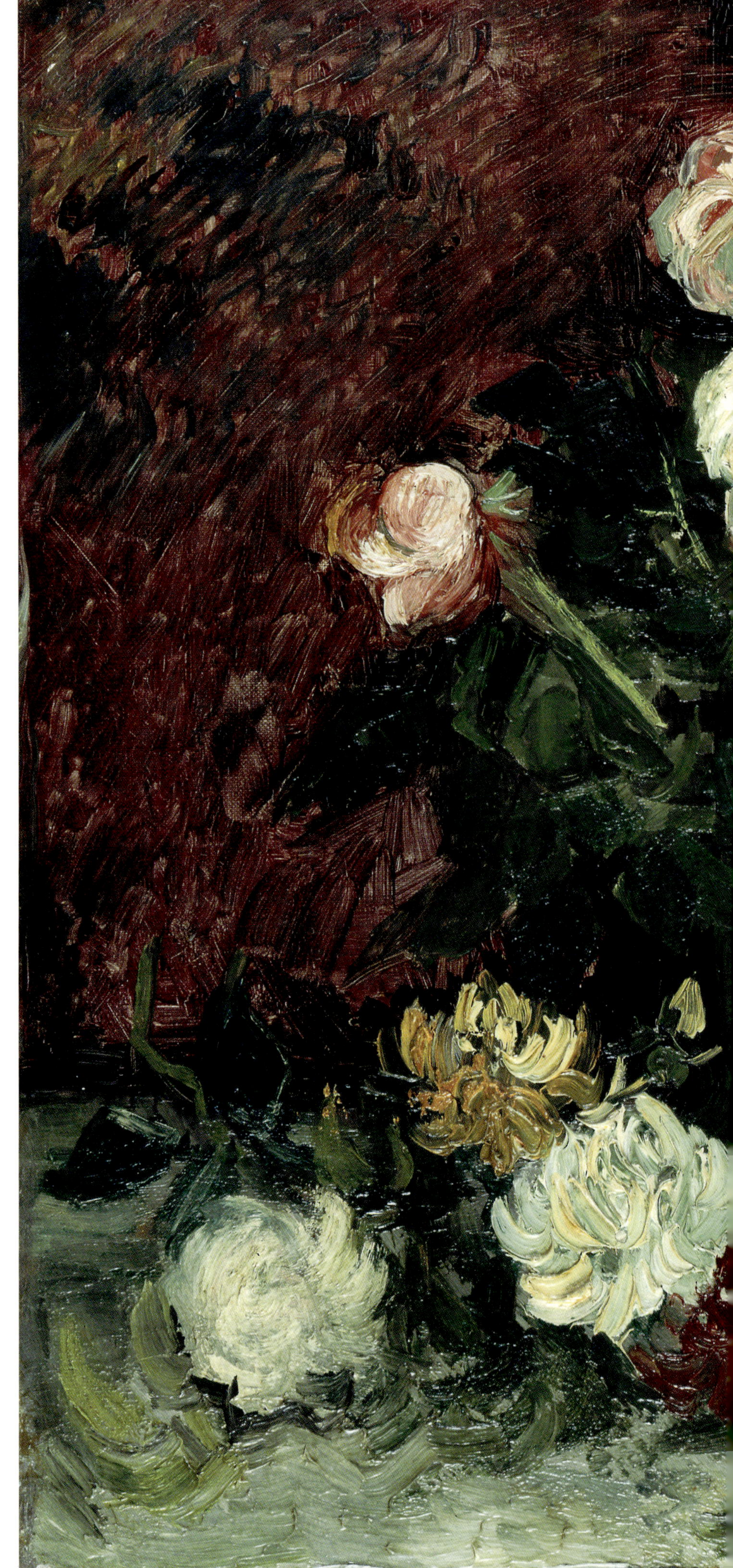

Cat. 10
Vincent van Gogh, *Roses and Peonies,*
Paris, June 1886
Oil on canvas, 59.8 × 72.5 cm

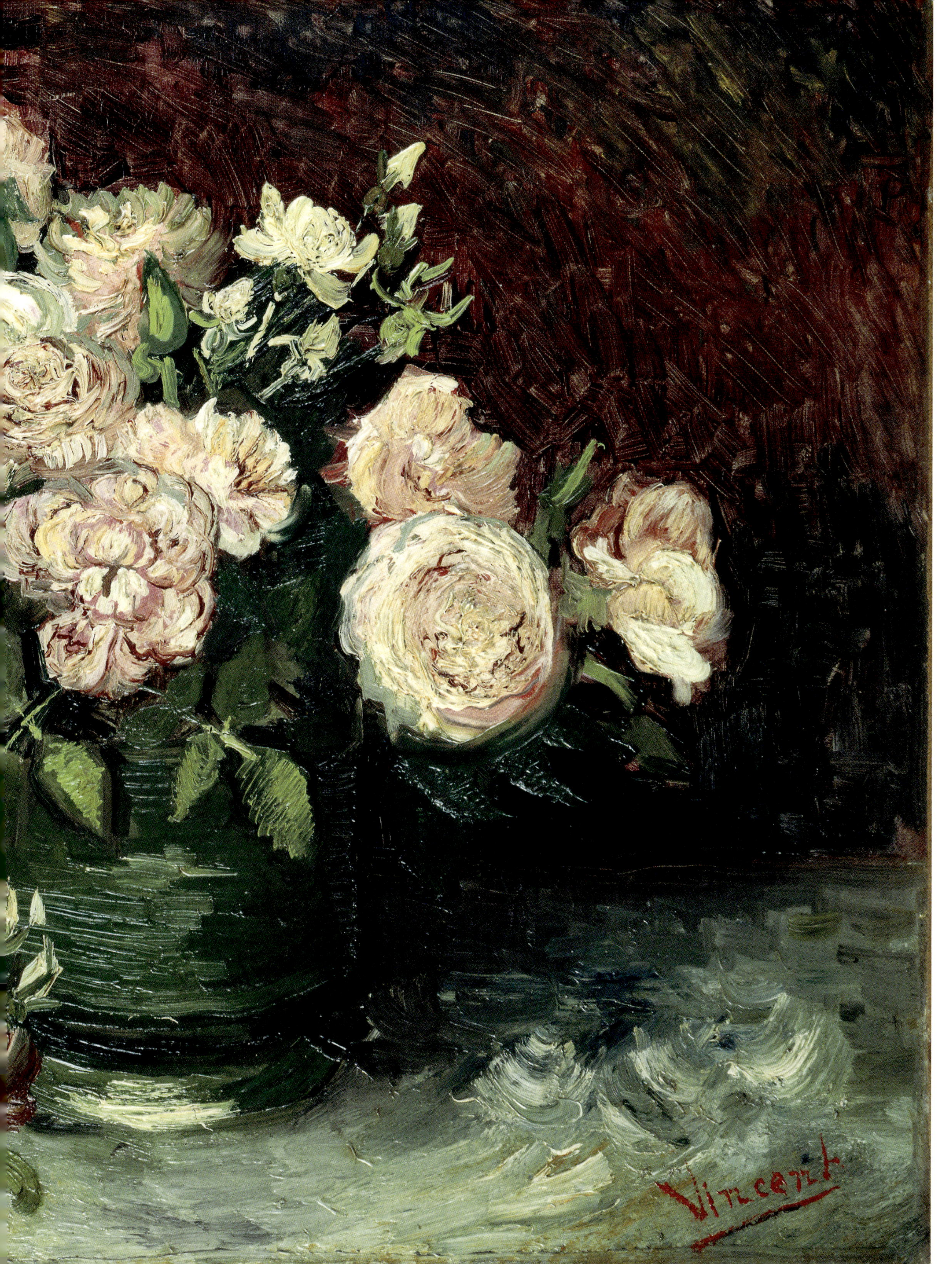
Vincent

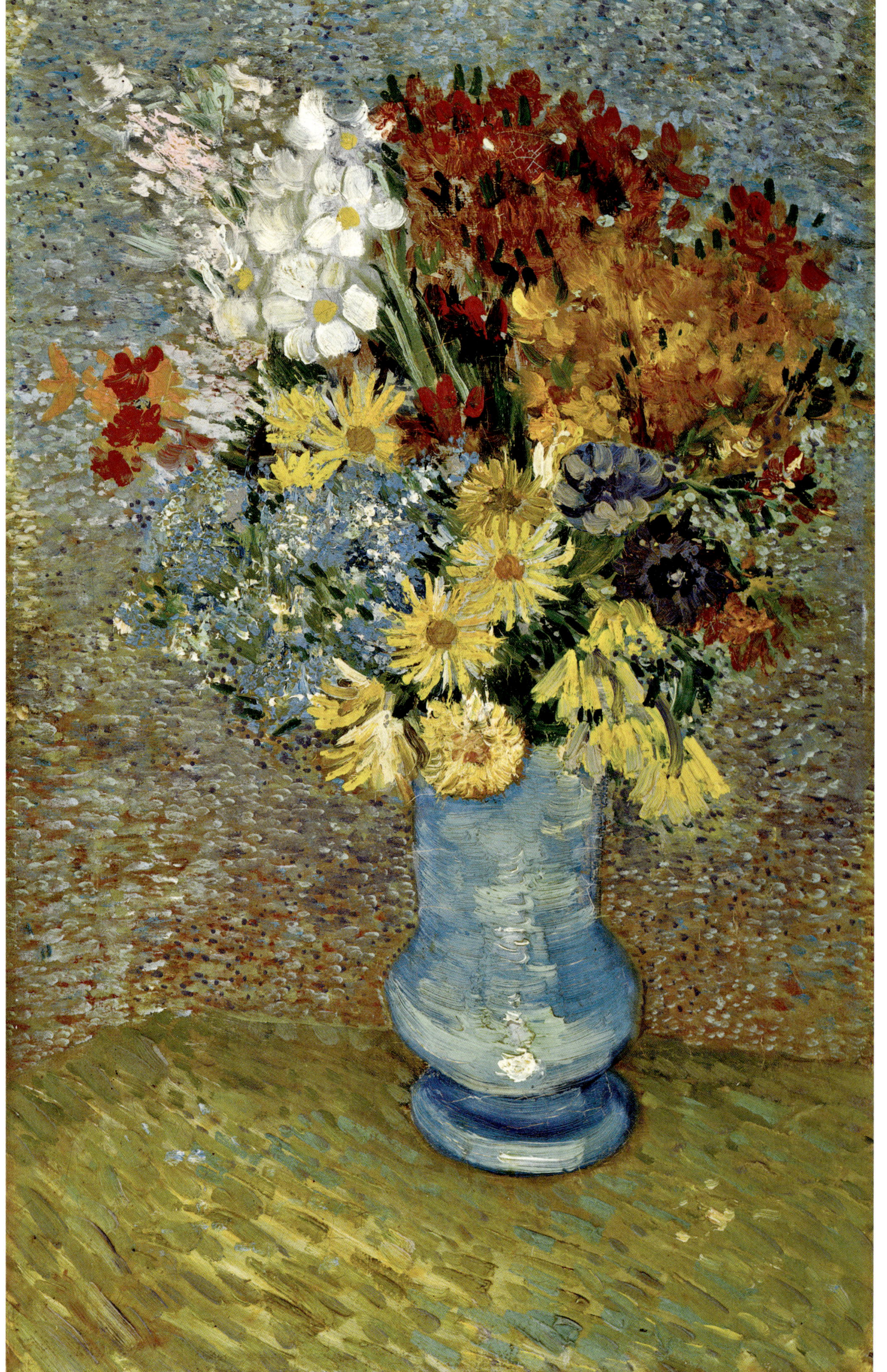

Cat. 11
Vincent van Gogh, *Flowers in a Blue Vase,*
Paris, June 1887
Oil on canvas, 61.5 × 38.5 cm

→
Cat. 12
Vincent van Gogh, *Kneeling Ecorché,*
Paris, June 1886
Oil on cardboard, 35.2 × 26.8 cm

→
Cat. 13
Vincent van Gogh, *Café Table with Absinthe,* Paris, February–March 1887
Oil on canvas, 46.3 × 33.2 cm

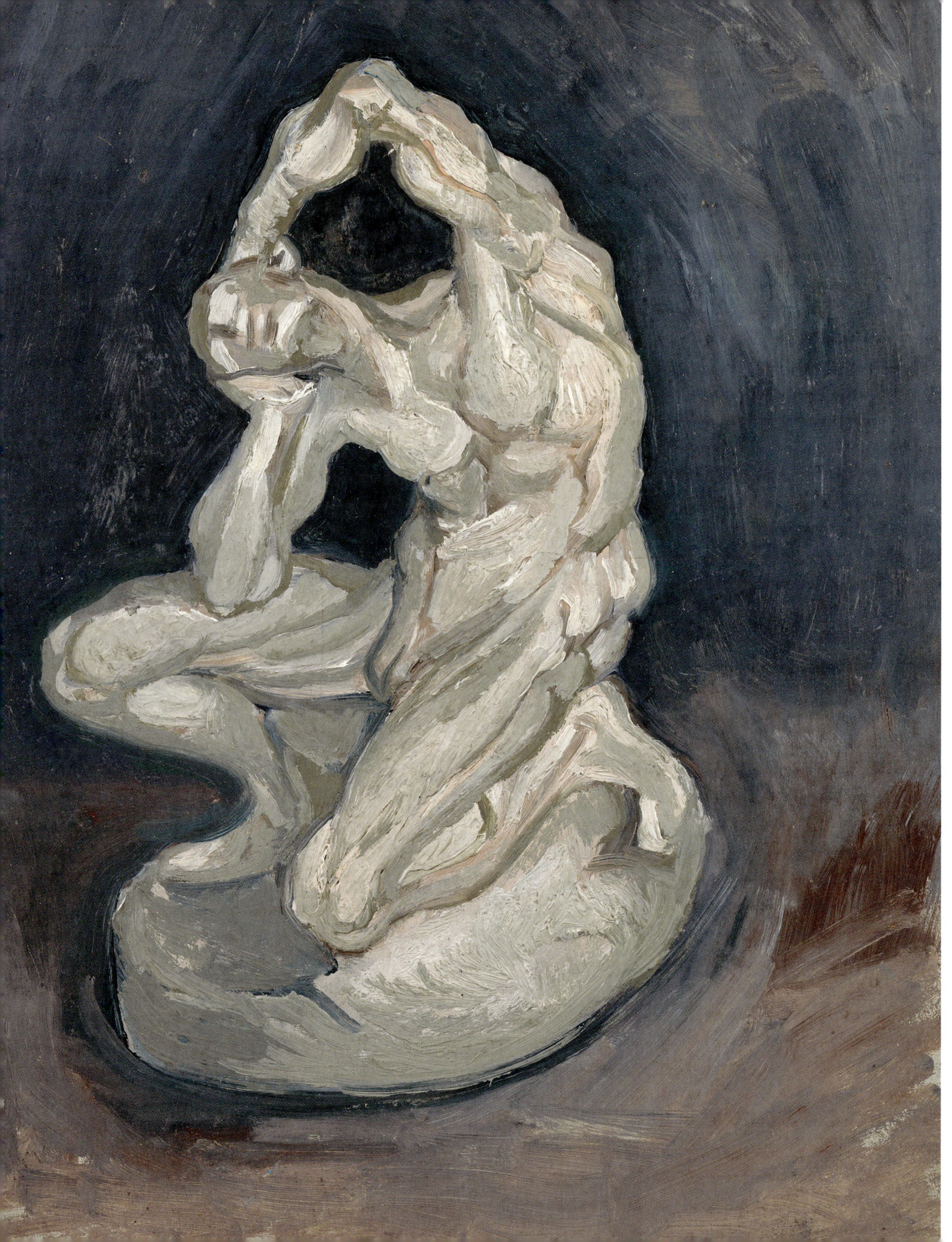

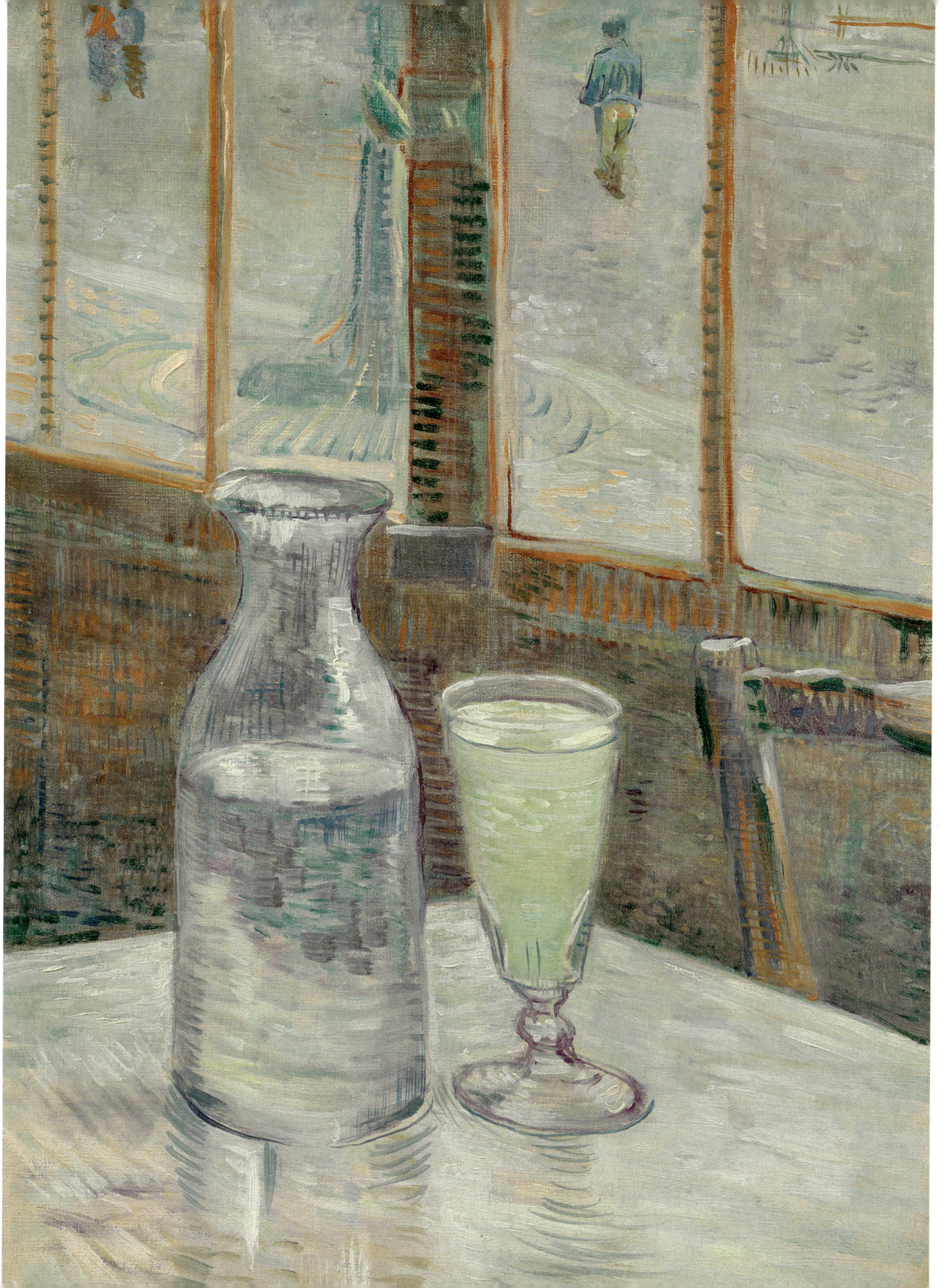

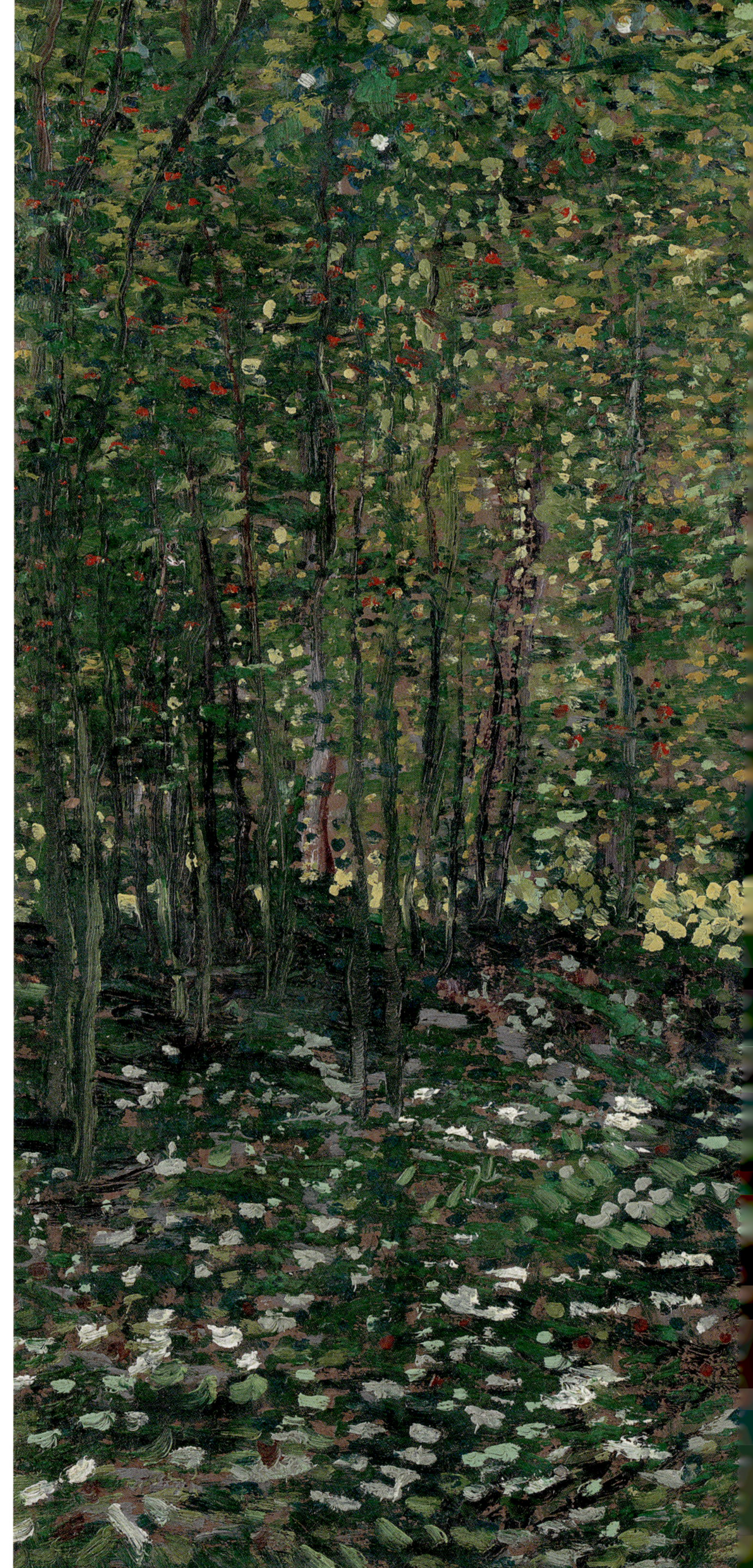

Cat. 14
Vincent van Gogh, *Trees and Undergrowth*,
Paris, July 1887
Oil on canvas, 46.2×55.2cm

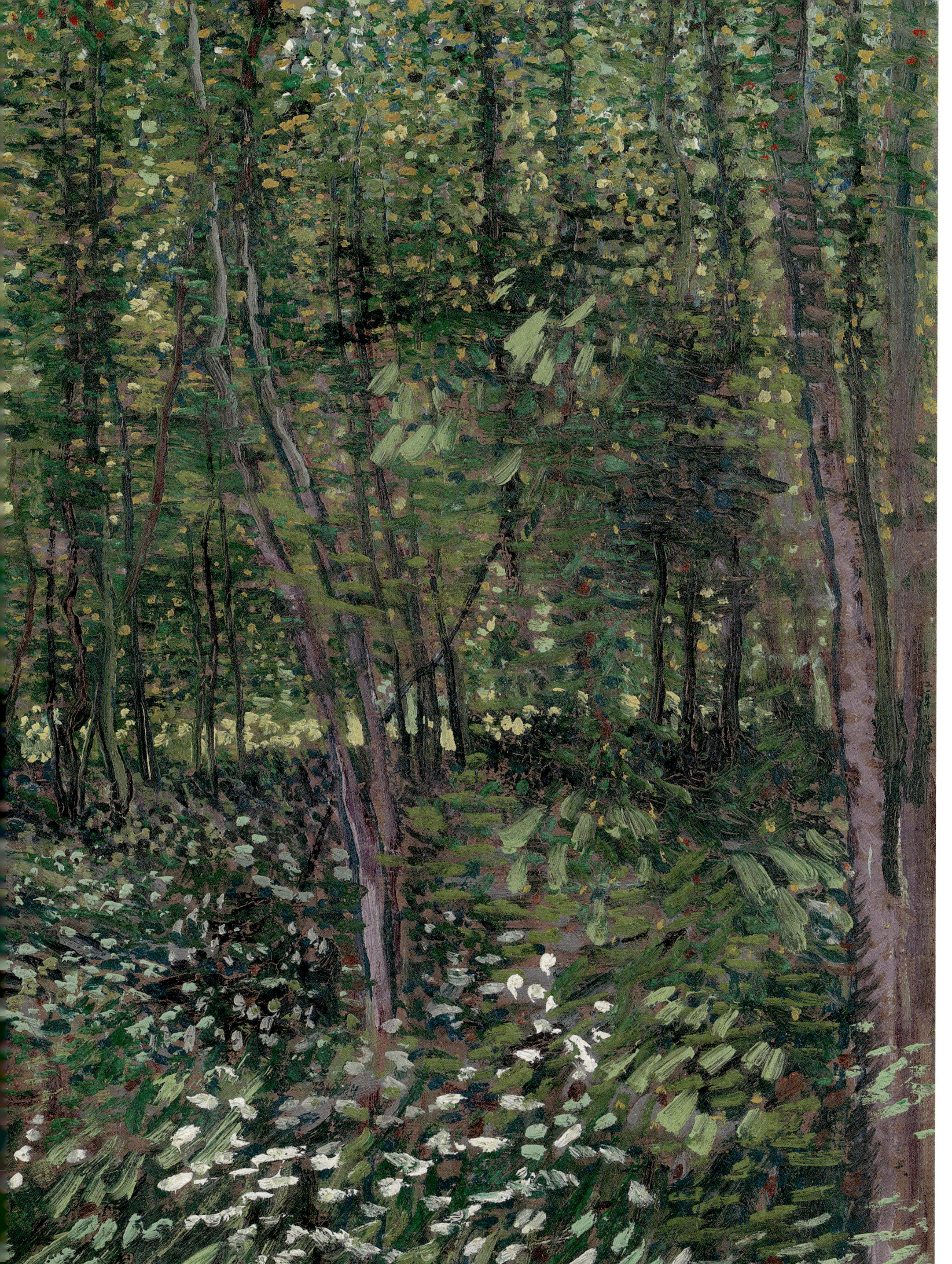

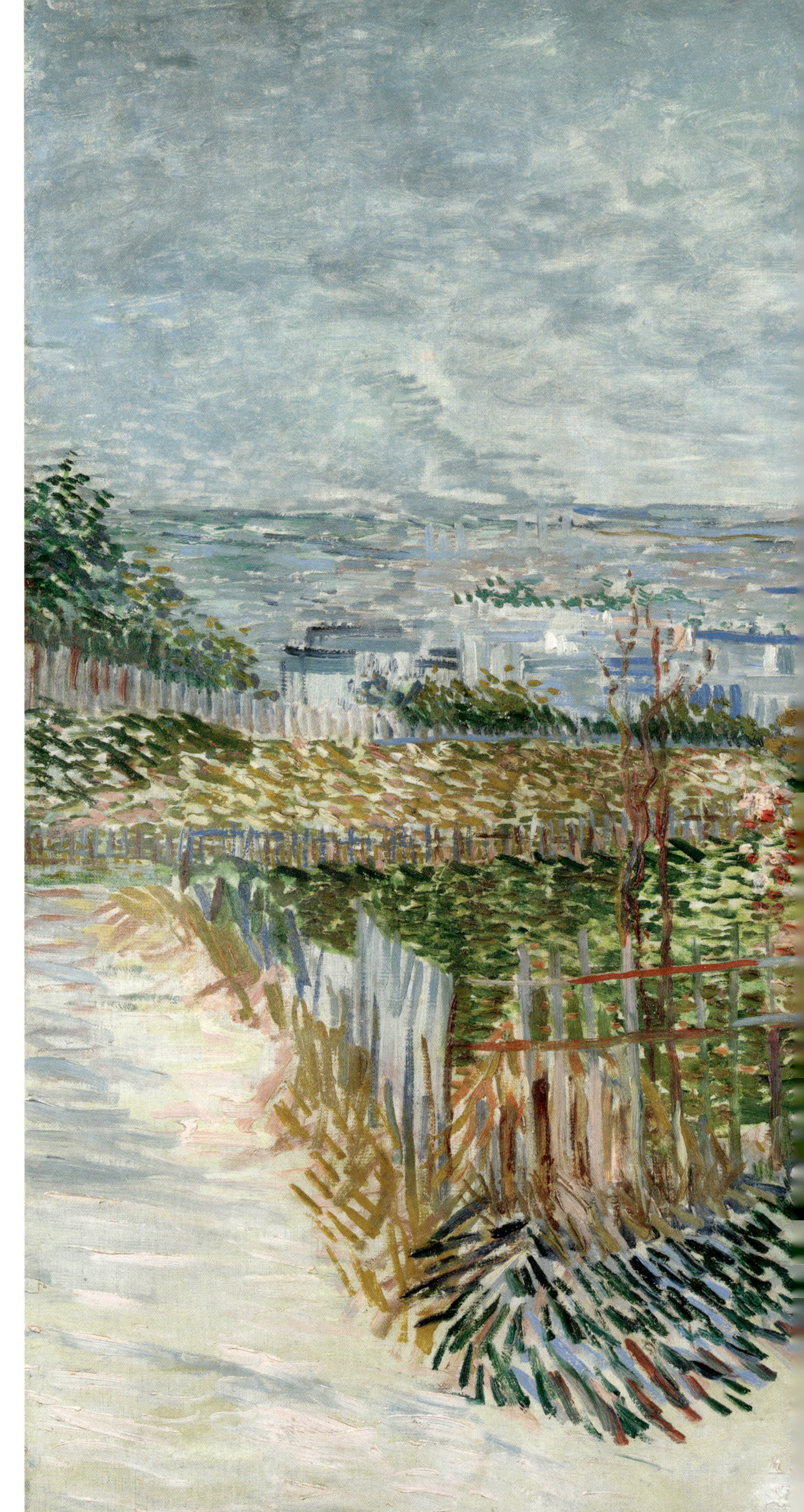

Cat. 15
Vincent van Gogh, *Montmartre: Behind the Moulin de la Galette,* Paris, July 1887
Oil on canvas, 81 × 100 cm

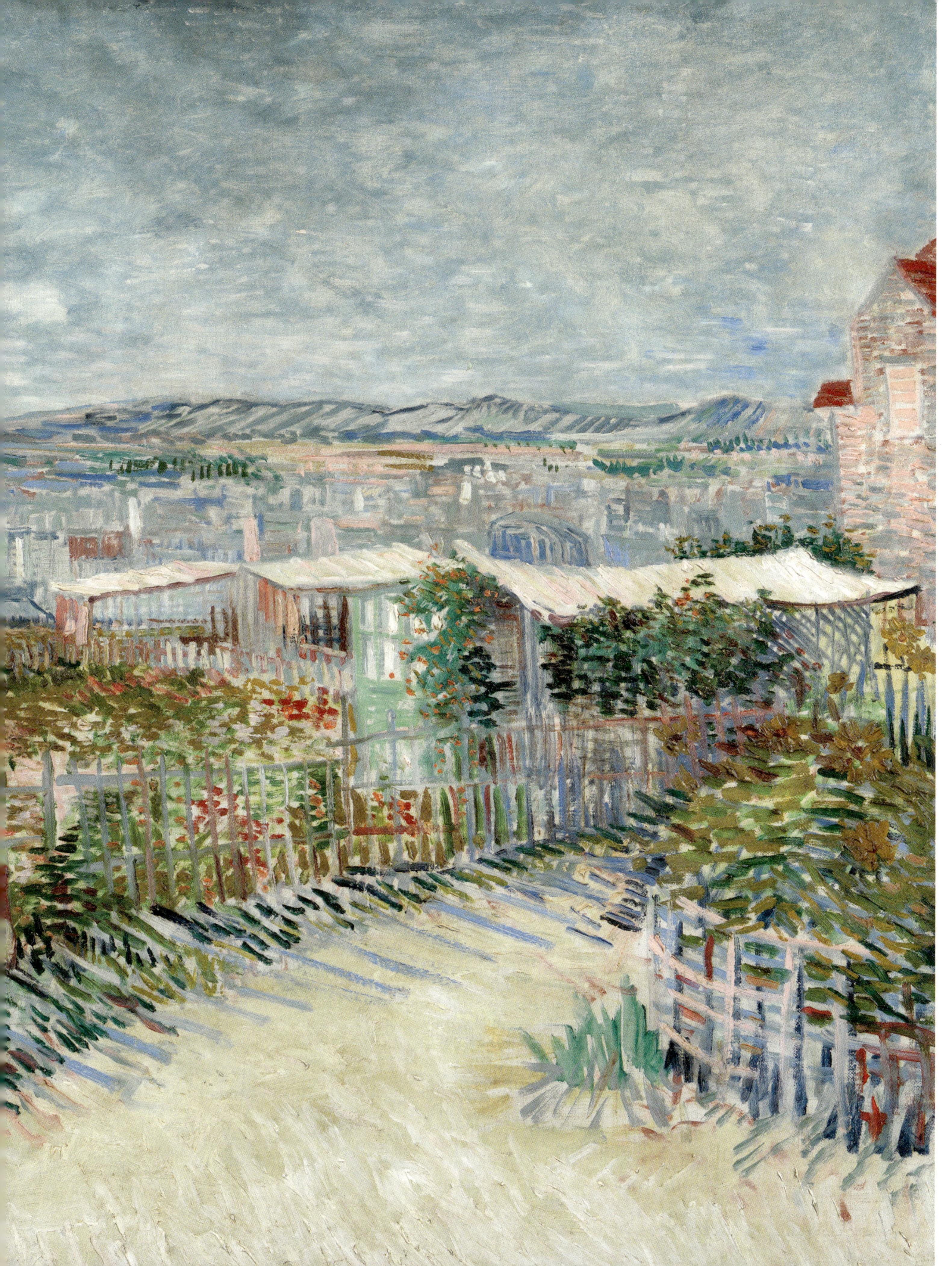

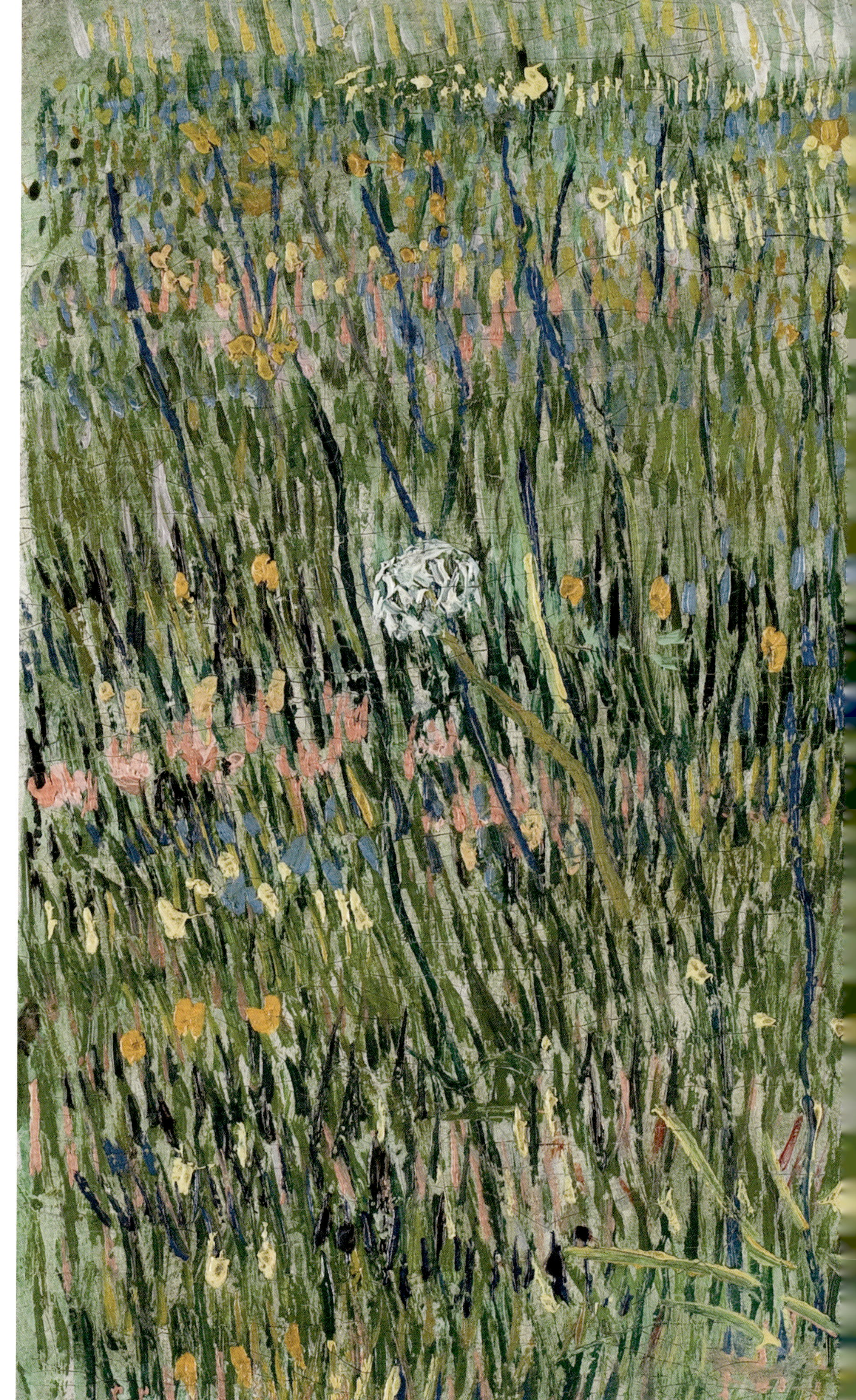

Cat. 16
Vincent van Gogh, *Patch of Grass*,
Paris, April–June 1887
Oil on canvas, 30.8×39.7 cm

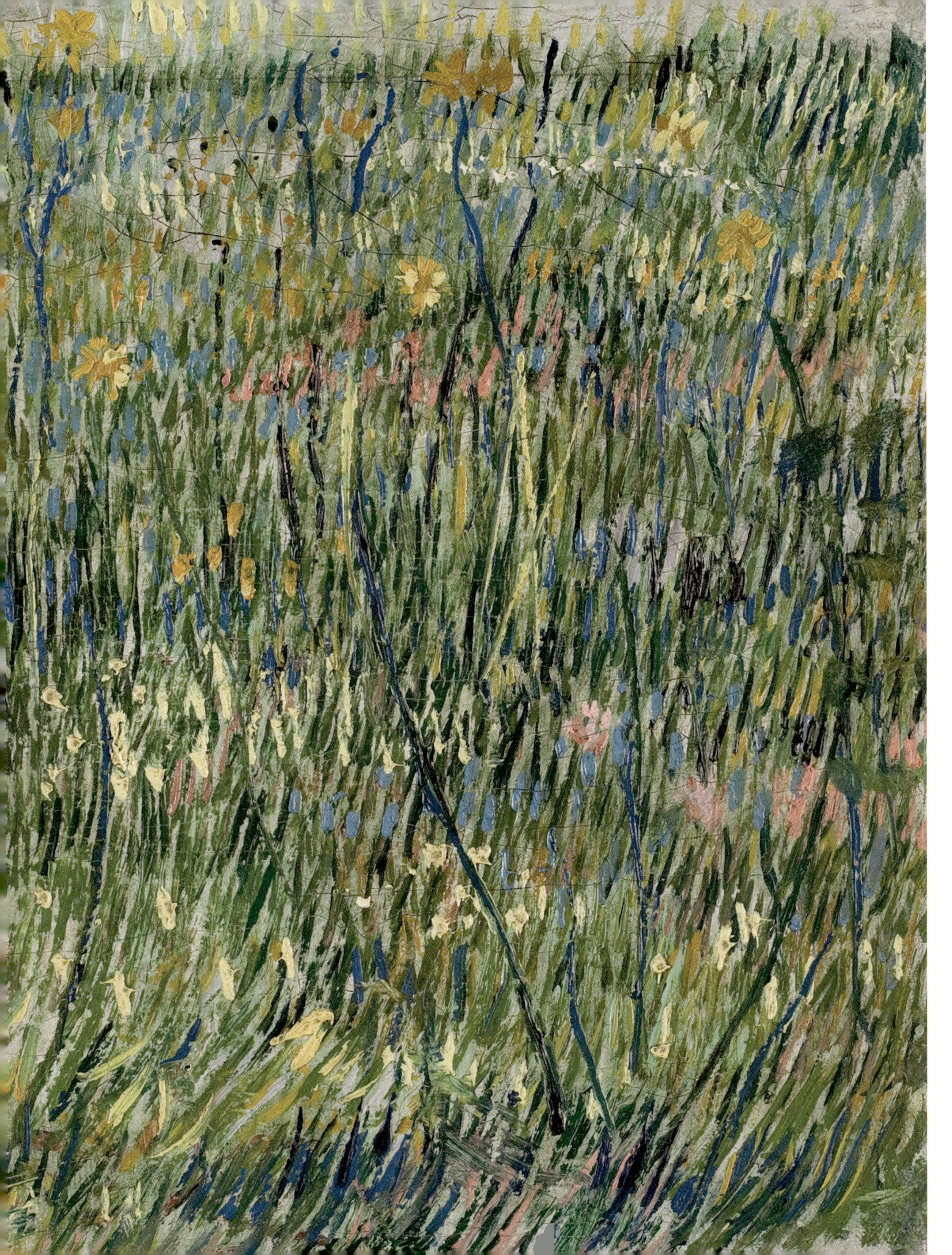

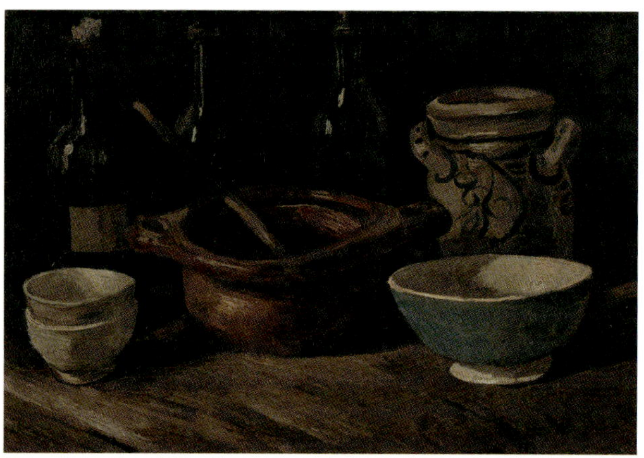

fig. 25

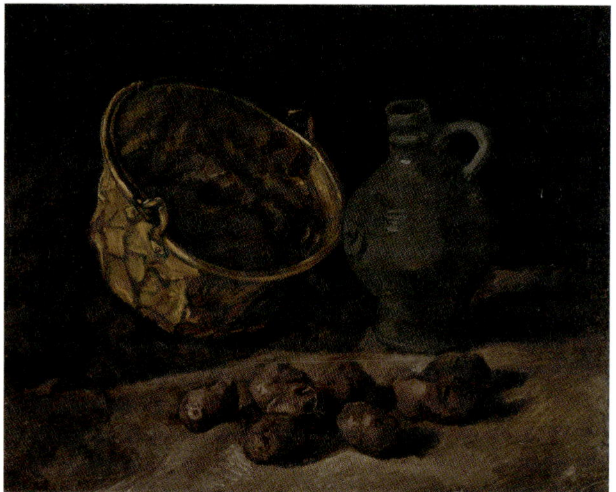

fig. 26

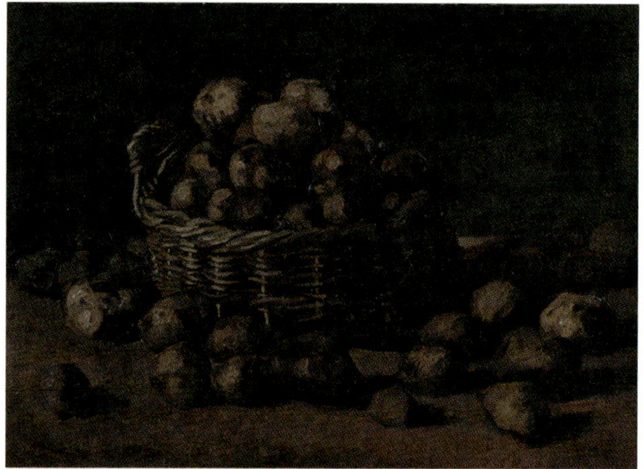

fig. 27

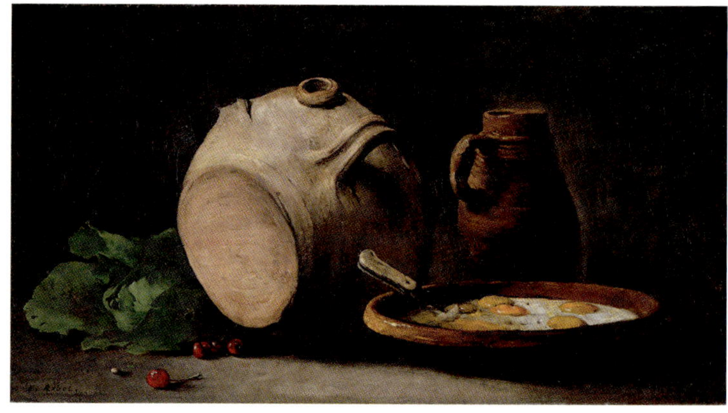

fig. 28

25 Vincent van Gogh, *Still Life with Earthenware and Bottles*, Nuenen, September–October 1885
Oil on canvas, 40.1×56.3 cm
Van Gogh Museum, Amsterdam
(Vincent van Gogh Foundation)

26 Vincent van Gogh, *Still Life with Brass Cauldron and Jug*, Nuenen, September 1885
Oil on canvas, 65.5×80.5 cm
Van Gogh Museum, Amsterdam
(Vincent van Gogh Foundation)

27 Vincent van Gogh, *Basket of Potatoes*, Nuenen, September 1885
Oil on canvas, 45×60.5 cm
Van Gogh Museum, Amsterdam
(Vincent van Gogh Foundation)

28 Théodule Ribot, *Still Life with Eggs*, c. 1865–1875
Oil on canvas, 53×92 cm
Van Gogh Museum, Amsterdam

More than ever before, Van Gogh—in his exploration of rural life—was now deliberately following Millet, and more than ever before, he was projecting an image of himself as a peasant painter by producing a work that afforded an intense and genuine inside look at peasant life. "I really have wanted to make it so that people get the idea that these folk, who are eating their potatoes by the light of their little lamp, have tilled the earth themselves with these hands they are putting in the dish, and so it speaks of manual labour and—that they have thus honestly *earned* their food. I wanted it to give the idea of a wholly different way of life from ours—civilized people. So I certainly don't want everyone just to admire it or approve of it without knowing why. I've had the threads of this fabric in my hands the whole winter long, and searched for the definitive pattern—and if it's now a fabric that has a rough and coarse look, nevertheless the threads were chosen with care and in accordance with certain rules. And it might well prove to be a real peasant painting. *I know that it is.* But anyone who would rather see insipidly pretty peasants can go ahead. For my part, I'm convinced that in the long run it produces better results to paint them in their coarseness than to introduce conventional sweetness" [497]. Pleased with the possibilities of the lithograph, Van Gogh considered making a series of prints depicting scenes of rural life, and he had already thought of a working title for it: "*les paysans chez eux*" [493]. In The Hague, he had intended to produce a similar series, but then, as now, his plan was not realized.[29]

The figure studies that followed *The Potato Eaters* were the previously mentioned large drawings that exuded the spirit of Millet's *Labours of the Fields* (*Travaux des champs*). Van Gogh worked on them for several months. In the summer, his passion for portraying folk types was given new impetus by his acquaintance with the work of Jean-François Raffaëlli, who painted scenes that focus on workers and everyday urban life. In a catalogue of his work, which Vincent received from Theo, Raffaëlli also recorded his thoughts about the expression of character and beauty. Van Gogh did not agree with everything, but it set him to thinking: "*Seemingly there's nothing simpler than painting peasants or rag-pickers and other labourers* but—*no subjects in painting are as difficult as those everyday figures!* There isn't—as far as I know—a single academy where one learns to draw and paint a digger, a sower, a woman hanging a pot over the fire, or a seamstress. But in every town of any consequence at all there's an academy with a choice of models for historical, Arab, Louis XV and, in a word, all figures, provided they don't exist in reality" [515]. But despite his enthusiasm for figures, Van Gogh was unexpectedly steered in the direction of the still life.

RUSTIC STILL LIFES

In September 1885, Van Gogh became the target of gossip. He was unjustly accused of getting Gordina de Groot pregnant, and a Nuenen priest actively discouraged his parishioners from posing for him. The sudden lack of models prompted him to focus on the still life. He had recently read a new book about colour, Félix Bracquemond's *Du dessin et de la couleur* (Paris 1885), and once again he had fallen completely under the spell of colour theories. The still life, so easy to manipulate, was the ideal vehicle for experimenting with colour and tone.

The still lifes that Van Gogh had made between November 1884 and April 1885 had been dictated by the objects in the collection of Antoon Hermans, but now he chose things that he himself thought suitable, and succeeded, more so than the first time, in finding objects that tied in with his study of peasant life. He painted simple objects of earthenware and glass, such as those found in the peasants' cottages—and in his own modest living quarters (fig. 25)—and on one occasion a more ambitious piece, *Still Life with Brass Cauldron and Jug* (fig. 26). In addition to being an exercise in colour, this work provides proof of his competence in the rendering of materials: the earthenware of which the jug is made contrasts nicely with the brass of the much-used and badly dented cauldron.

Of particular interest is a group of seven works that may justifiably be called peasant still lifes. The potatoes and apples that were harvested in September and October were subsequently kept in coarsely woven baskets, and these were all rustic motifs that evoked the atmosphere of rural life that Van Gogh sought to document (fig. 27). Having sent one of the canvases to Theo, he then wrote about it in terms that recall his descriptions of *The Potato Eaters*: "You'll get a large still life of potatoes—where I've tried to get *body* into it—I mean express the material. Such that they become lumps that have weight and are solid, which you'd feel if they were thrown at you, for instance" [533]. One of the rustic still lifes that Van Gogh painted that autumn was *Still Life with Apples and Pumpkins* (cat. 7). Here the fruits of the harvest are freely grouped around a full basket. The result evidently pleased him, because it is one of the few works of this period to bear his signature.

Still lifes featuring simple utilitarian objects, vegetables, fruit and other foodstuffs, whether or not prepared, had become an established genre among the realists. Although such subjects had been depicted in earlier times too, around the mid-nineteenth century this genre became popular with serious buyers. François Bonvin, Théodule Ribot (fig. 28) and Antoine Vollon were a few of the painters who regularly produced such work, and Van Gogh must have seen a considerable number of their paintings.

Later in September and in October, Van Gogh worked on another still-life motif with a distinctly rural character: birds' nests (fig. 29). He had begun to collect these and even paid small sums for certain nests brought to him by the youngsters in the village. Anton Kerssemakers noted that Van Gogh had no fewer than thirty nests, which he stored in two cupboards in his studio. According to Elisabeth (Lies) Van Gogh, her brother even kept them in the branches of a dead tree that stood in his studio.[30]

Van Gogh was an admirer of the work of the writer Jules Michelet and had read, among other things, his *L'Oiseau* (*The Bird*) of 1856, in which Michelet wrote about many aspects of birds, including their ingenious nest-making.[31] An 1881 edition, which Van Gogh possibly knew, contained illustrations by Hector Giacomelli that included depictions of a number of birds' nests.[32] Moreover, Van Gogh associated them with peasants' cottages, for which he had such a weakness. In the winter of 1885–86, Vincent, who was planning to make drawings of birds' nests, sent Theo a charming sketch of what he had in mind (fig. 30), along with the note: "I feel for *the brood and the nests*—particularly those *human* nests, those cottages on the heath and their inhabitants" [533].

Van Gogh made five still lifes of birds' nests. These, together with the still lifes of baskets of potatoes and apples (and a few other still lifes of "uncontained" fruit and vegetables), meant that his initially rather pragmatic approach to the genre had now taken on a very personal touch and had become integrated into the rest of his work, which drew so heavily upon everyday rural life.

NEW AUTUMN LANDSCAPES

In late October and early November 1885, Van Gogh was again in thrall to the autumn. On 3 or 4 November, he wrote in a letter to Theo: "You'll shortly receive two studies of the autumn leaves, one in yellow (poplars)—and the other in orange (oaks)" [538]. These two paintings are now in the Museum Boijmans Van Beuningen and the Kröller-Müller Museum (fig. 31).

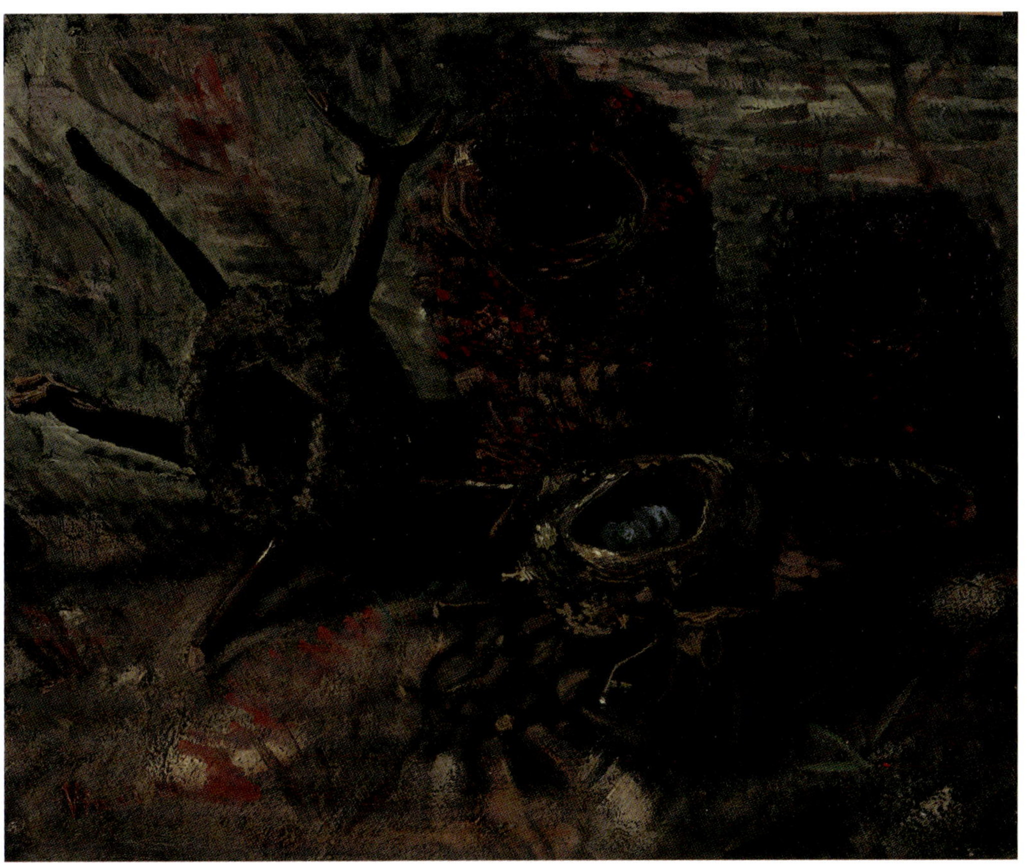

fig. 29

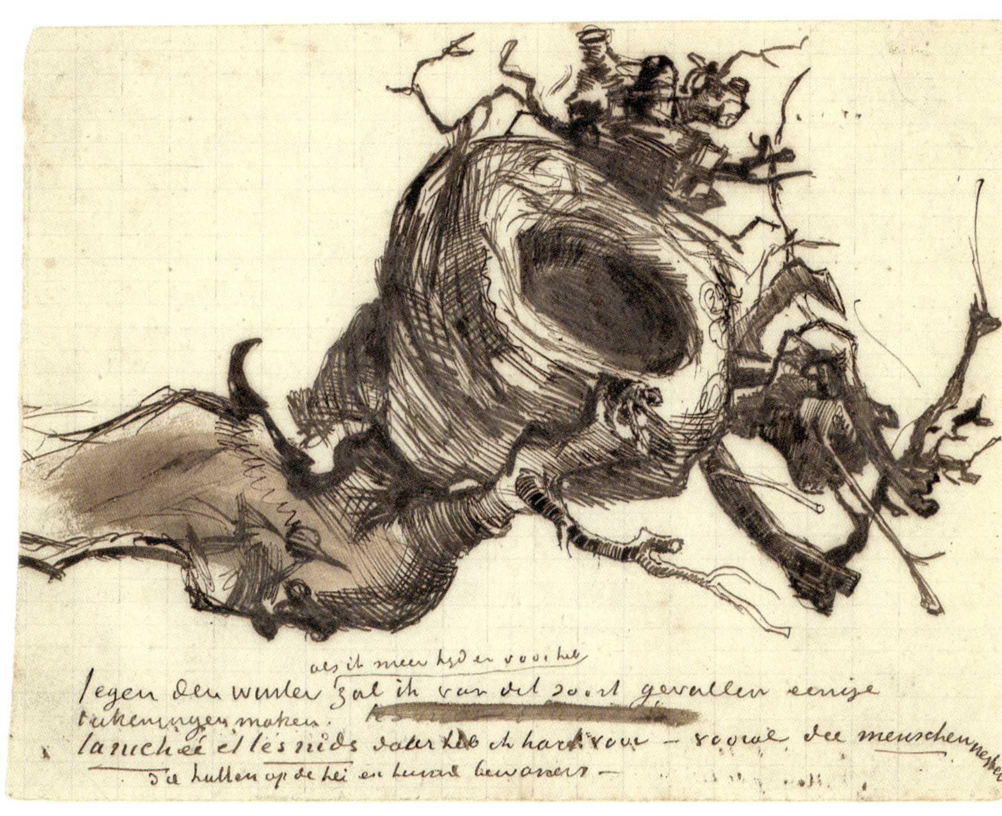

fig. 30

29 Vincent van Gogh, *Birds' Nests*, Nuenen, September–October 1885
Oil on canvas, 39.3×46.5 cm
Van Gogh Museum, Amsterdam
(Vincent van Gogh Foundation)

30 Vincent van Gogh, sketch of a bird's nest in letter 533, Nuenen, 4 October 1885
Pen and ink on paper, 13.4×16.8 cm
Van Gogh Museum, Amsterdam
(Vincent van Gogh Foundation)

In the same letter he reported: "I've also made another autumn study of the pond in the garden at home. There's definitely a painting in that spot. I did already try to get it out once last year. The one I've made now is something of a stiff composition; two trees (orange and yellow) on the right, two bushes (grey-green) in the middle, two trees (brownish yellow) on the left. In front—the pond, black—foreground of withered grass. Background, a glimpse over the hedge onto a very bright green. A sky to harmonize with this in terms of power, in slate-grey and dark blue." Van Gogh does not say whether this study is drawn or painted, nor does he mention the presence of figures. The passage quoted has always been connected with a painting that was lost in 1944 during the Second World War.[33] Its size (92 × 104 cm) puts it among the largest paintings in Van Gogh's œuvre. It was an ambitious work, precisely because the scene was populated by numerous figures, which Van Gogh would certainly not have failed to mention. Although they are also present in a drawing, on close inspection they appear to be a later addition, so he is probably referring in the letter to this drawn version and not to the painting (fig. 32). Before that intervention, the sheet was an autumn study that closely corresponded to the description given by Van Gogh. In addition to the figures, he also inserted the tower standing in the distance in the field, thus adding a completely different layer of meaning to the scene. The drawing subsequently served as the example for the now lost painting, a work he more or less anticipated in the letter.

Although Van Gogh had previously depicted figures in nature or in a park, the above-mentioned drawing and lost painting are the first mature versions of a subject that would become an important, poetically charged motif in his work: people strolling and couples courting in a park. To be sure, the garden in question is a private garden, but it is clear that Van Gogh transformed it into a place with an entirely different character than it had in reality. Not only was the parsonage garden enclosed, but it was not a setting where six people could stroll at the same time—seven, if we count the child with the woman in the lower part of the painting. Four of the figures form two pairs, and this lends the scene an intimate character, owing in particular to the contemplative couple who seem to be enjoying the view of the pond from their place on the landing-pier.

The works that originated at this time were largely influenced, in terms of colour, by a short trip to Amsterdam that Van Gogh had taken in October to visit the newly opened Rijksmuseum. He was overwhelmed by the Old Masters' rich use of colour, and realized that his own dark palette was in danger of becoming very grey indeed. The autumn landscapes of October and November, with their captivating colour contrasts, obviously profited from this new insight.

ANTWERP AND PARIS: IN SEARCH OF MODELS

In November 1885, Van Gogh left Nuenen and travelled to Antwerp, mainly for the purpose of studying more frequently from the model. He enrolled at the academy, where he could draw from plaster casts, and in the evenings he visited two drawing clubs where one could draw from live models. He even succeeded in persuading several women and one man to pose for painted studies of heads (fig. 33).

The instruction at the academy was not to his liking, however, and after three months he was so disheartened that he decided to go to Paris. There he hoped to have more luck in the studio of Fernand Cormon (where he worked from early March to early June 1886). Yet again, he was disappointed, because Cormon's approach to life drawing did not fit in with what had meanwhile become Van Gogh's own uncompromising principles. In both Antwerp and Paris, the instructors had insisted on proceeding

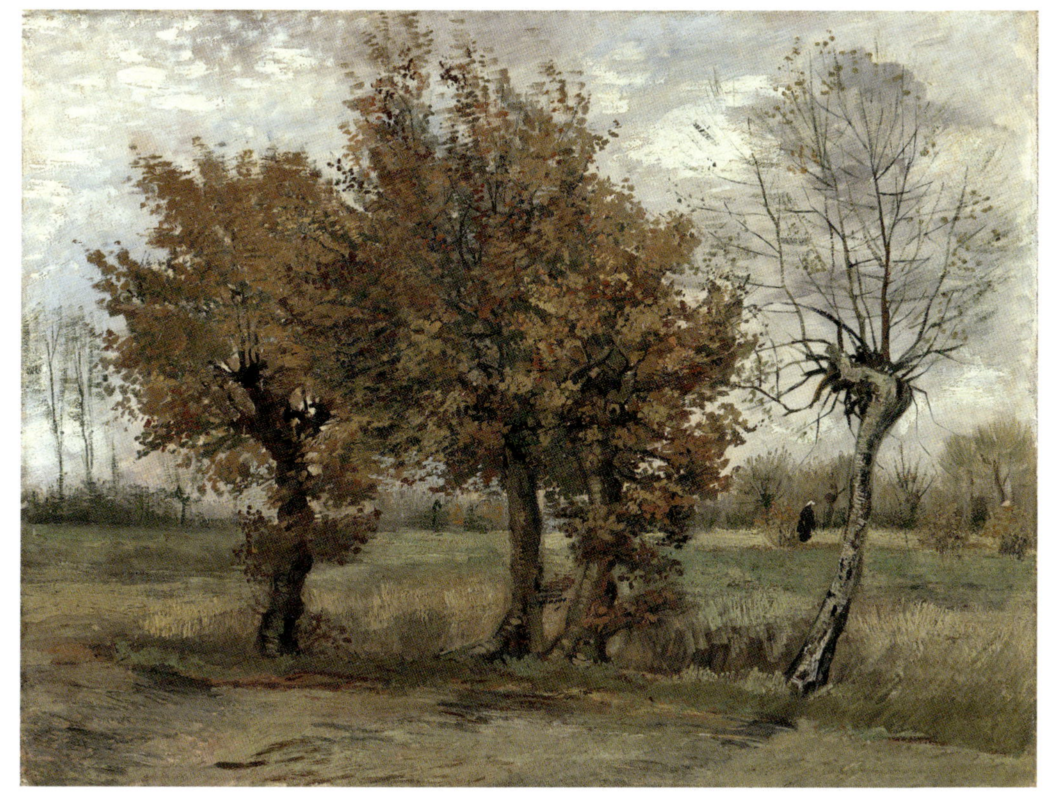

fig. 31

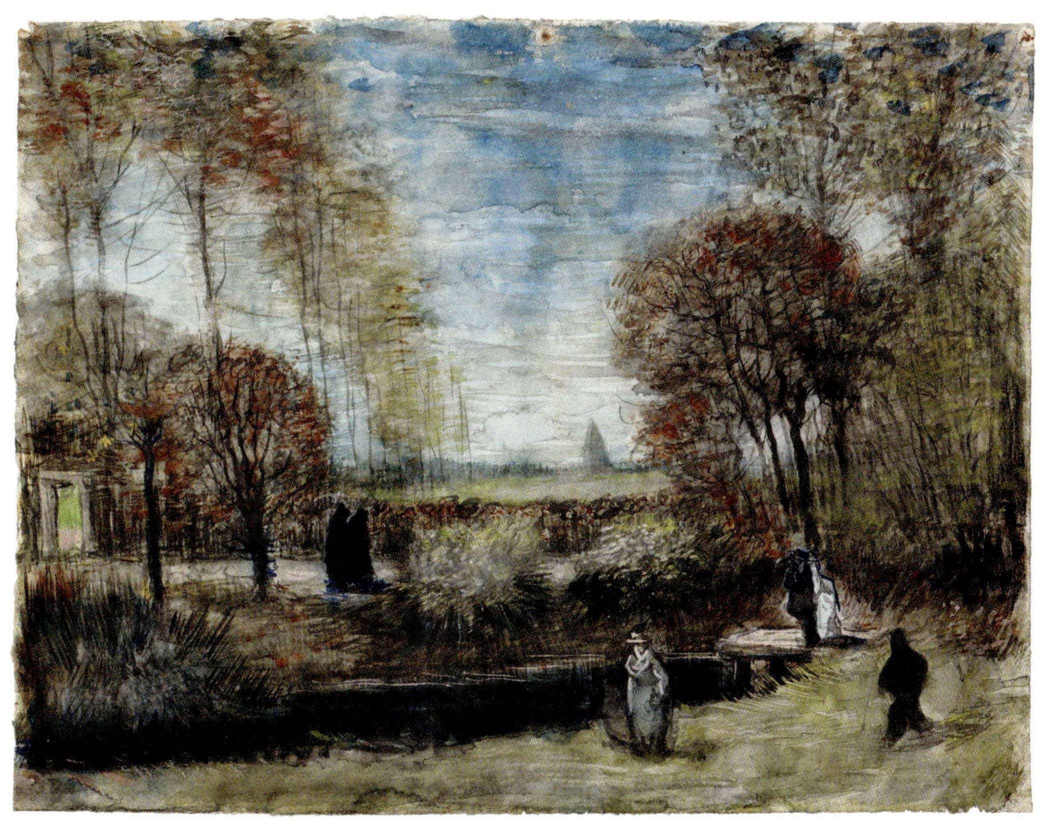

fig. 32

31 Vincent van Gogh, *Autumn Landscape*, November 1885
Oil on canvas, 69 × 87.8 cm
Kröller-Müller Museum, Otterlo

32 Vincent van Gogh, *The Parsonage Garden with Figures*,
late October–early November 1885
Brush and opaque and transparent watercolour on paper, 38 × 49 cm
Private collection

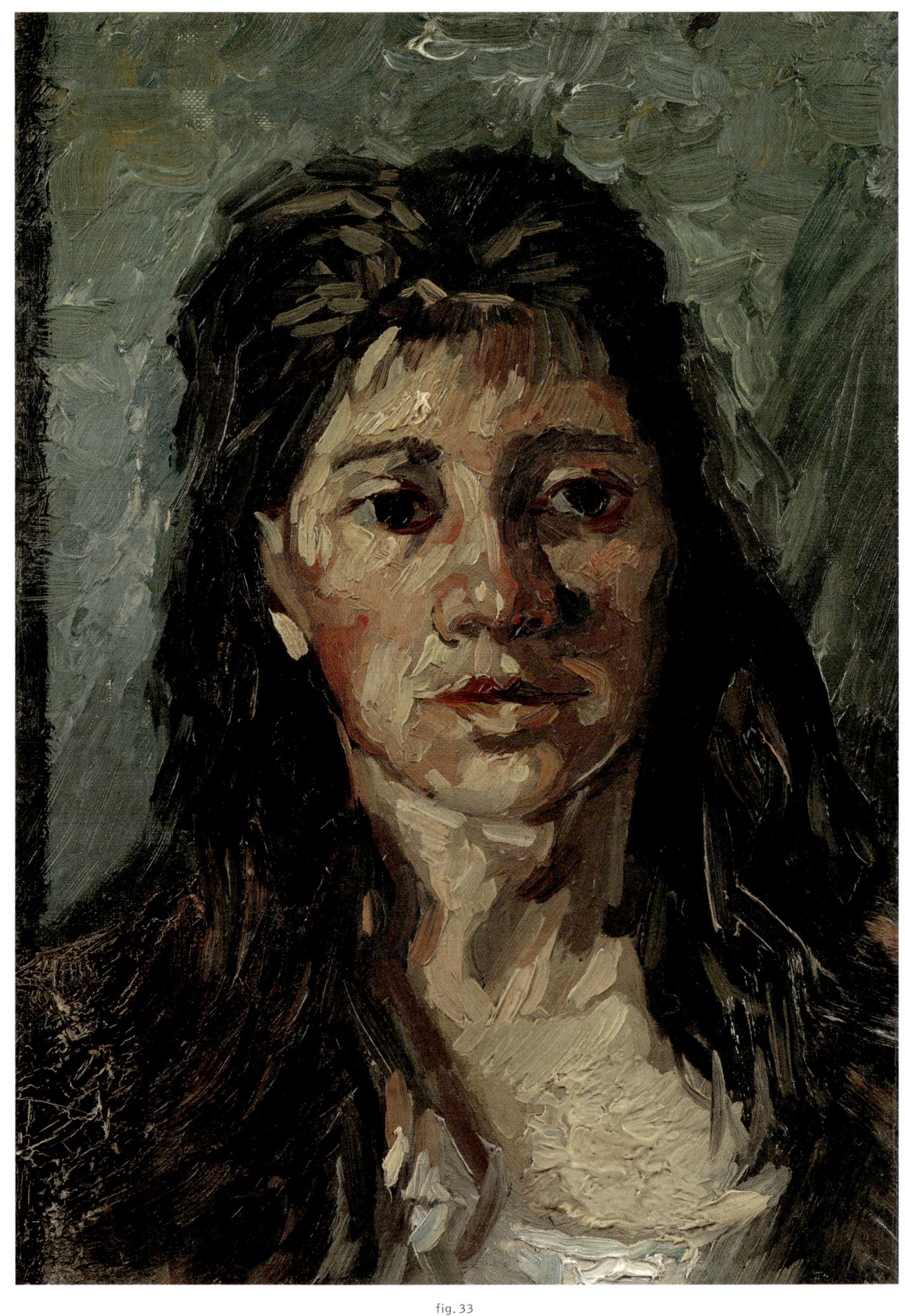

fig. 33

33 Vincent van Gogh, *Head of a Prostitute*, Antwerp, December 1885
Oil on canvas, 35.2 × 24.4 cm
Van Gogh Museum, Amsterdam
(Vincent van Gogh Foundation)

from the contours, whereas Van Gogh had taught himself to start with large volumes. The two working methods were irreconcilable.[34]

Throughout his career, Van Gogh never gave up hope of becoming a figure painter above all else. In a letter of mid-June 1888 to his sister Wil, he recalled the peasants who had posed for him in Nuenen and his difficulty in finding models ever since: "*I still miss* my models who were made for me and whom I still adore; if only I had them here now—I'm sure my 50 paintings would hit the mark. Do you understand that I'm not angry with the human race because they think I'm this or that—I freely admit in advance that they're absolutely right, but it saddens me that I don't have enough power to get what I want to pose for me, where I want and for as long or as short as I want. The problem I have to bring to an end, to overcome, lies *there* and not in the technical difficulty. And today I'm a landscape painter whereas I'm actually more suited to portraits" [626]. When he was living and working in Paris, he wrote the following to Horace Livens, a painter friend: "I have lacked money for paying models, else I had entirely given myself to figure painting" [569]. Later his brother Theo also wrote to his fiancée, Johanna (Jo) Bonger, about the difficulties Vincent was having in finding models: "In Paris he saw masses of things he wanted to paint, but time and again he was prevented from doing so. Models didn't want to pose for him, he was forbidden to sit and work in the street and because of his volatile disposition this repeatedly led to scenes, which upset him *so* much that he became completely unapproachable and by the end of it all he'd had more than enough of Paris."[35]

Even taking into account Van Gogh's lack of both money and social skills, the effort it cost him to find models in Paris is really quite surprising. In The Hague and Nuenen, he had not had much difficulty in persuading people to pose for him, usually for a small remuneration. Later on, in Arles, Van Gogh again complained about the difficulty of finding models, yet in 1888, in the ten months before the first attack of his illness prevented him from working, he made nearly thirty portraits and figure pieces (not including replicas). No doubt (professional) models were considerably more expensive in Paris, but his living expenses were lower there since he had moved in with Theo, who was, moreover, generally willing to give him money. Vincent's difficult character certainly made it hard for him to persuade potential models to pose for him, but other factors must also be taken into account. In Nuenen, his foray into large-format figure painting had not been an unqualified success: he had overpainted some of his more ambitious works, such as the bust of a shepherd, and *The Potato Eaters* had not become the masterpiece he had hoped for. In many of his paintings and drawings of weavers, the loom was in effect the protagonist, and the figures were relegated to supporting roles. By contrast, he had become very good at depicting landscapes and had found his niche within the still life, which might explain why he frequently gravitated to them. Moreover, both genres, in particular the still life, offered excellent opportunities to overcome the artistic barrier with which he had collided head-on early in 1886 upon his arrival in Paris, where he had been confronted with the necessity of forsaking his old dark palette for bright and powerful colours. In any event, the more than two hundred works that Van Gogh painted during his two years in Paris include—apart from an impressive series of self-portraits—only around eighteen figure pieces and portraits, among them likenesses of people from his own circle of friends and acquaintances, such as Julien Tanguy, who sold artists' supplies, and Agostina Segatori, a café owner with whom he had a brief affair (fig. 34, 35). However, those numbers must be revised slightly, for beneath some of the existing paintings are previously executed portraits and a figure painting, which have become visible in X-radiographs.[36] One of these is the portrait of a woman (fig. 36), which was found under the *Self-Portrait with Pipe* (cat. 8).

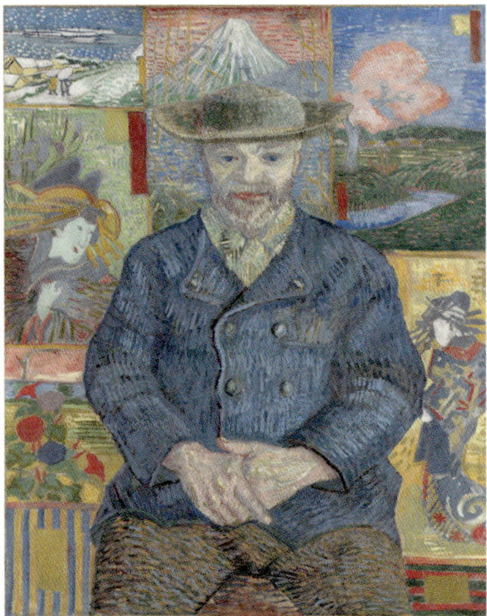

fig. 34

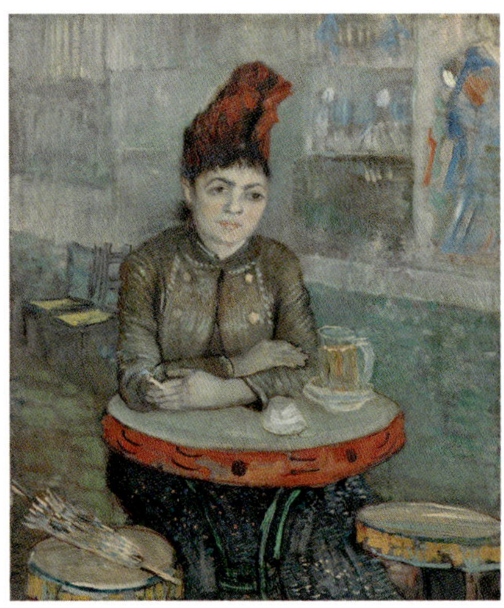

fig. 35

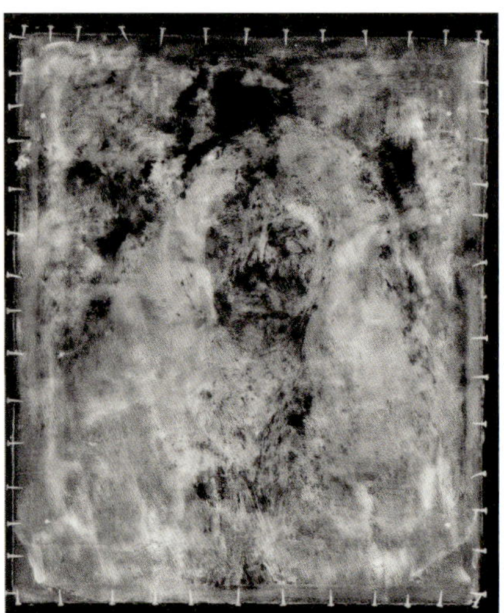

fig. 36

fig. 37

34 Vincent van Gogh, *Portrait of Père Tanguy*, autumn 1887
Oil on canvas, 92 × 73 cm
Musée Rodin, Paris

35 Vincent van Gogh, *In the Café: Agostina Segatori in Le Tambourin*, Paris, January–March 1887
Oil on canvas, 55.5 × 47 cm
Van Gogh Museum, Amsterdam
(Vincent van Gogh Foundation)

36 X-radiograph of *Self-Portrait with Pipe* (cat. 8), September–November 1886, revealing the portrait of a woman painted earlier that year
Oil on canvas, 46 × 38 cm
Van Gogh Museum, Amsterdam
(Vincent van Gogh Foundation)

37 Vincent van Gogh, *Self-Portrait with Straw Hat*, Paris, July–August 1887, painted on the back of a Nuenen still life
Oil on canvas, 41.8 × 31.5 cm
Van Gogh Museum, Amsterdam
(Vincent van Gogh Foundation)

SELF-PORTRAITS

Before his time in Paris, Van Gogh had never painted a self-portrait, which is remarkable, considering that he painted his own likeness there some thirty times. A pragmatic explanation for this is the likely presence in Theo's apartment of a mirror of reasonable size—a prerequisite to self-portraiture—and the fact that Van Gogh even portrayed himself half-length (fig. 38) means that the mirror must have been fairly large. Certainly his studio in Nuenen would have had nothing of the kind, so it would not have occurred to him to make a self-portrait there, even when he found himself without models in September 1885. Of course, this alone does not explain the large number of self-portraits he painted in Paris. Attempts have been made to give psychological reasons for that long series of self-likenesses, attributing them to a period of profound introspection. Another explanation is that a lack of models prompted him to portray himself frequently, as a way of studying the figure and experimenting with colour and technique. But it is difficult to generalize about these self-portraits, because they were not all equally ambitious works by any means. A number of them, for example, were painted on the backs of canvases already used in Nuenen (for still lifes, for instance). Those heads were usually painted rapidly with loose brushstrokes, and without much detail (fig. 37). It is unlikely that Van Gogh intended these as anything but studies. *Self-Portrait with Pipe* (cat. 8), on the other hand, a work painted between September and November 1886, is carefully worked out and shows him as a self-assured, well-dressed and even rather distinguished man. *Self-Portrait with Grey Felt Hat* (cat. 9), painted a year later, is also very accomplished and depicts a more elegant Van Gogh. It is a well-considered experiment, executed in complementary colours and deliberate brushstrokes, and shows him with a kind of halo around his head. The last painting that Van Gogh made in Paris was also a self-portrait, the most ambitious of this long series (fig. 38). He described it several months later, in June 1888, writing from Arles to his sister Wil: "A portrait that I painted in the mirror, and which Theo has: a pink-grey face with green eyes, ash-coloured hair, wrinkles in forehead and around the mouth, stiffly wooden, a very red beard, quite unkempt and sad, but the lips are full, a blue smock of coarse linen, and a palette with lemon yellow, vermilion, Veronese green, cobalt blue, in short all the colours, except of the orange beard, on the palette, the only whole colours, though. The figure against a grey-white wall. You'll say that this is something like, say, the face of—death—in Van Eeden's book or some such thing—very well, but anyway isn't a figure like this—and it isn't easy to paint oneself—in any event *something different* from a photograph? And you see—this is what Impressionism has—to my mind—over the rest, it isn't banal, and one seeks a deeper likeness than that of the photographer" [626]. The detailed description and long list of colours indicate the importance of this canvas. The power of expression Van Gogh tried to achieve in it—a power that transcends the possibilities of photography—betrays the great potential he saw in portrait painting.

THE STILL LIFE AND COLOUR

While in Nuenen, Vincent had carried on discussions about colour with Theo, which, even though they had given him food for thought, had not led to the rejection of his predominantly earth-coloured palette. His visit to the Rijksmuseum in October 1885 had made him realize that a more lively use of colour was essential, but it had not prepared him for the modern treatment of colour which confronted him in Paris in 1886 in the work of the Impressionists, the young avant-garde and the Japanese prints that he had begun to collect. The significance of the colour theories he had studied so zealously in Nuenen—but could not apply convincingly with his grey palette—now began to dawn on him. Another stimulus was the opportunity to see at first hand the work of Delacroix, his supreme guide in the field of colour. Visits to the Louvre deepened his knowledge of the Old Masters, and at the Musée du Luxembourg he studied the more classical modern art of his day (academic artists, realists and the Barbizon masters), which the state had acquired.

Van Gogh did not immediately shake off his Dutch habits, but he did realize the value of patiently exploring the possibilities. The flower still life was a suitable genre in this regard, for it enabled him to experiment with the strong complementary contrasts he had learned about: red against green, blue against orange, yellow against purple. At the same time, he could create subtle contrasts between closely related hues. In October of the following year, he wrote about this to his sister Wil: "Last year I painted almost nothing but flowers to accustom myself to a colour other than grey, that's to say pink, soft or bright green, light blue, violet, yellow, orange, fine red. And when I painted landscape in Asnières this summer I saw more colour in it than before. I'm studying this now in portraits" [574]. Aside from Delacroix, there was another painter who proved to be of great importance to Van Gogh in his exploration of colour: Adolphe Monticelli, who died in June 1886. Van Gogh was bowled over by Monticelli's use of colour and his pastose manner of painting.

After leaving Cormon's studio, Van Gogh began to paint flower still lifes with his usual exacting discipline: he made between thirty-six and forty of them, and they occupied him from June until sometime in September 1886, judging from the flowering time of the blooms in the bouquets. *Roses and Peonies* is one of the works made in June, the month when these flowers bloom (cat. 10). It is an apt example of Van Gogh's approach to colour: the green of the vase and foreground forms a complementary contrast to the red background and the pink of the flowers, while the flowers and background present a subtle interplay of shades of red.

In the summer of 1887, when flowers were again in plentiful supply, Van Gogh resumed painting flower still lifes, to practise using ever-brighter colours, as seen in *Flowers in a Blue Vase* (cat. 11). This work also testifies to his experimentation with Impressionistic and Neo-Impressionistic handling of colour and brushwork. The background is built up of dots and short strokes, a technique he had learned from such artists as Georges Seurat and Paul Signac, though he did not apply it in their dogmatic manner.

Another kind of still life also features prominently in Van Gogh's Paris œuvre. To continue his study of the human figure despite his lack of models, he acquired plaster casts after old sculptures (the surviving casts are preserved in the Van Gogh Museum, fig. 39). He copied these in June 1886, in both drawings and paintings. In addition to exercises in proportions and anatomy, these paintings were also experiments in colour and brushwork. Considering when they were made, they are remarkably bright in colour. As shown by the kneeling figure, a so-called écorché (a "muscleman", or anatomical statuette, cat. 12), Van Gogh used mainly blue, off-white and greyish shades in lively variations. The brushwork is similar to the pastose style also seen in the flower still lifes of that time. In February and March 1887, Van Gogh turned again to these plaster casts, but then in the more Neo-Impressionistic manner he was trying out at that time.

By now the still life had become a fixture in the artist's repertoire, and he continued to develop this genre for the rest of his career. In addition to the still lifes mentioned above, he also painted simple objects. One very realistic motif consists of one or more pairs of heavy shoes of the type workers wear, which he depicted in four Paris paintings, while a fifth displays slightly more elegant footwear. By portraying such extremely humdrum objects, he was following the realistic course he had charted in the Netherlands. *Café Table with Absinthe* (cat. 13) and *Flowerpot with Garlic Chives* (fig. 40) of 1887 also reflect his preference for mundane subjects. The former clearly shows the influence of the Japanese prints which Van Gogh had come to value, and which stimulated him to make daring compositions with bold truncations, as seen, for

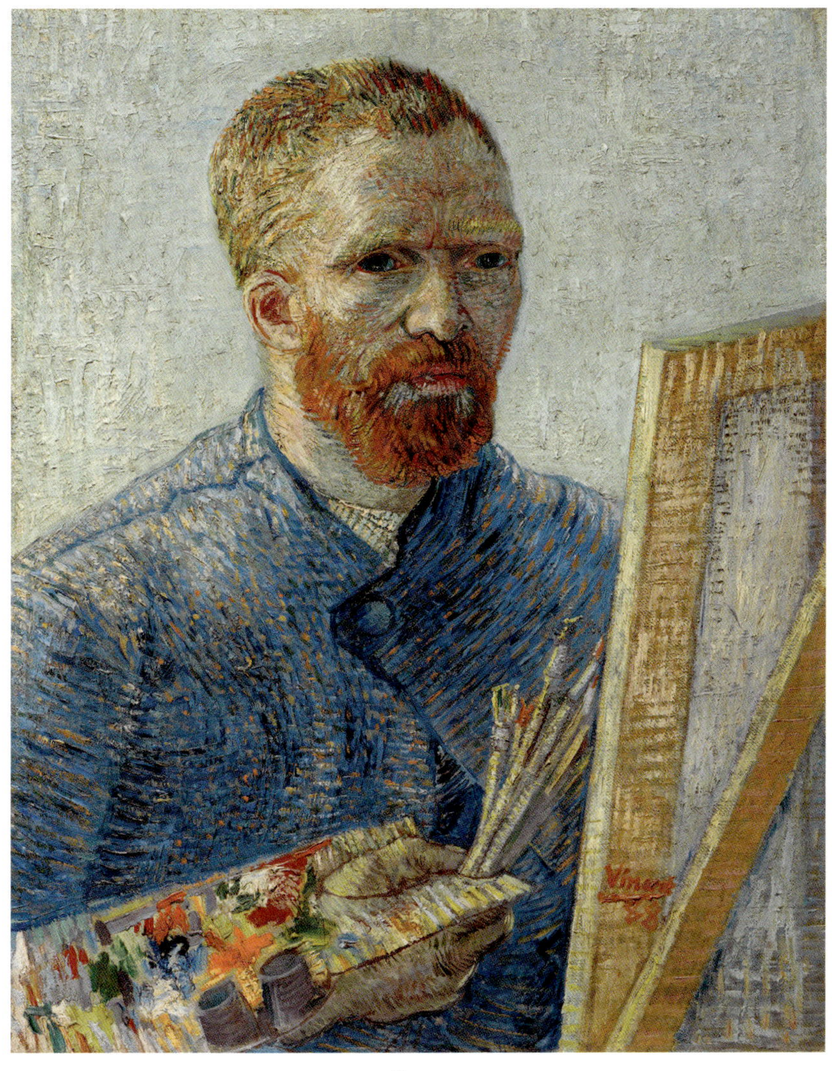

fig. 38

38 Vincent van Gogh, *Self-Portrait as a Painter*, Paris, December 1887–February 1888
Oil on canvas, 65.1 × 50 cm
Van Gogh Museum, Amsterdam
(Vincent van Gogh Foundation)

39 Vincent van Gogh, *Kneeling Ecorché*
Plaster statuette
Van Gogh Museum, Amsterdam
(Vincent van Gogh Foundation)

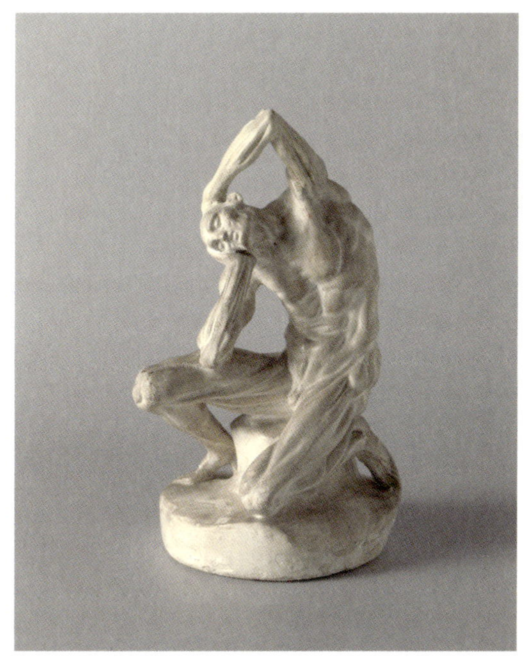

fig. 39

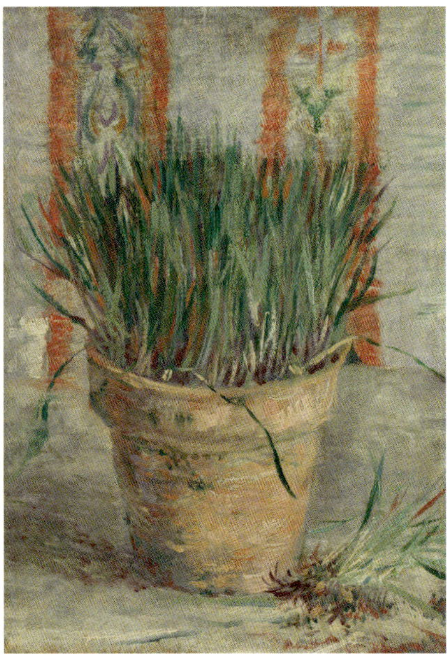

fig. 40

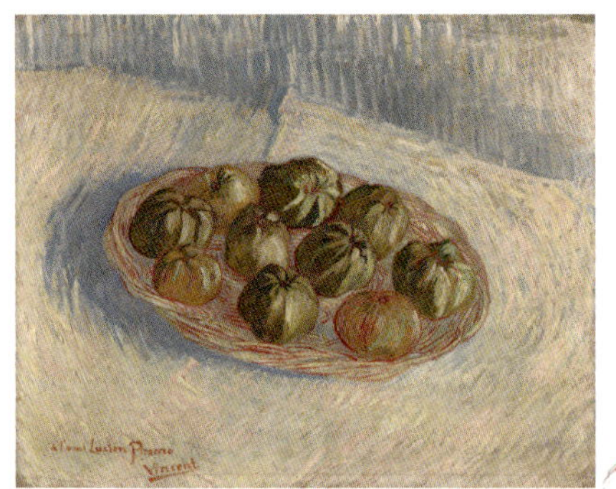

fig. 41

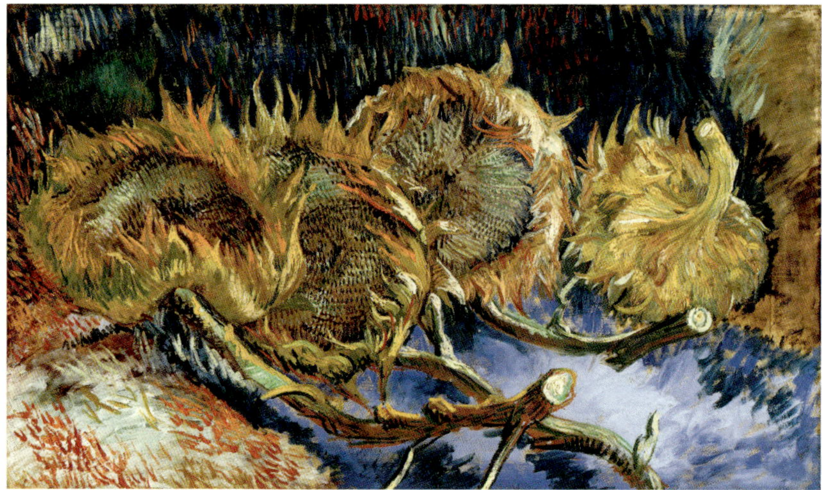

fig. 42

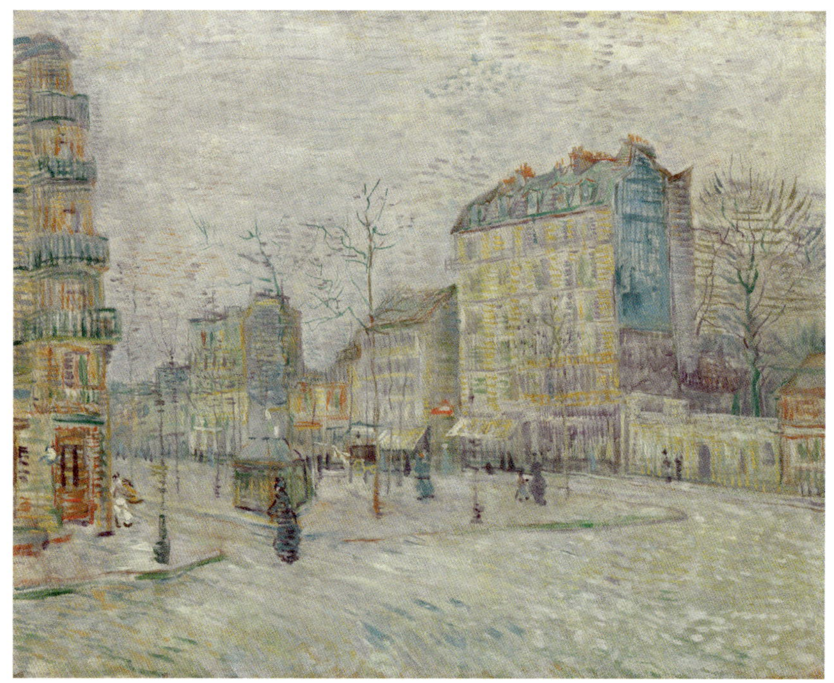

fig. 43

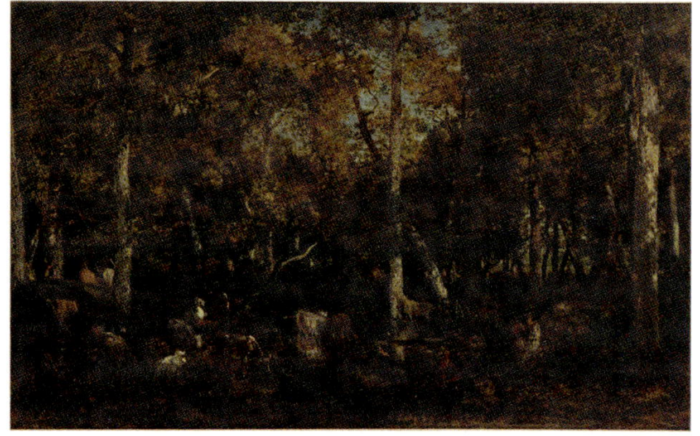

fig. 44

40 Vincent van Gogh, *Flowerpot with Garlic Chives*, Paris, January–February 1887
Oil on canvas, 31.9 × 22 cm
Van Gogh Museum, Amsterdam (Vincent van Gogh Foundation)

41 Vincent van Gogh, *Basket of Apples*, September–October 1887
Oil on canvas, 54 × 65 cm
Kröller-Müller Museum, Otterlo

42 Vincent van Gogh, *Four Sunflowers Gone to Seed*, August–October 1887
Oil on canvas, 59.5 × 99.5 cm
Kröller-Müller Museum, Otterlo

43 Vincent van Gogh, *Boulevard de Clichy*, Paris, March–April 1887
Oil on canvas, 46 × 55.5 cm
Van Gogh Museum, Amsterdam (Vincent van Gogh Foundation)

44 Théodore Rousseau, *Forest Interior*, 1836–1837
Oil on canvas, 65 × 103 cm
Musée d'Orsay, Paris

example, in the chair at right. Both works illustrate his success in inventing modern variants within the realistic tradition. With his modern idiom he continued to paint flowers, fruit (fig. 41) and simple objects. In Nuenen, he had contemplated making a somewhat more serious still life for his brother with the help of the "Gothic" objects in Hermans's collection; now, however, he resolutely clung to the everyday. By this time, the increased importance of the still life in his work was obvious: not only was he painting more of them, but they were beginning to display larger formats and more studied compositions, as seen in *Four Sunflowers Gone to Seed* (fig. 42). That he had meanwhile begun to win recognition from his fellow artists emerges from the fact that Paul Gauguin traded two of Van Gogh's smaller still lifes of sunflowers for a landscape he had done in Martinique.

THE LANDSCAPE INSIDE AND OUTSIDE THE CITY

In Paris, a favourite theme of the Impressionists and their successors had been images of metropolitan life. The boulevards and the new apartment buildings that had sprouted up in recent decades, the cafés, restaurants and nightlife became themes well suited to modern art. Van Gogh also chose such subjects now and then (fig. 43), but they were not a defining feature of his work from this period. Painter friends such as Henri de Toulouse-Lautrec, Émile Bernard and Louis Anquetin depicted the more dissolute aspects of Parisian life, such as cabarets and brothels. Van Gogh made no effort whatsoever to portray such scenes in Paris, and only one half-hearted attempt in Arles,[37] where *The Night Café* (fig. 49) became his most explicit depiction of squalid nightlife.

If life in the big, modern city did not succeed in captivating him, it is none the less striking how often Van Gogh succeeded in his quest for landscape motifs and rustic subjects. He found them outside Paris, in Asnières, and in an otherwise unspecified forest (cat. 14). Such *sous-bois* were a type of wooded view, defined by the forest floor, undergrowth and tree trunks. Van Gogh knew such woodscapes from the Barbizon painters, an example being a canvas by Rousseau that he could have seen at this time in the Louvre (fig. 44).[38]

Close to home, too, in the city itself, Van Gogh found patches of countryside, since he and Theo lived in Montmartre. For centuries this had been a horticultural area, dotted with windmills. In Van Gogh's day, the advance of the city was noticeable mainly on the hill's southern slope, where many very old windmills had already disappeared. Van Gogh documented this state of affairs in a small sketch: at right, new houses are covered in scaffolding; at left, the distant view extends past vegetable gardens, sheds and windmills (fig. 45). He made more than thirty drawings and paintings of this piece of urban countryside. One of his most impressive depictions of it—and a principal work of his Paris œuvre—demonstrates his ability to imbue a relatively simple subject such as vegetable gardens with quiet grandeur (cat. 15). This was, after all, the environment in which he felt most at home.

Van Gogh also documented the windmills of Montmartre in a number of paintings, and while doing so, he must have been thinking of Georges Michel—a forerunner of the School of Barbizon for whom he had great respect—who had painted Montmartre and its environs at a time when Paris had not yet encroached upon this picturesque hill (fig. 46). By the time of Van Gogh's stay in Paris, the three windmills remaining in Montmartre had lost their original function, and two of them, Le Blute-fin and Le Radet, were part of the Moulin de la Galette, a centre of entertainment and nightlife. Evidently this did not bother the artist, for the Blute-fin, a characteristic structure built in 1622, occurs frequently in his work and easily dominates these compositions with its robust appearance (fig. 47). The windmill and vegetable gardens combine to form a compelling image of rusticity.

Thematically related to some extent are the gardens and parks that Van Gogh portrayed throughout his career. In these havens of artificial nature inserted into a town or village setting, he often experienced an intoxicating poetry. In Paris, too, he painted several park views, which are not always easy to pin down to a specific place. One view whose location he did spell out is *Garden with Courting Couples: Square Saint-Pierre* (fig. 48). With this fairly large canvas painted in a Neo-Impressionist style, he again featured lovers in consoling surroundings, a theme he had already portrayed in Nuenen (fig. 32).

Typical of Van Gogh's preferred subject matter is a type of painting that he developed in Paris and continued to vary upon in later years. From a raised vantage point in nature or in a garden, he gazed down on his motif to paint a close-up of a grass-covered patch, a flowerbed or some spot in the woods. *Patch of Grass* (cat. 16) is one such painting, which consists of nothing but blades of grass and small flowers, tinged with a simplicity that recalls, once again, the Japanese prints that had come to play such a significant role in his work.

MODERNIZING TRADITION

In the south of France, Van Gogh transformed himself into one of the most original painters of his time, having equipped himself with a very personal idiom, not only in terms of style and technique, but also with regard to choice of subject. *The Bedroom* (fig. 69), *The Night Café* (fig. 49), *Starry Night* (fig. 50) and a woman reading in a library (fig. 63) are good examples of original subjects. Yet much of his work also displays the great continuity in his art and thought. In the summer of 1888, Van Gogh was hard at work in Arles, portraying the colourfulness of the season in his modern palette, but in a letter to Theo of 8 August, he again writes admiringly about his old heroes: "Millet gave us the essence of the peasant, and now, yes, there's Lhermitte, it's true there are one or two more, *Meunier*... and have we now more generally learned how to see peasants—*no,* hardly anyone knows how to polish one off. Isn't it partly the fault of Paris and the Parisians, fickle and disloyal like the sea? Well then, you're damned right to say, let's go quietly on our way, working for ourselves. You know, whatever becomes of sacrosanct Impressionism, I'd still myself have the wish to do the things that the *previous* generation, Delacroix, Millet, Rousseau, Diaz, Monticelli, Isabey, Decamps, Dupré, Jongkind, Ziem, Israëls, Meunier, a heap of others, Corot, Jacque... could understand" [657]. A short time later, he sent instructions to his sister Wil, who was visiting Theo in Paris: "I hope that you'll often go and look at the [Musée du] Luxembourg and the modern paintings in the Louvre so that you get an idea of what a Millet, a Jules Breton, a Daubigny, a Corot is. You can keep the rest. Except—Delacroix. Although people are now working in yet another very different manner, the work of Delacroix, of Millet, of Corot, that remains and the changes don't affect it" [667].

At this time, Van Gogh himself was working on his series of sunflowers, whose colour, style of painting and idiom made them marvels of modernity. He had acquired his contemporary idiom in Paris by studying the modern movements there and exploring Japanese art. This had opened his eyes to powerful colours, expressive brushwork and bold compositions. His appreciation of the work of the Impressionists and the Paris avant-garde was sincere. Japan had become a shining example, and he hoped to find its equivalent in Provence. The Japanese masters had sharpened his gaze and taught him to look at things with a "Japanese eye".[39] Yet in spite of all

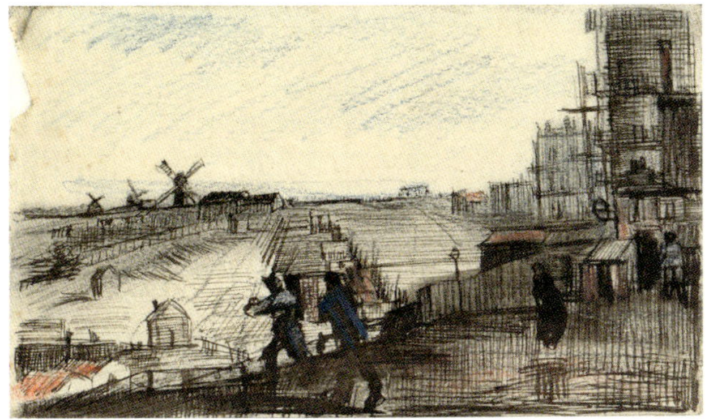

fig. 45

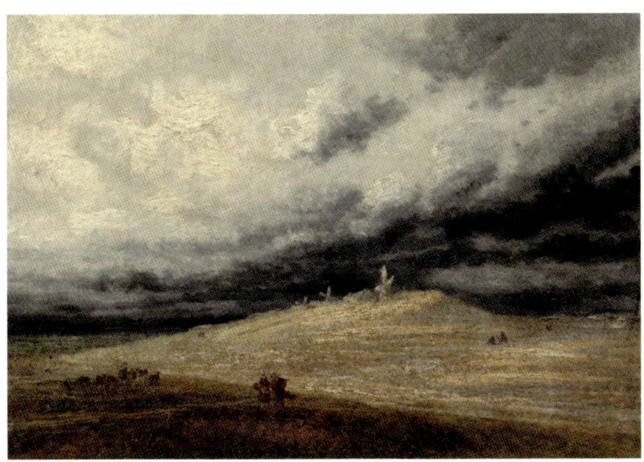

fig. 46

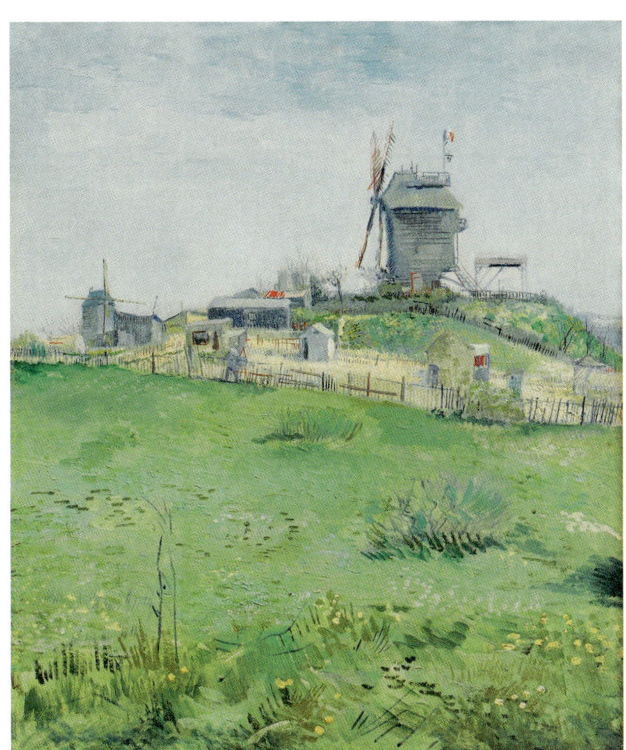

fig. 47

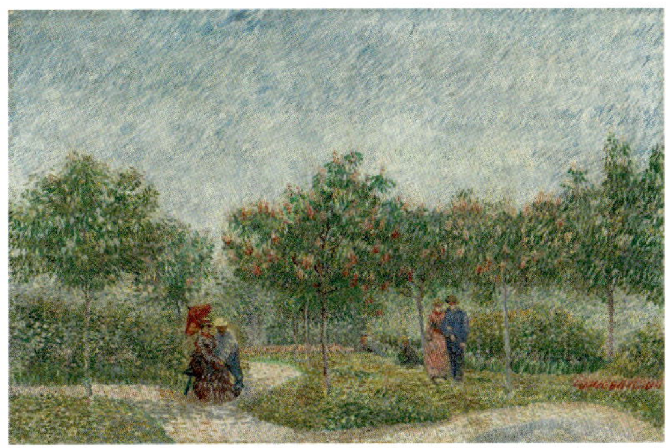

fig. 48

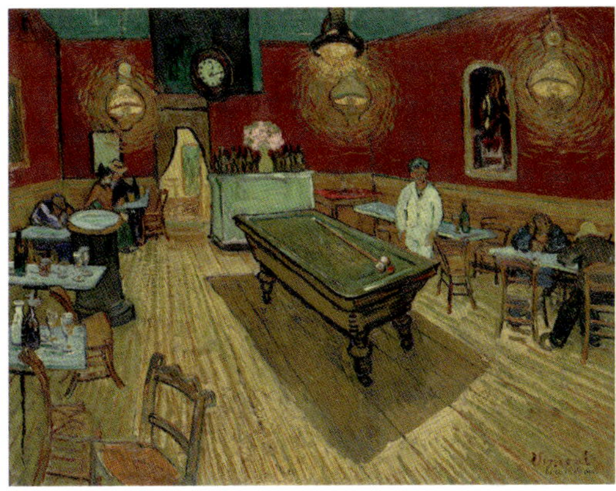

fig. 49

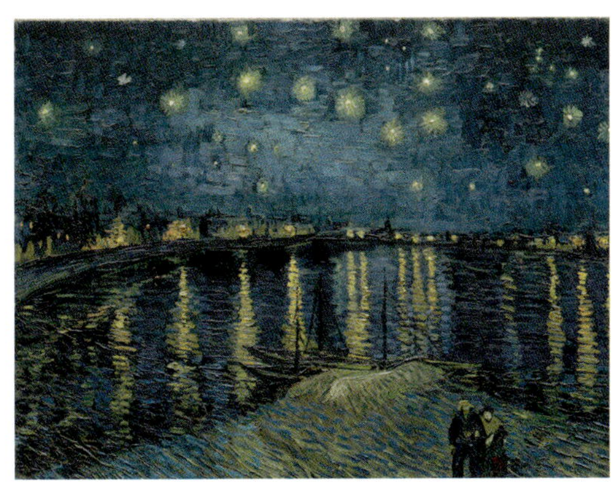

fig. 50

45 Vincent van Gogh,
View of Montmartre, Paris,
May–September 1886
Chalk, pen and brush and ink on paper,
10.1 × 16.8 cm
Van Gogh Museum, Amsterdam
(Vincent van Gogh Foundation)

46 Georges Michel,
Three Windmills, c. 1814–1843
Oil on paper on canvas, 50.3 × 69.4 cm
The Mesdag Collection, The Hague

47 Vincent van Gogh, *Le Moulin de la Galette*, 1886–1887
Oil on canvas, 47.3 × 39.4 cm
Carnegie Museum of Art, Pittsburgh.
Acquired through the generosity
of the Sarah Mellon Scaife Family

48 Vincent van Gogh, *Garden with Courting Couples: Square Saint-Pierre*,
Paris, May 1887
Oil on canvas, 75 × 113 cm
Van Gogh Museum, Amsterdam
(Vincent van Gogh Foundation)

49 Vincent van Gogh,
The Night Café, September 1888
Oil on canvas, 72.4 × 92.1 cm
Yale University Art Gallery, New Haven.
Bequest of Stephen Carlton Clark

50 Vincent van Gogh,
Starry Night, 1888
Oil on canvas, 72.5 × 92 cm
Musée d'Orsay, Paris

that, Van Gogh's thinking was still shaped by his old loves, although he had shaken off the grey palette of the Hague School.[40] Even without mentioning them frequently, he kept the painters of Barbizon and the older masters such as Rembrandt, Van Goyen and Koninck firmly in mind, and although he was sometimes unaware of it, they continued to guide his choices.

When Van Gogh arrived in Arles on 20 February 1888, he was dismayed at the cold and snow that was afflicting a large part of France at the time and had been one of his reasons for fleeing Paris. When milder weather finally arrived in the second week of March, he began to explore the surrounding countryside in earnest.

It is remarkable to see how Van Gogh primarily sought, certainly in the first six months, subjects that were already familiar to him. This is definitely the case with *Pollard Willows at Sunset* (cat. 17), which must be one of the first works that he made in March 1888.[41] The trees are still bare and hardly any green is visible in the ground cover, which had been blanketed with snow for weeks. Willows, whether or not pollarded, do indeed grow in Provence, but they are not its most characteristic tree. Remarkably, the cypresses so typical of the region figure in works from Arles only as accessories; they did not arouse Van Gogh's interest until Saint-Rémy, when olive groves, too, finally became a main motif.[42] Pollard willows, on the other hand, are a very familiar sight in the Dutch landscape in particular, and they were a popular subject among artists. Van Gogh was extremely fond of them, and had depicted them (as well as pollarded birches, which look similar) a number of times in the Netherlands. Just as in the Hague drawing of tree roots (fig. 12), he saw their resemblance to people, in this case old men.[43]

A spring motif in the form of blossoming orchards soon presented itself with a power that Van Gogh had never experienced in the Netherlands. He embarked on a long series of works depicting this subject, which was popular in both Western and Japanese art. Back in 1875, he had admired a spring landscape by Daubigny in the Musée du Luxembourg,[44] and had seen it again in Paris only recently (fig. 51). His partiality for seasonal landscapes had been strengthened by the blossoming orchards in his collection of Japanese prints.

In the Netherlands and Paris, Van Gogh had drawn and painted blossoming trees only rarely; he had probably never seen orchards like the ones he now encountered in Provence. He eagerly seized upon this traditional motif and set to work in his modern style of painting: "At present I'm busy with the fruit trees in blossom: pink peach trees, yellow-white pear trees. I follow no system of brushwork at all; I hit the canvas with irregular strokes which I leave as they are, impastos, uncovered spots of canvas—corners here and there left inevitably unfinished—reworkings, roughnesses; well, I'm inclined to think that the result is sufficiently worrying and annoying not to please people with preconceived ideas about technique" [596].

In that letter to Émile Bernard, he strongly emphasized his free approach, since the two men were involved in a discussion about painting from the imagination—which Bernard advocated—as opposed to painting from life. Van Gogh was an ardent champion of the latter method, and was seeking a new approach to it in style and technique. He described this manner of working in more detail with regard to one of his orchard paintings—probably the variation on *Orchard Bordered by Cypresses* (cat. 18), now in a private collection[45]—and accompanied the text with a sketch (fig. 52): "Here's a croquis, by the way, the entrance to a Provençal orchard with its yellow reed fences, with its shelter (against the mistral), black cypresses, with its typical vegetables of various greens, yellow lettuces, onions and garlic and emerald leeks. While always working directly on the spot, I try to capture the essence in the drawing—then I fill the spaces demarcated by the outlines (expressed or not) but felt in every case, likewise with simplified tints, in the sense that everything that will be

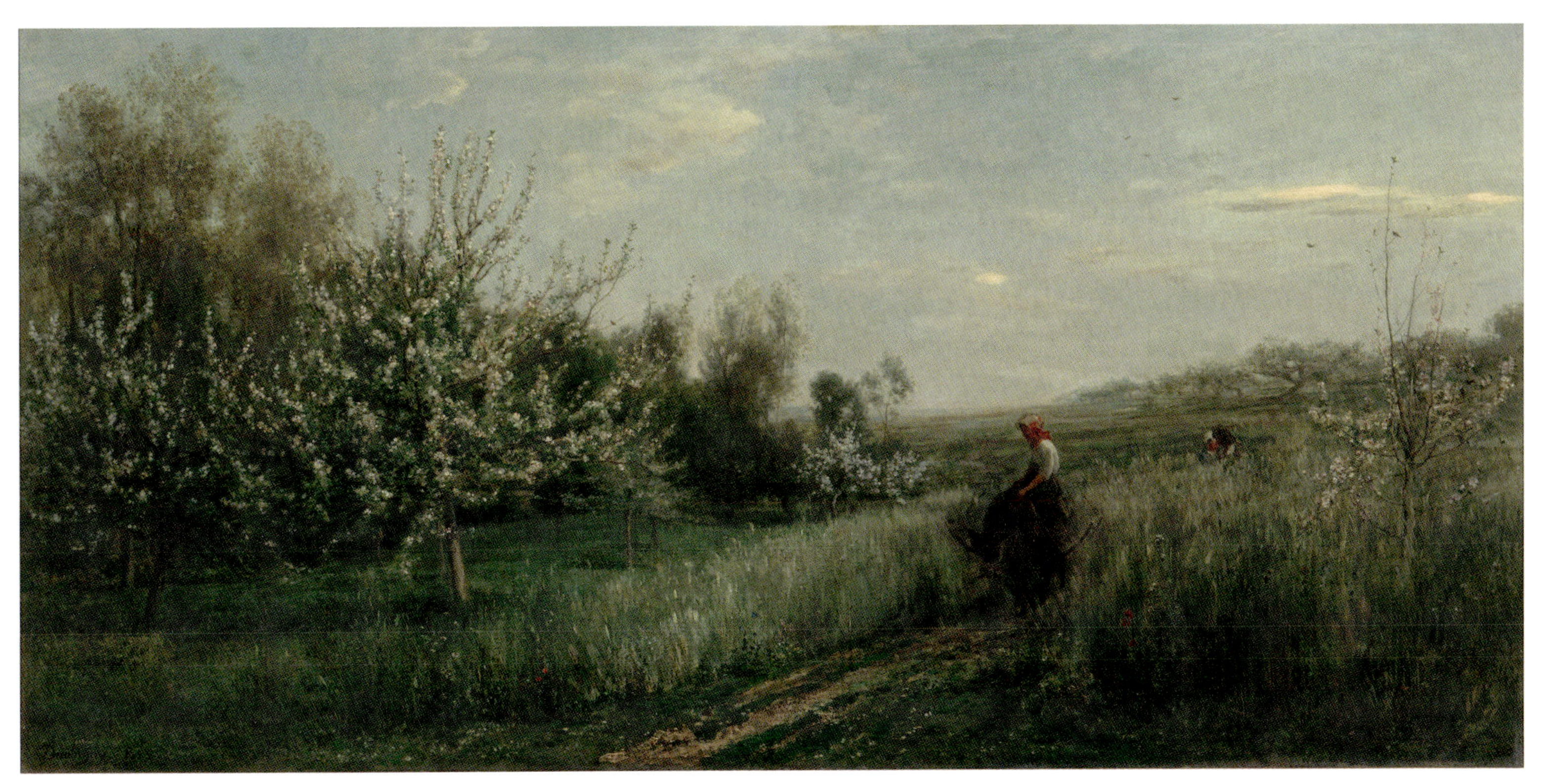

fig. 51

51 Charles-François Daubigny,
Spring, 1857
Oil on canvas, 96 × 193 cm
Musée des Beaux-Arts, Chartres

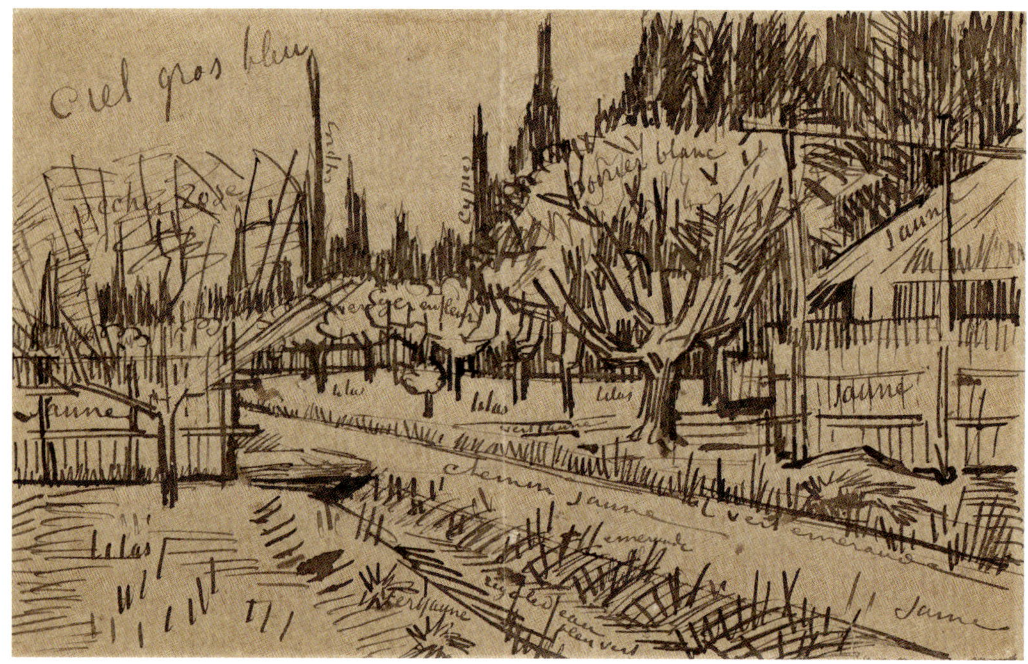

fig. 52

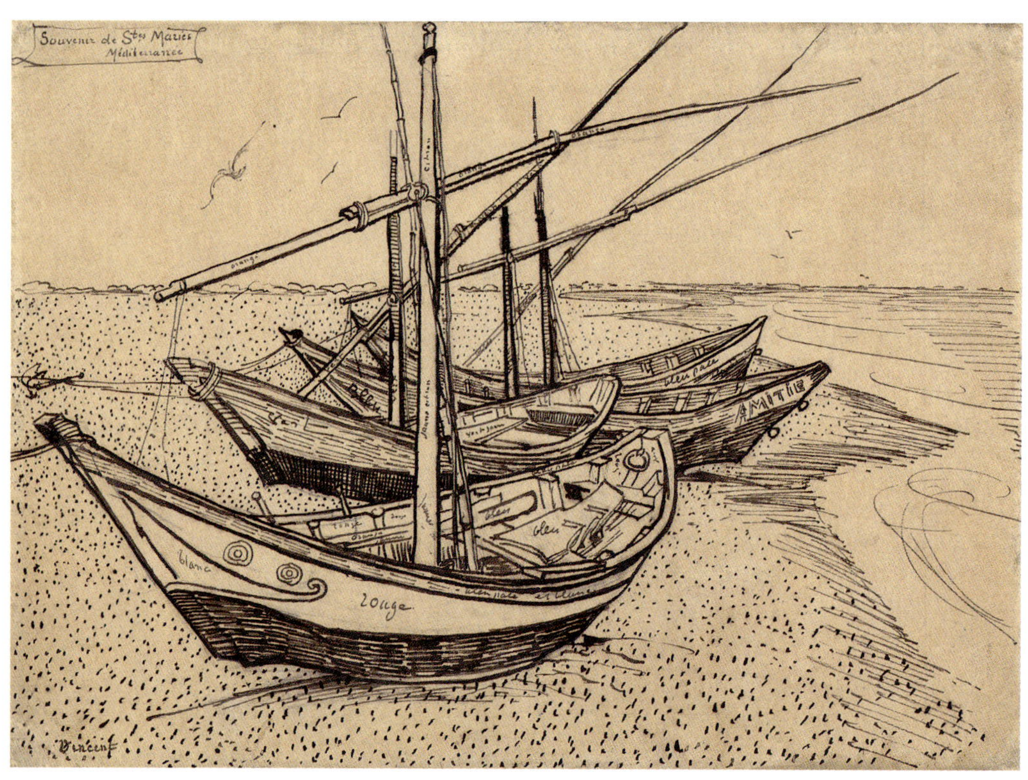

fig. 53

52 Vincent van Gogh, sketch in letter 596, *Orchard boardered by cypress trees*, c. 12 April 1888
Thaw Collection, The Pierpont Morgan Library, New York

53 Vincent van Gogh, *Fishing Boats on the Beach at Les Saintes-Maries-de-la-Mer*, June 1888
Pencil, pen and ink on paper, 39.5 × 53.3 cm
Private collection, New York

earth will share the same purplish tint, that the whole sky will have a blue tonality, that the greenery will either be blue greens or yellow greens, deliberately exaggerating the yellow or blue values in that case." Colour, technique and the quest for expression were the means by which he sought to revamp traditional motifs. In describing the vegetables—lettuce, onions, leeks—he seems to be emphasizing the ordinariness and rusticity of the subject.

The enthusiasm that had taken hold of Van Gogh resulted not only in a series of fourteen paintings and two drawings, but also in thoughts about the connection between certain canvases. He made a copy of *Pink Peach Trees*, which he considered one of his best landscapes,[46] in order to combine it with two other orchard paintings to form a triptych.[47] The work discussed just above (cat. 18) was given a pendant, and those two were intended to form a diptych.[48] The fact that diptychs and triptychs are frequently seen in churches lends a devotional touch to this form of presentation.

In the second half of April, the flowering season of the fruit trees came to an end, and Van Gogh had to go in search of other landscape motifs. One of these, *Field with Irises near Arles* (cat. 19), painted in May, is a powerfully colourful rendering of a highly original composition, which clearly shows what he meant by looking with a Japanese eye. The irises, which brazenly cut a diagonal through the image, are the actual subject of the picture, while the town of Arles in the background is a mere detail. Van Gogh described the motif as "a Japanese dream" [609].

ON THE MEDITERRANEAN COAST

During his years in The Hague, Van Gogh had often visited Scheveningen, where he had depicted seascapes, a genre with an age-old tradition. In late May and early June 1888, His Dutch seascapes were given Mediterranean sequels, when he travelled to the fishing village of Saintes-Maries-de-la-Mer to study the sea and the fishermen. Though he spent less than a week there, he made a series of drawings and paintings on which he elaborated after returning to Arles by making paintings after some of the drawings and drawings after paintings.

Vincent painted and drew boats at sea and on the beach, and wrote to Theo, proudly telling him about a drawing of boats on the beach (fig. 53). For many years Van Gogh had made use of a perspective frame, an instrument that helped him to translate three-dimensional space and perspective into a convincing, two-dimensional image. The frame, which he placed between himself and his subject, contained a horizontal, a vertical and two diagonal threads. That same pattern was transferred to the paper or canvas, making it possible to reproduce the correct proportions and perspective. For the boats with their complicated play of lines, however, Van Gogh had not needed it, thanks to his ever-increasing proficiency: "I'm also convinced that it's precisely through a long stay here that I'll bring out my personality. The Japanese draws quickly, very quickly, like a flash of lightning, because his nerves are finer, his feeling simpler. I've been here only a few months but—tell me, in Paris would I have drawn *in an hour* the drawing of the boats? Not even with the frame. Now this was done without measuring, letting the pen go" [620]. Back in Arles, he made a painting after this sheet (cat. 20). He must have had the painting in mind while making the drawing, because he supplied it with colour notations.

Saintes-Maries-de-la-Mer offered Van Gogh not only the sea but also another traditional motif that was very dear to him: the simple cottages in which the fishermen and shepherds lived with their families. These humble dwellings strongly resembled the cottages he had painted in Nuenen. In fact, depictions of the simple living quarters of peasants and labourers run like a thread through his œuvre.

PEN DRAWINGS

Throughout his time in Arles, Van Gogh did a great deal of drawing, mainly with the pen. He had found a type of reed that was well suited to making pens, and he discovered that he had a real aptitude for this instrument. The body of drawings from Arles (and later from Saint-Rémy) is exceptionally impressive. The pen drawings are mainly of landscapes, but he also drew figures from life. In addition, he made a small number of works in watercolour and in mixed techniques.[49]

THE PLAIN OF LA CRAU, SUMMERY LANDSCAPES

Four kilometres north of Arles lies the plain of La Crau and a rocky hill with the abbey of Montmajour, which Van Gogh saw in ruins, though it has since been restored. La Crau is a steppe-like area that had largely been given over to agriculture by Van Gogh's time.[50] In May 1888, on and near Montmajour, he made a series of modestly sized pen drawings and one larger sheet, followed in July by another six large ones. The series of seven large works is a spectacular example of his abilities as a draughtsman (fig. 54).

The wheat harvest on La Crau began in June, and Van Gogh embraced this opportunity to paint one of his favourite subjects. In his eyes, the growth cycle of wheat, culminating in the harvest, stood for the glory of life itself and made him think of the infinite, the everlasting, of which the sower and the wheat sheaf were symbols.[51] He composed a panoramic landscape which he executed in two drawings and a painting (fig. 55). "I have a new subject on the go, green and yellow fields as far as the eye can see, which I've already drawn twice and am starting again as a painting, just like a Salomon Koninck," he wrote to Theo, though he was a bit confused, because he meant Philips Koninck, the seventeenth-century painter of panoramic landscapes [623]. He went on to say that the painting also resembled "something by Michel or like Jules Dupré", thereby making all the more clear which painters he was trying to emulate. That month he painted another half-dozen landscapes with wheatfields.

The summer also brought gardens into bloom. Van Gogh, immediately fascinated, captured them in drawings and paintings in July and August (fig. 56). In July, he found a garden near Montmajour, and later he was guided by a local resident to other gardens in exuberant bloom, which he would never have found on his own.

ONCE AGAIN, THE HUMAN FIGURE

Shortly after arriving in Arles, Vincent reported to Theo that he had made three studies, including "an old woman of Arles" [578]. This signalled a good start, since he hoped to devote a great deal of attention in his new surroundings to the human figure. The identity of the woman in the painting is not known, but in any case she was the kind of model he preferred: with a furrowed face, simply dressed with a shawl and a scarf wrapped around her grey hair (cat. 21). There were no other figure pieces for the time being, because Van Gogh could not find anyone else to pose for him, until June: "I have a model at last—a Zouave—he's a lad with a small face, the neck of a bull, the eye of a tiger, and I started doing one portrait and started again on another. The bust-length I painted of him was terribly hard. In a uniform the blue of blue enamel saucepans, with dull orange-red trimmings and two lemon-yellow stars on his chest, a common blue and very hard to do. I've stuck his very tanned, feline

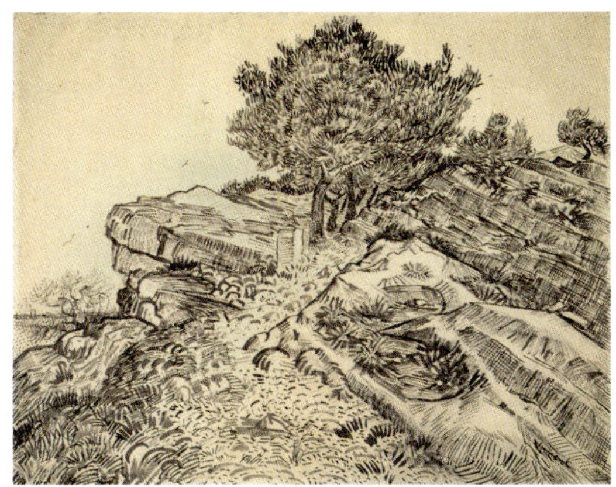

fig. 54

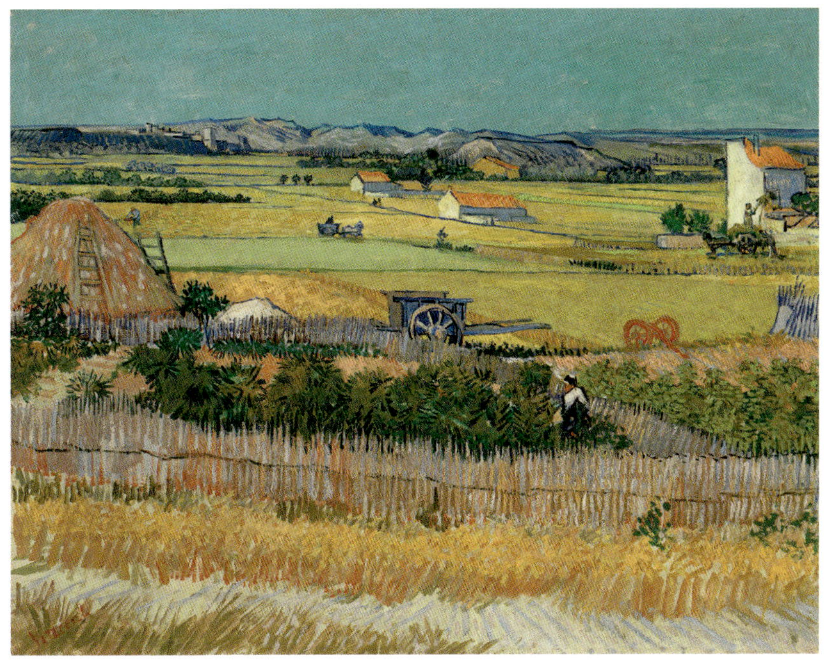

fig. 55

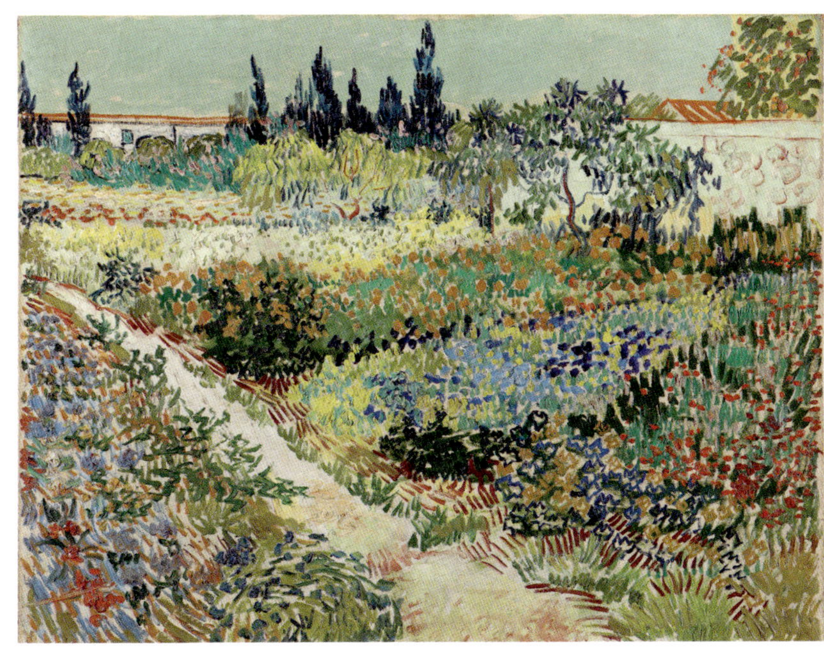

fig. 56

54 Vincent van Gogh, *The Rock of Montmajour with Pine Trees*, Arles, July 1888
Pencil, pen and reed pen and brush and ink, on paper, 49.1 × 61 cm
Van Gogh Museum, Amsterdam
(Vincent van Gogh Foundation)

55 Vincent van Gogh, *The Harvest*, Arles, June 1888
Oil on canvas, 73.4 × 91.8 cm
Van Gogh Museum, Amsterdam
(Vincent van Gogh Foundation)

56 Vincent van Gogh, *Garden at Arles*, July 1888
Oil on canvas, 73 × 92 cm
Gemeentemuseum Den Haag, The Hague—Loan Cultural Heritage Agency of the Netherlands

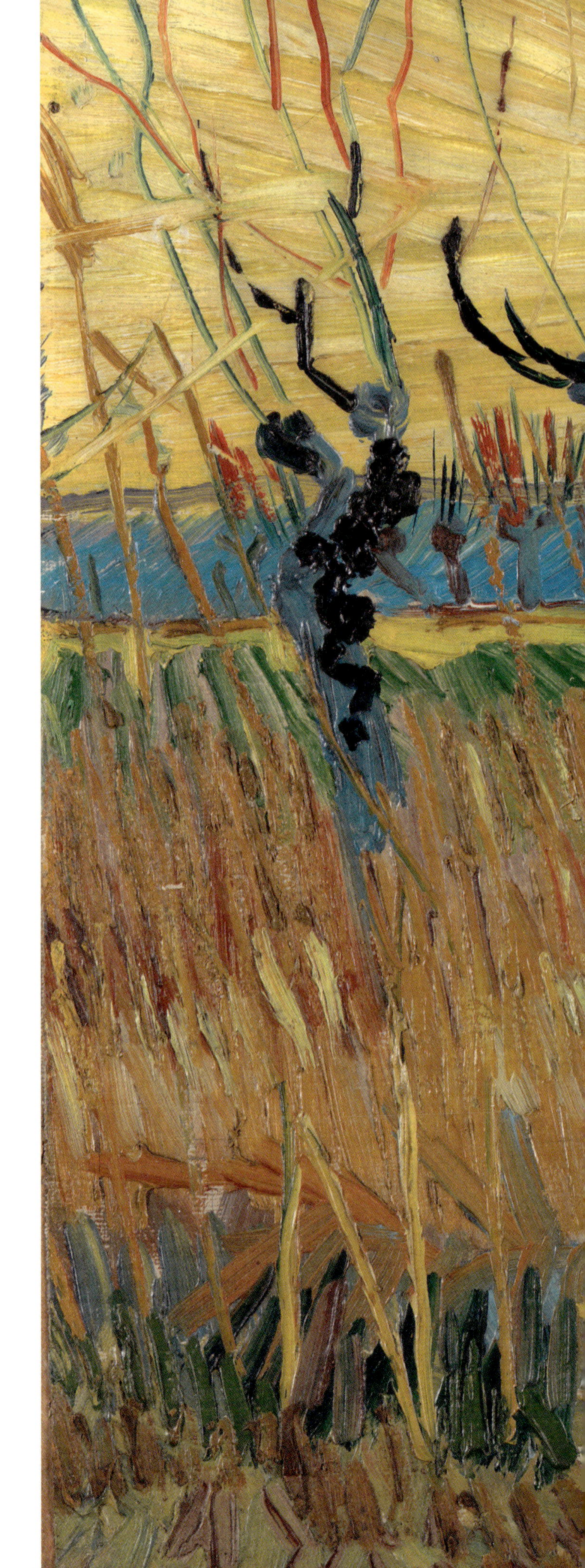

Cat. 17
Vincent van Gogh, *Pollard Willows at Sunset,* Arles, March 1888
Oil on canvas mounted on cardboard, 31.6 × 34.3 cm

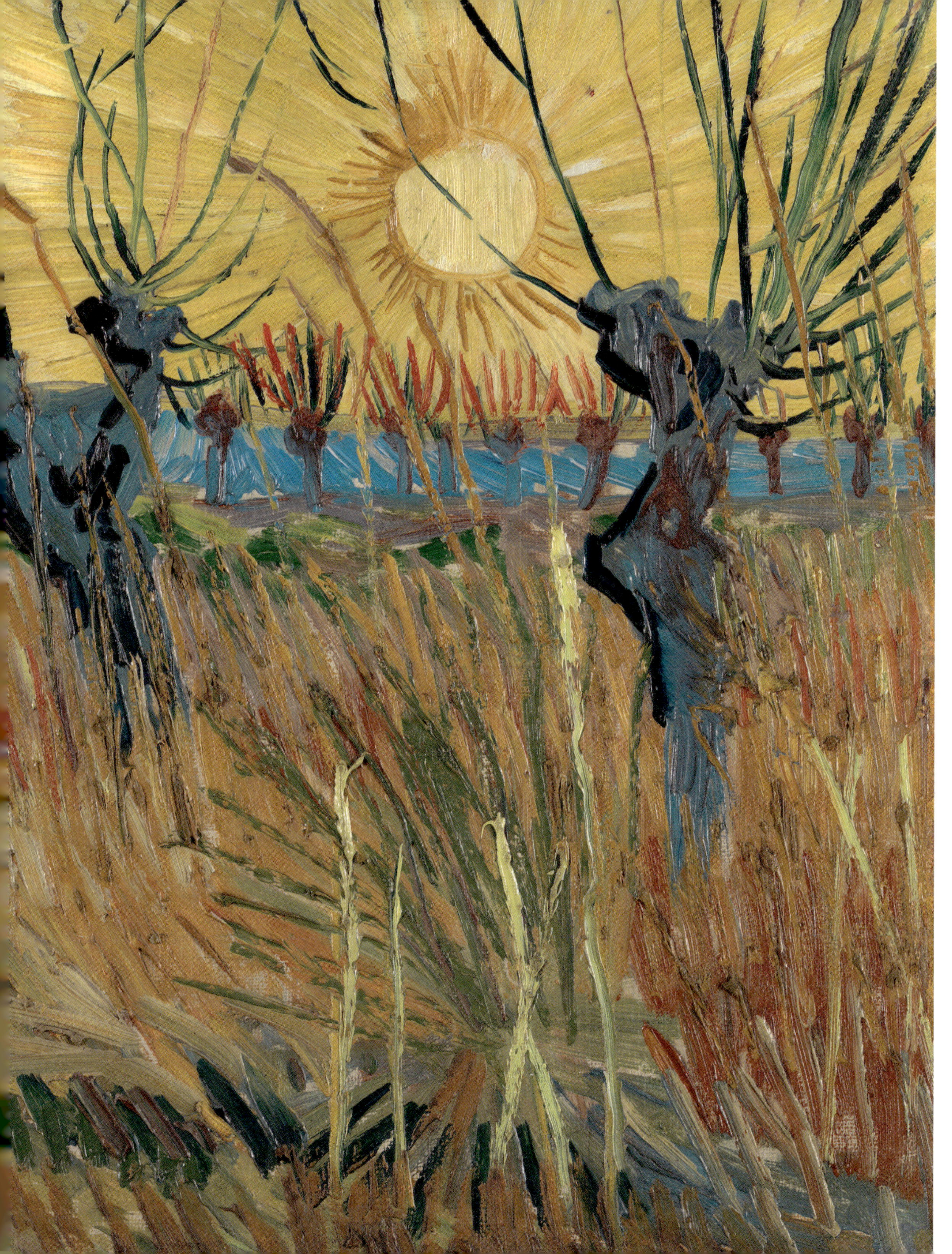

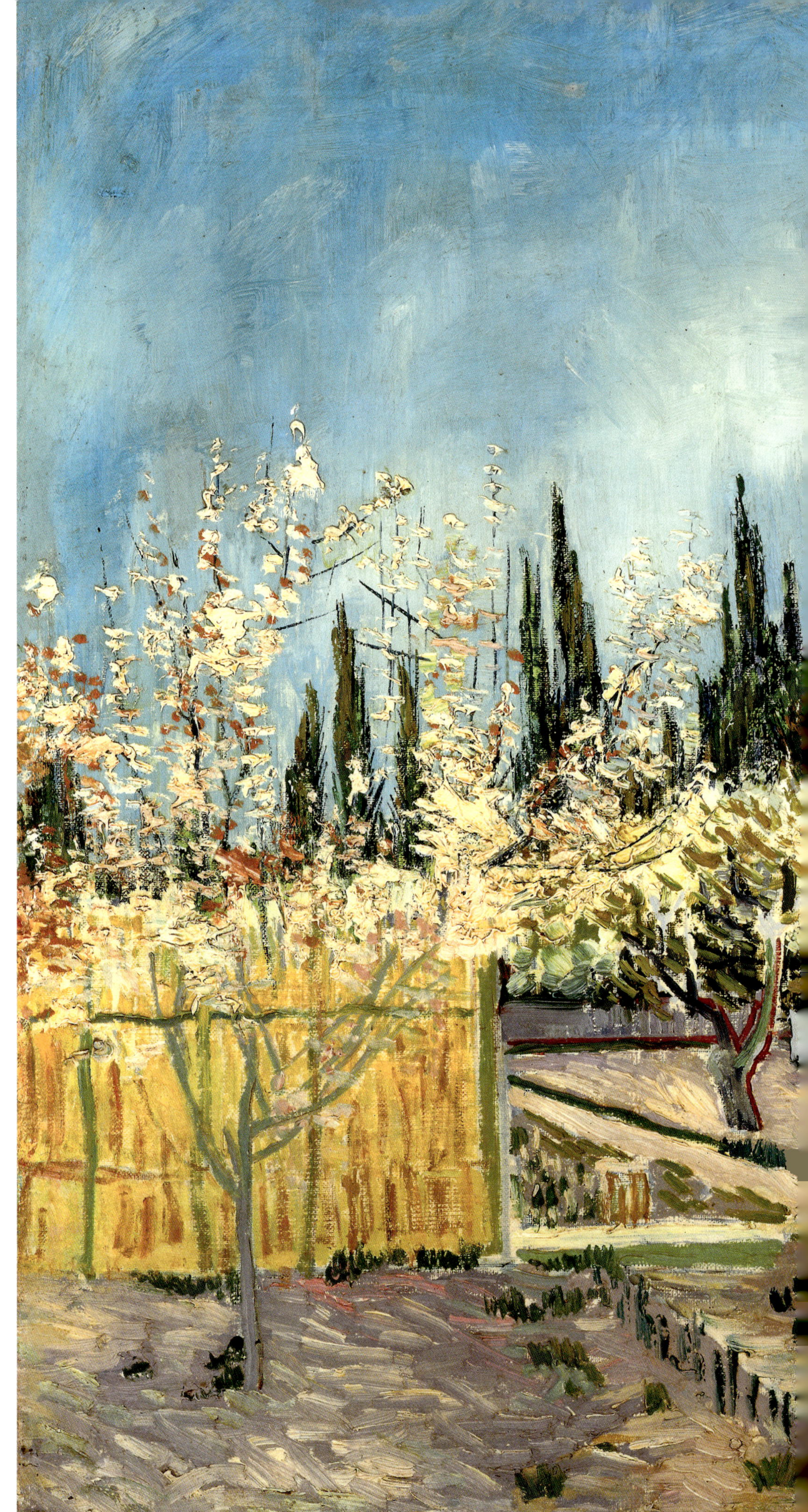

Cat. 18
Vincent van Gogh, *Orchard Bordered by Cypresses,* Arles, April 1888
Oil on canvas, 64.9 × 81.2 cm

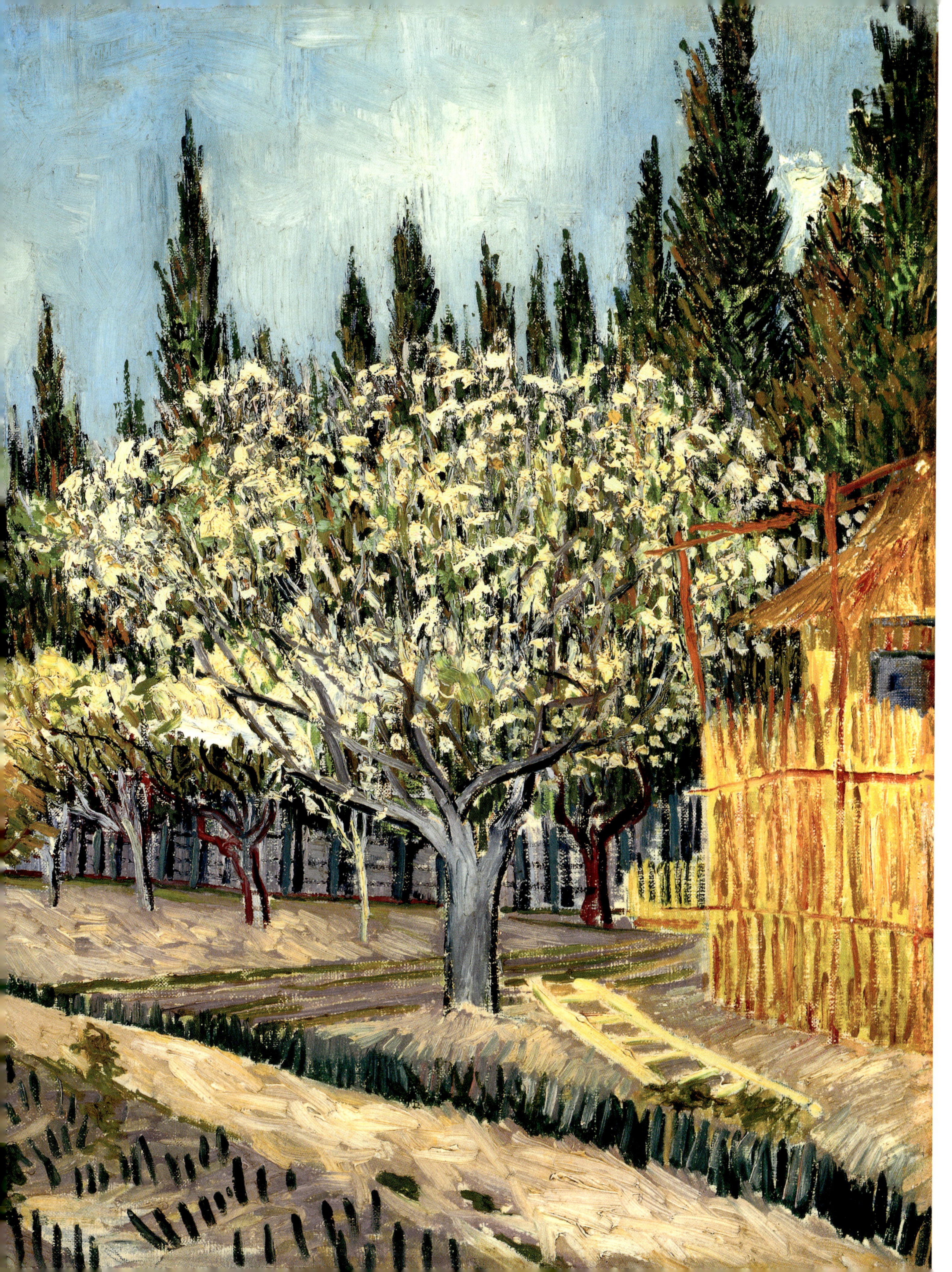

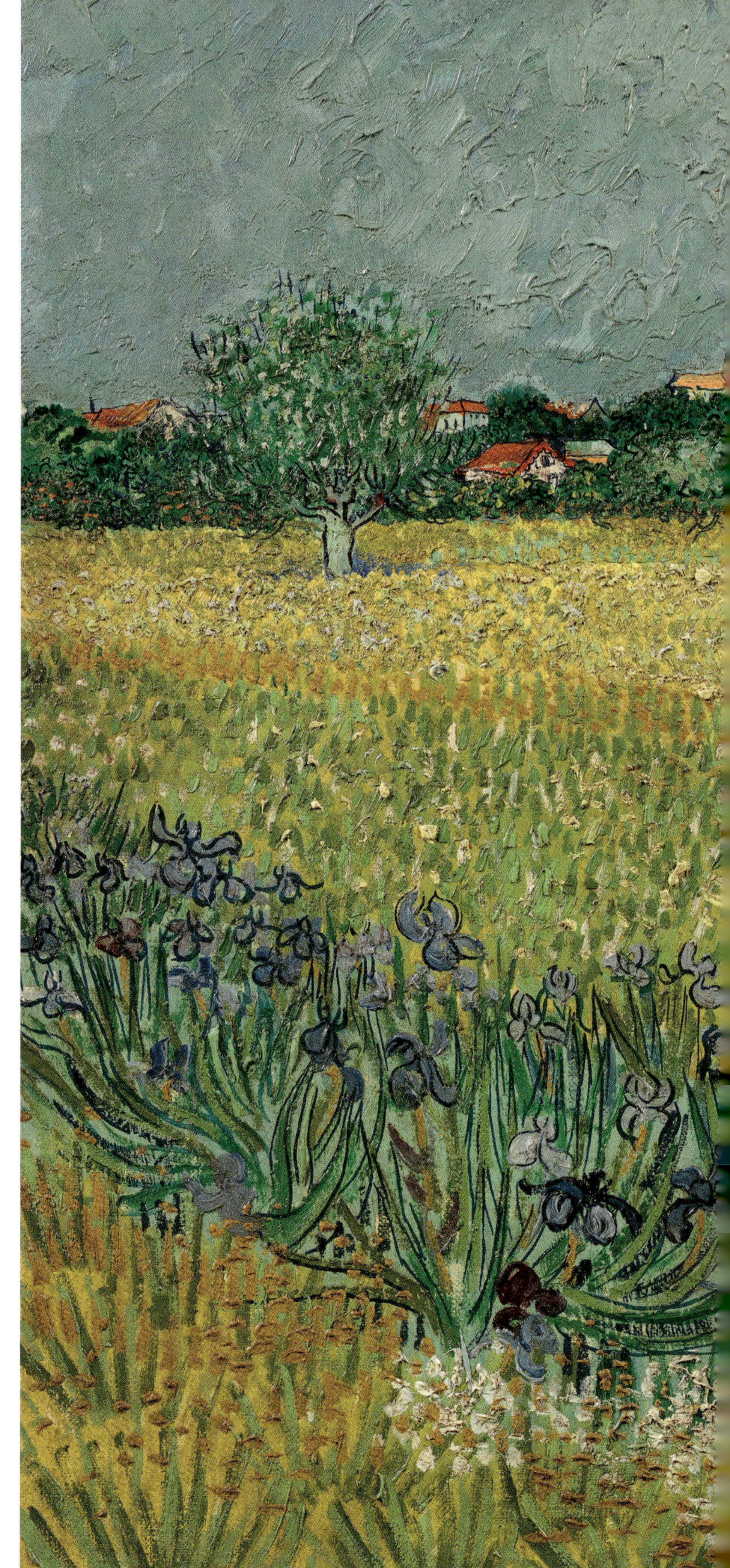

Cat. 19
Vincent van Gogh, *Field with Irises near Arles,* Arles, May 1888
Oil on canvas, 54 × 65 cm

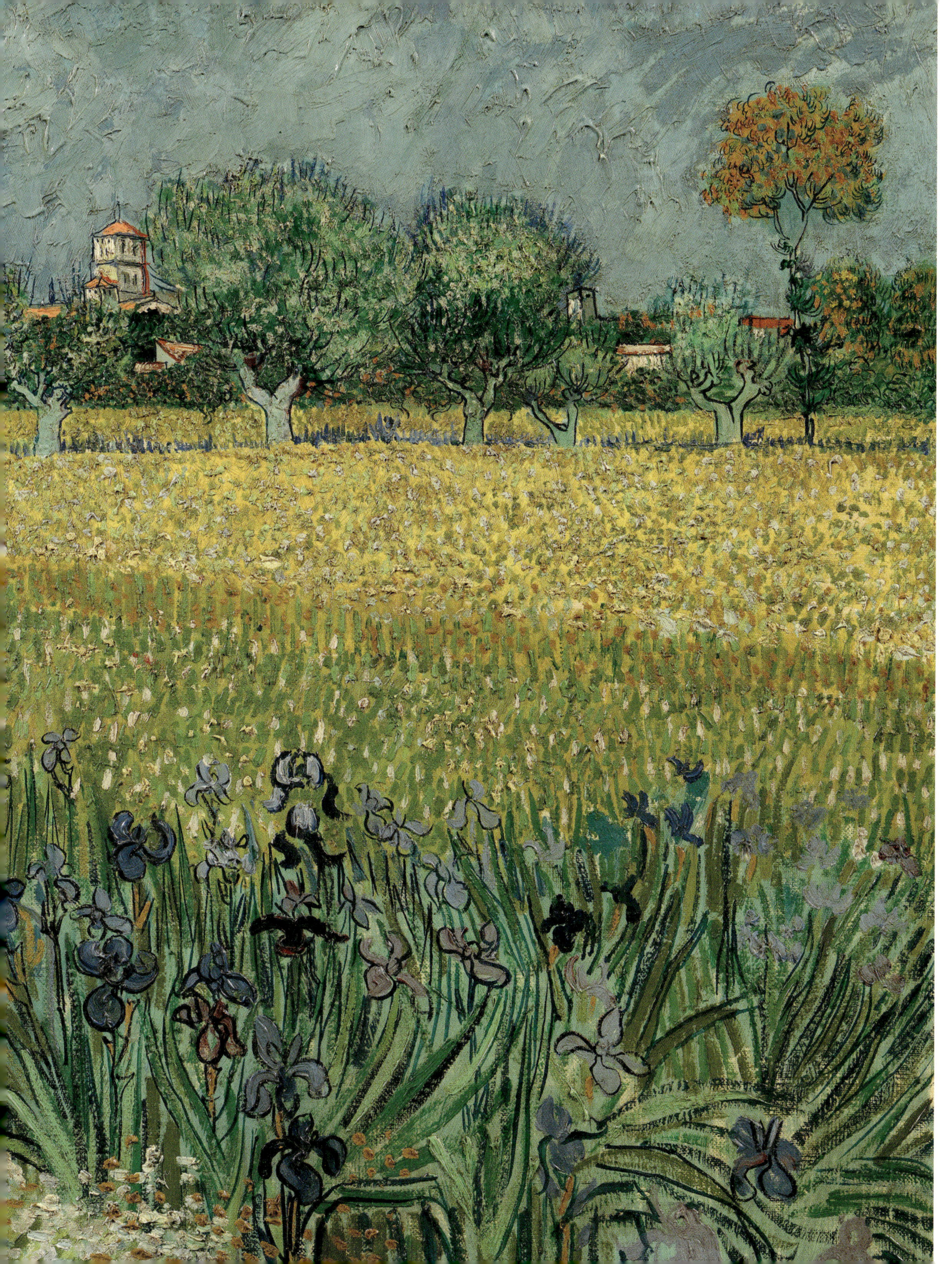

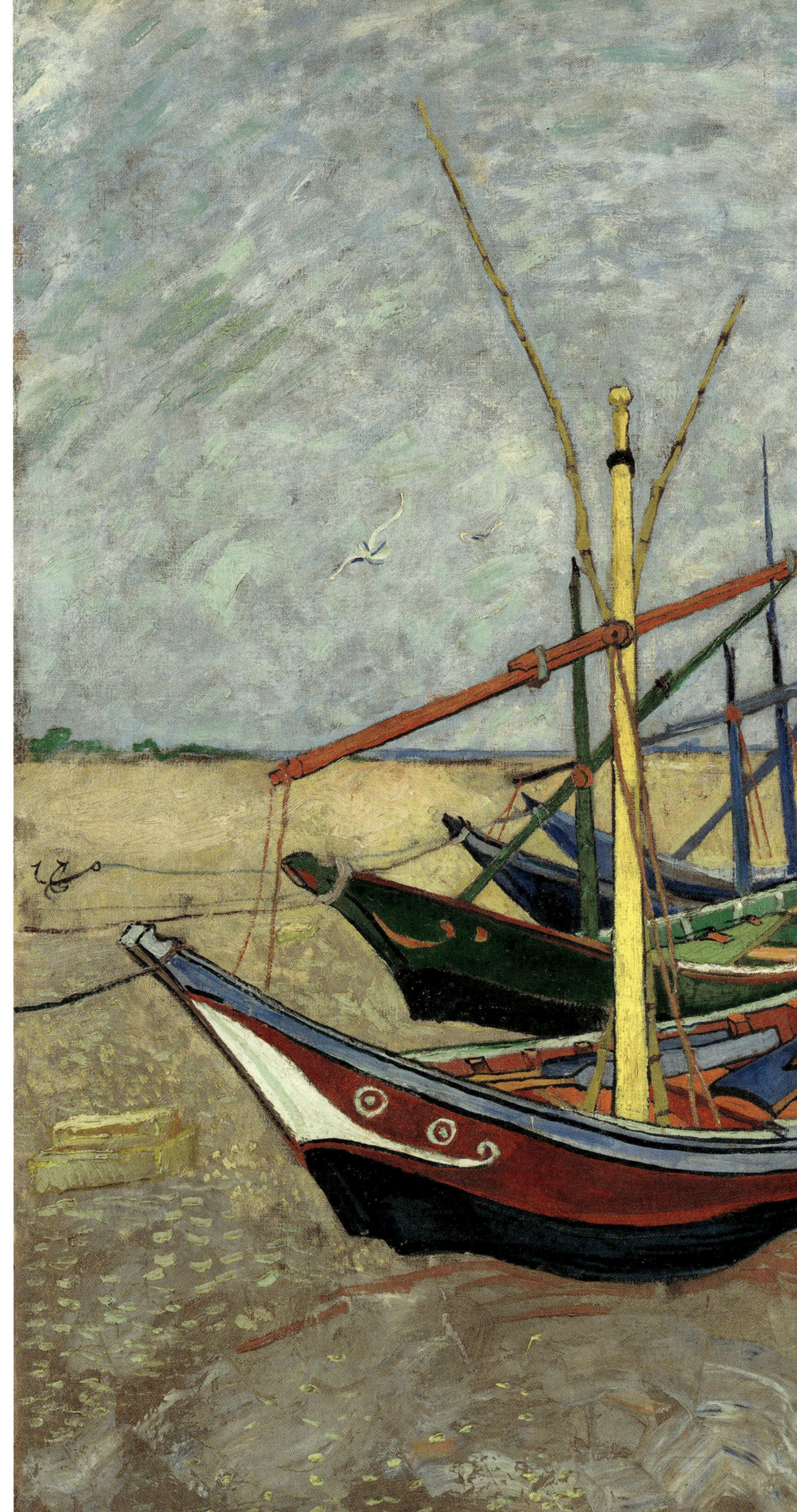

Cat. 20
Vincent van Gogh, *Fishing Boats on the Beach at Les Saintes-Maries-de-la-Mer,* Arles, June 1888
Oil on canvas, 65 × 81.5 cm

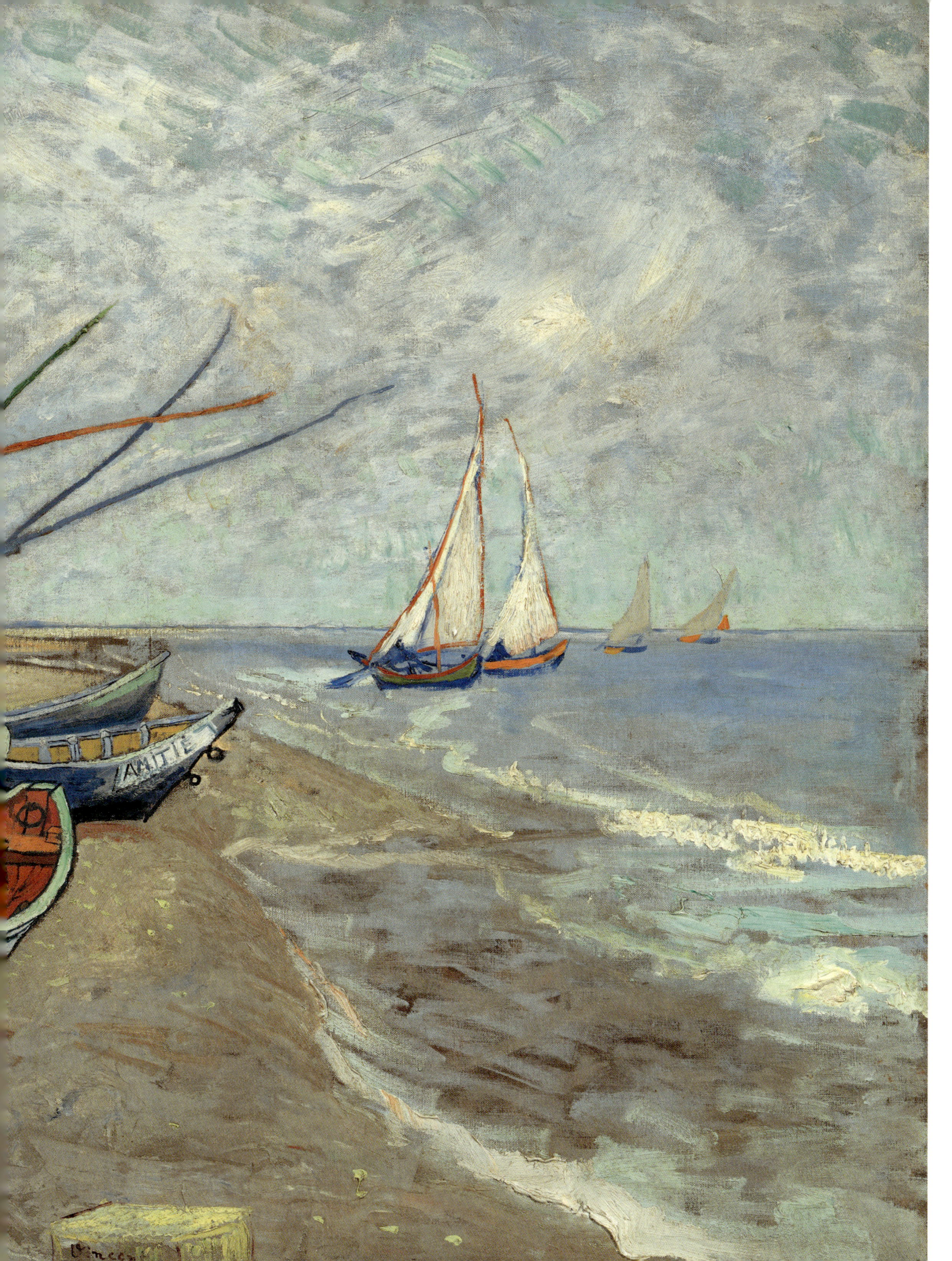
AMITIE

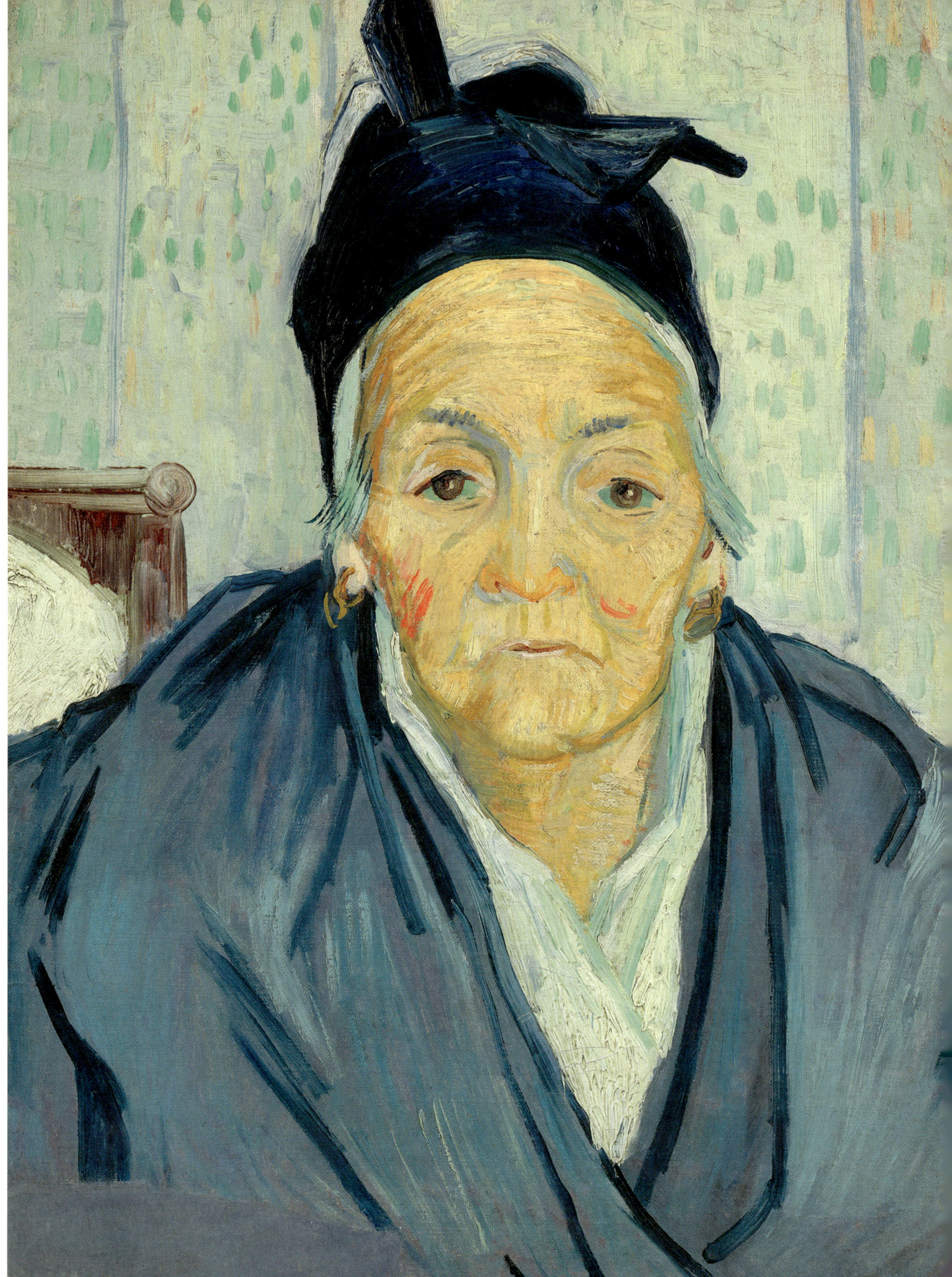

Cat. 21
Vincent van Gogh, *An Old Woman of Arles*,
Arles, February 1888
Oil on canvas, 58 × 42 cm

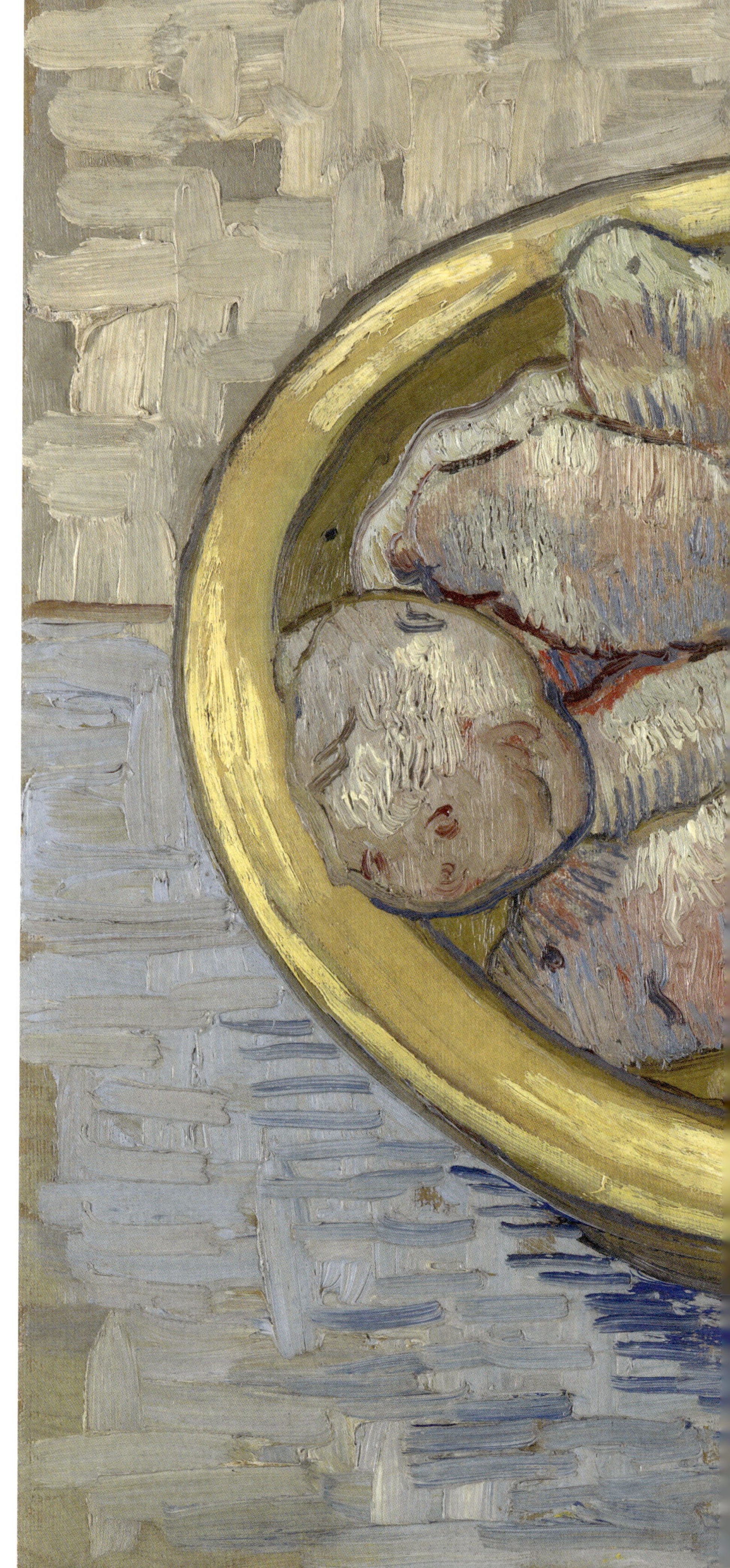

Cat. 22
Vincent van Gogh, *Still Life with Potatoes,*
Arles, mid-January 1889
Oil on canvas, 39.5 × 47.5 cm

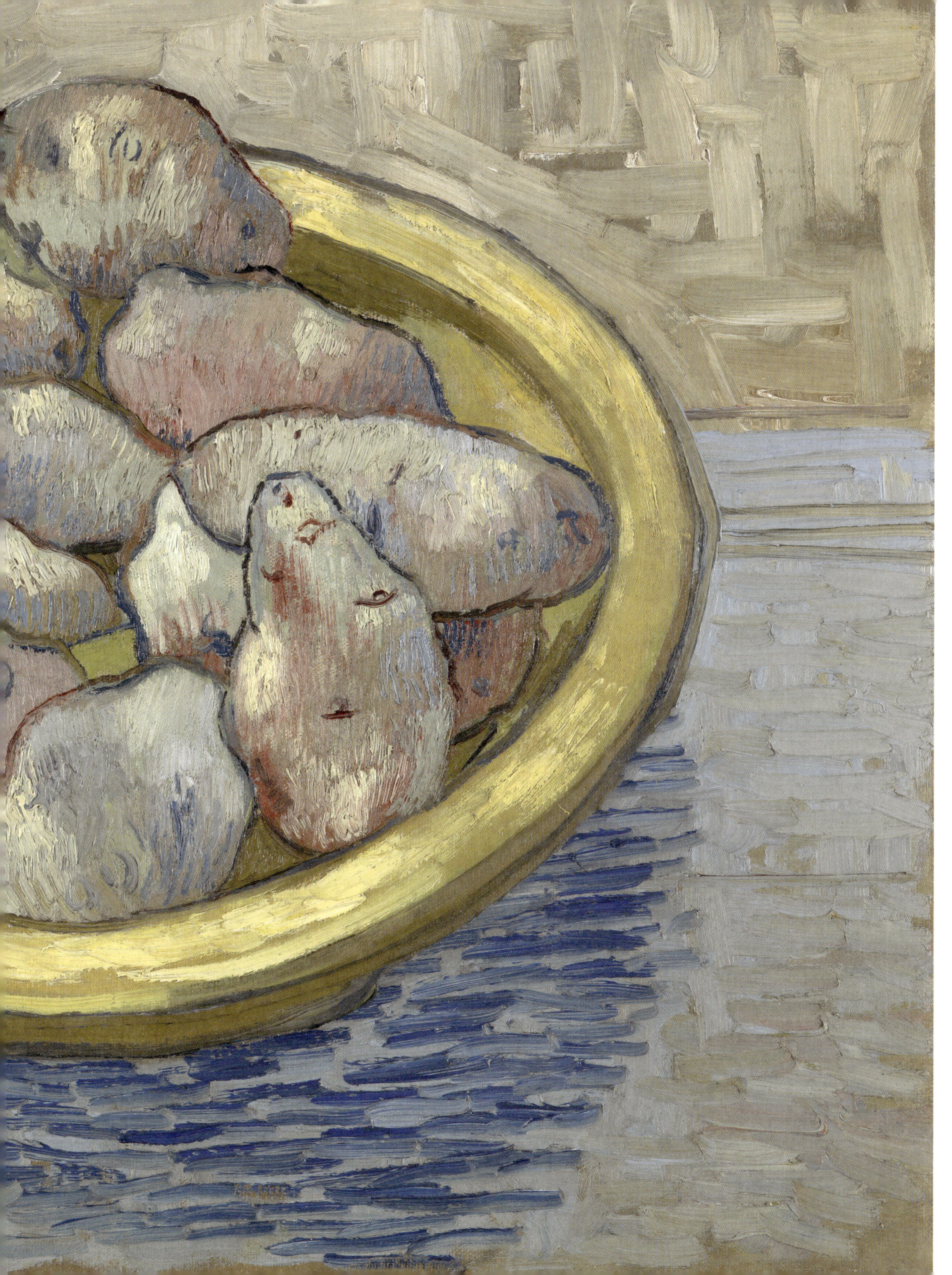

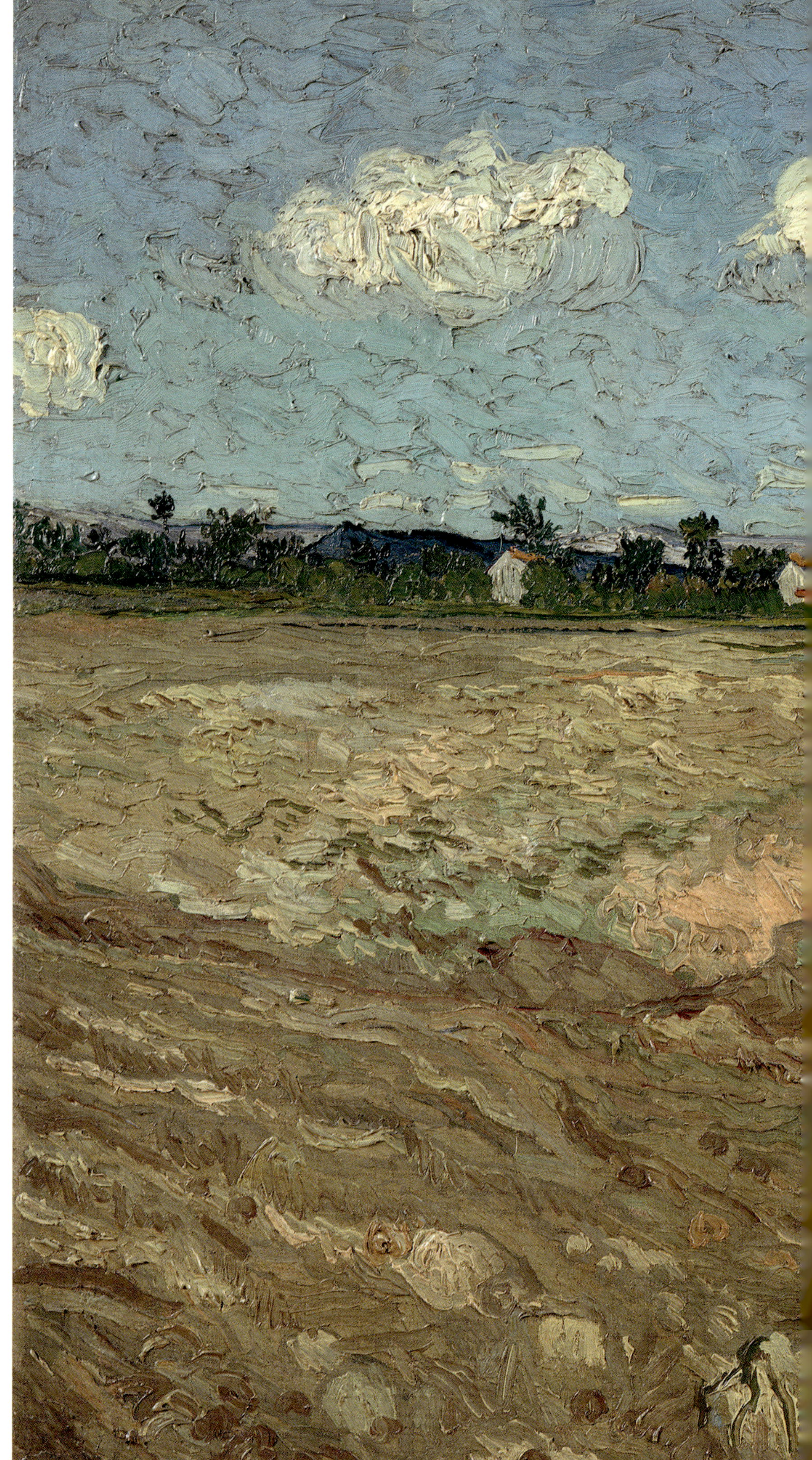

Cat. 23
Vincent van Gogh, *Ploughed Fields ('The Furrows')*, Arles, September 1888
Oil on canvas, 72.5×92.5 cm

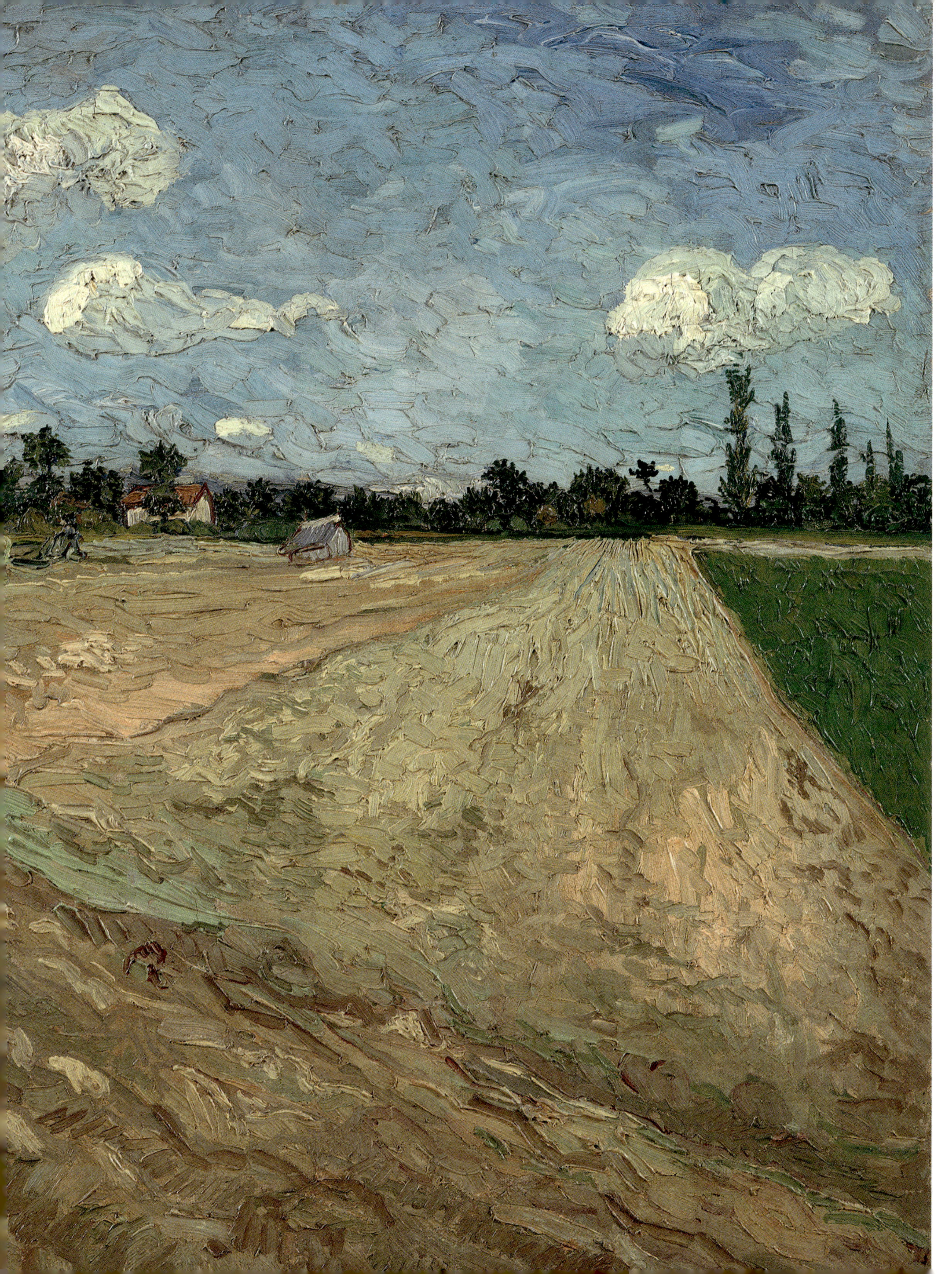

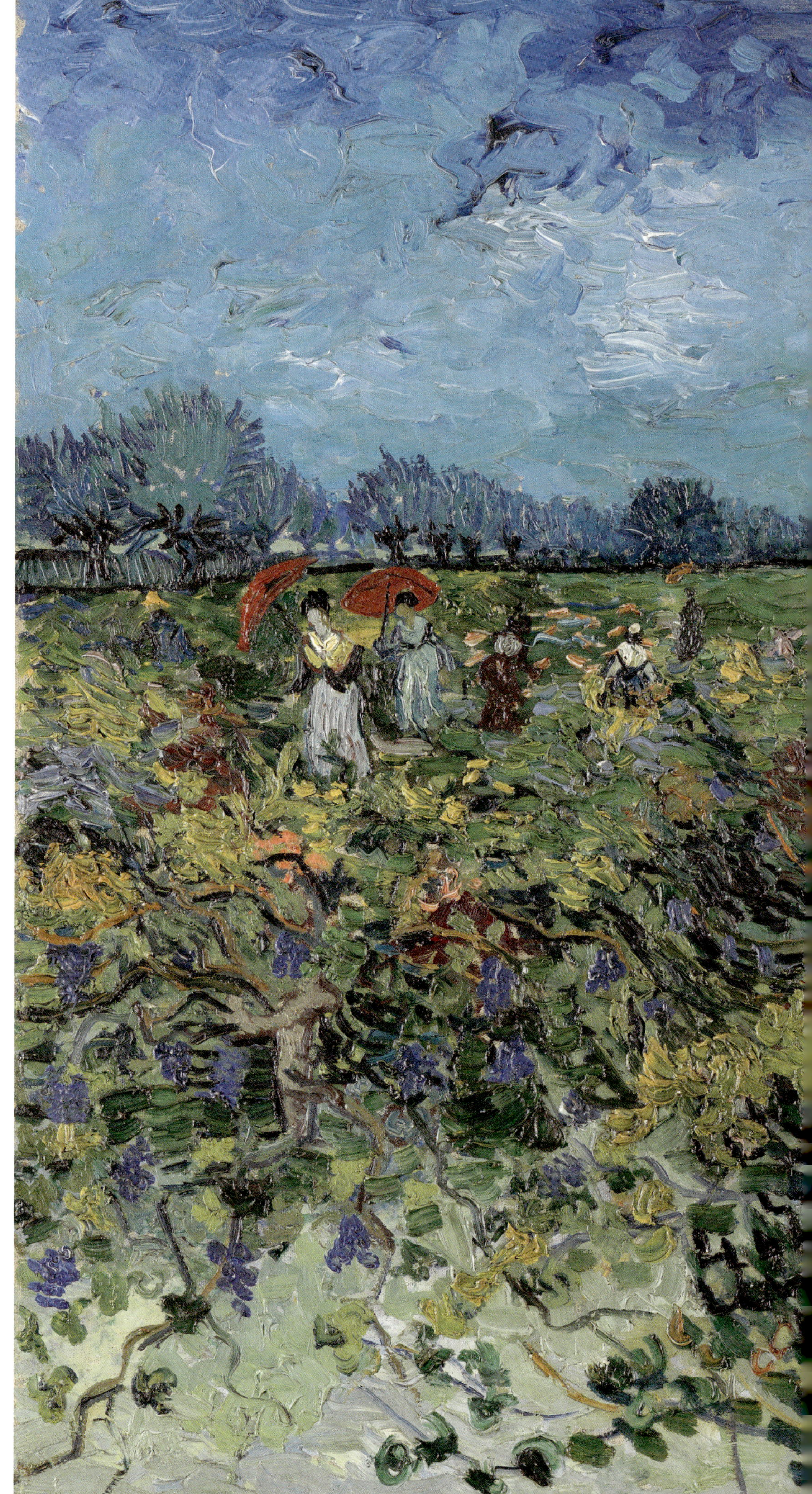

Cat. 24
Vincent van Gogh, *The Green Vineyard*,
Arles, 3 October 1888
Oil on canvas, 73.5 × 92.5 cm

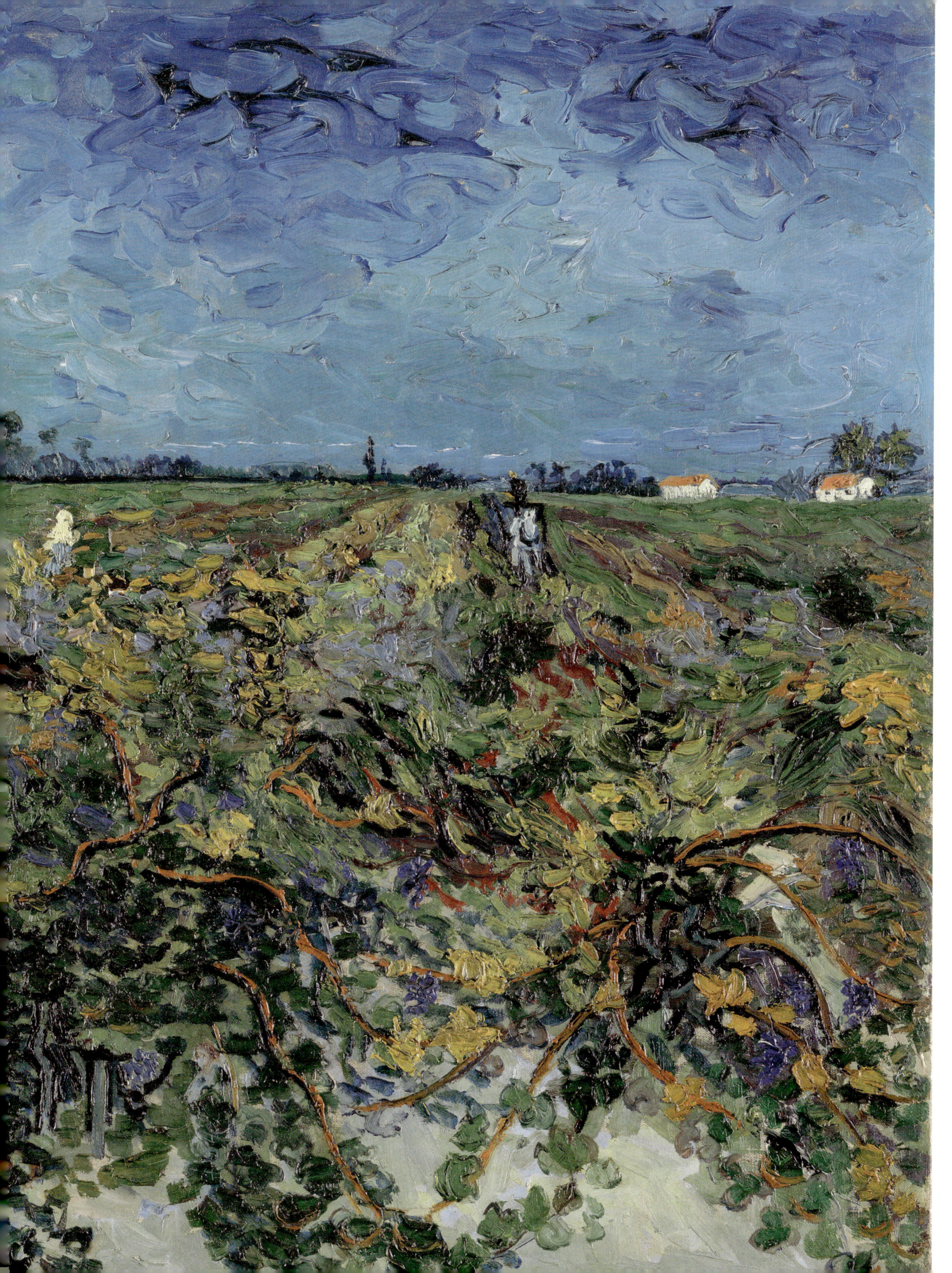

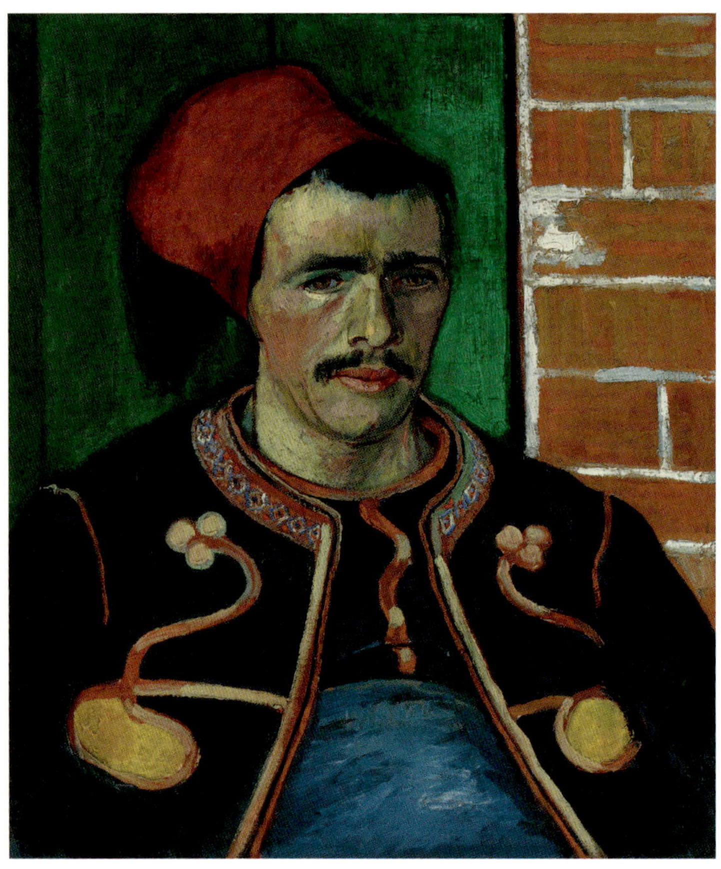

fig. 57

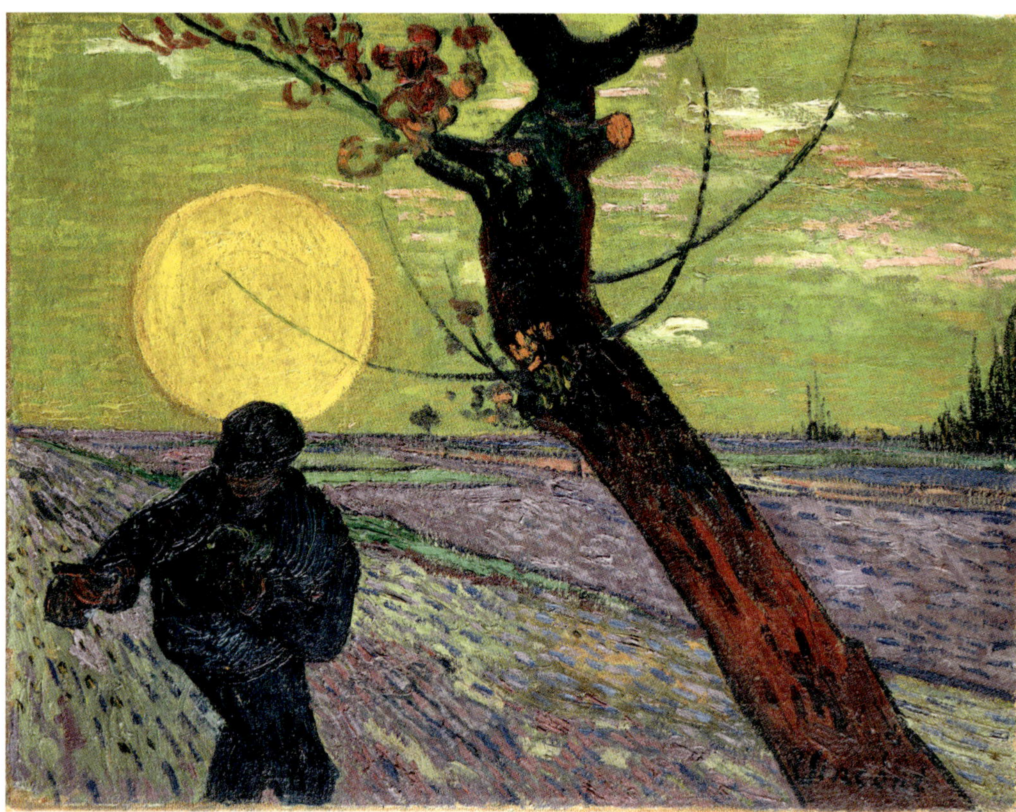

fig. 58

57 Vincent van Gogh,
The Zouave, Arles, June 1888
Oil on canvas, 65.8×55.7 cm
Van Gogh Museum, Amsterdam
(Vincent van Gogh Foundation)

58 Vincent van Gogh,
Sower with Setting Sun, November 1888
Oil on jute, 73×92 cm
Foundation E.G. Bührle Collection, Zürich

head, wearing a bright red cap, in front of a door painted green and the orange bricks of a wall. So it's a coarse combination of disparate tones that isn't easy to handle—the study I did of it seems very hard to me, and yet I'd always like to work on portraits that are vulgar, even garish like that one. It teaches me, and that's what I ask of my work above all" [629]. Van Gogh's description of the Zouave—bull's neck, tiger eyes, cat-like features—shows that he still observed his models with an eye trained by theories of physiognomy and phrenology. He captured the Zouave in three drawings and two paintings: a bust-length portrait (fig. 57) and a full-length likeness of him seated on the ground.

In June, Van Gogh also embarked on what was for him an extremely important undertaking: a truly modern figure piece. His high expectations are clear from his choice of motif: a sower, an imitation of Jean-François Millet's iconic *Sower*, no less. In his use of colour, he adhered to the colour theories of Delacroix, which had guided him since his time in Nuenen. As he explained in the letter quoted above, he had painted a sower in "a ploughed field, a large field of clods of purple earth—rising towards the horizon—a sower in blue and white. On the horizon a field of short, ripe wheat. Above all that a yellow sky with a yellow sun. You can sense from the mere nomenclature of the tonalities—that *colour* plays a very important role in this composition. And the sketch as such... also worries me a lot, in the sense that I wonder whether I shouldn't take it seriously and make a tremendous painting out of it. My God, how I'd love to do that. But I just wonder whether I'll have the necessary power of execution. I'm putting the sketch aside just as it is, hardly daring to think about it. For such a long time it's been my great desire to do a sower, but the desires I've had for a long time aren't always achieved. So I'm almost afraid of them. And yet, after Millet and Lhermitte what remains to be done is... the sower, with colour and in a large format."

In the end Van Gogh was dissatisfied with the study painted in June, but he did not give up hope. He made two more attempts, but still failed to achieve the desired result.[52] Only in November did he manage to create a composition that pleased him (fig. 58). He put the sower in the immediate foreground, his legs cut off by the lower edge, which makes it seem as though he is striding out of the picture. The sun forms a kind of nimbus behind his head, thereby enhancing the figure's grandeur. Because he wanted to depict the effect of dusk, he used complementary colours, but in a slightly subdued—rather than bright—colour scheme.

Van Gogh gradually got to know people in Arles, and a few of them agreed to sit for him. The postman Joseph Roulin, with his impressive beard and striking head, posed for him on various occasions from the end of July onwards (fig. 59), and late that year he painted portraits of every member of Roulin's family: his wife, Augustine, the sons, Armand and Camille, and even the baby, Marcelle. In December, Madame Roulin became the subject of *La Berceuse*, a woman holding a rope used to rock a cradle outside the picture (fig. 60). It pays homage to motherhood, and Van Gogh later developed the idea to hang it with a painting of sunflowers on either side. He made no fewer than five variations of it.

In August, Van Gogh met a shepherd, Patience Escalier, whom he painted twice (fig. 61). Although he mentioned the man by name in his letters, he did not intend these pictures primarily as portraits. He gave them the title *The Peasant*, which betrays his intention of portraying, above all, a characteristic type. The peasant heads painted in Nuenen had not been intended as portraits either, but as figure types. In Arles, however, Van Gogh took such studies even further, turning them into well-nigh allegorical representations of a figure type. In September he portrayed his friend, the painter Eugène Boch, as a poet, against the backdrop of a starry night. In a letter he associated another of his models—Paul Eugène Milliet, Second Lieutenant of the Zouaves—with the type of "the lover".[53] Characterizing the portraits in this way bestows them with a timeless quality and a significance greater than a person's mere appearance.

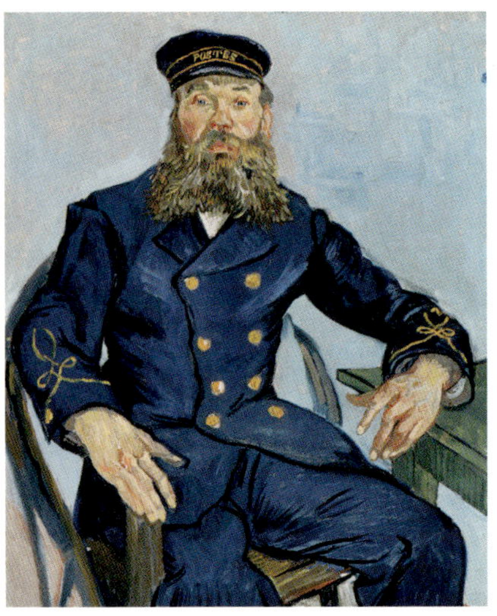

fig. 59

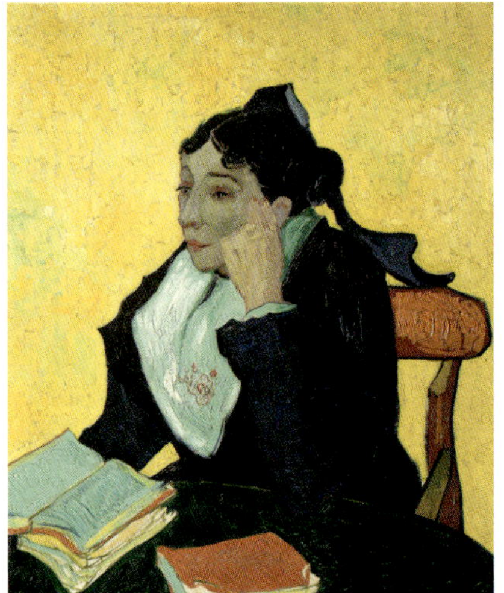

fig. 62

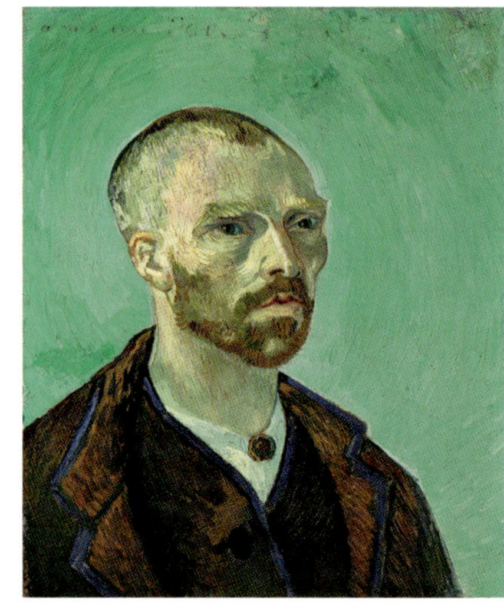

fig. 64

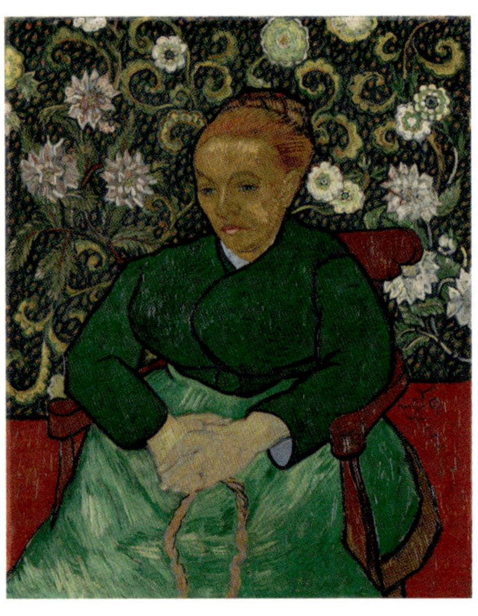

fig. 60

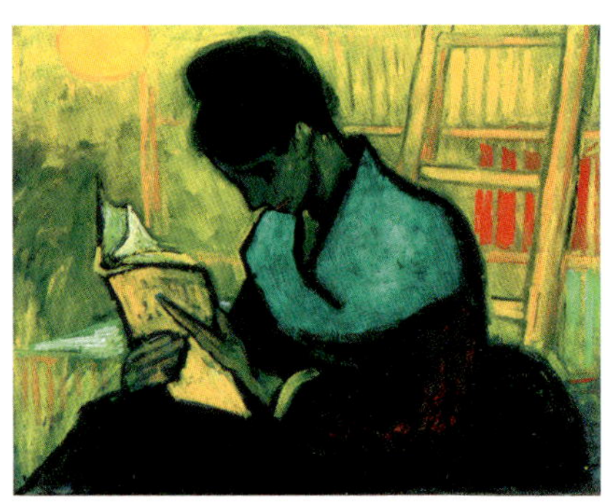

fig. 63

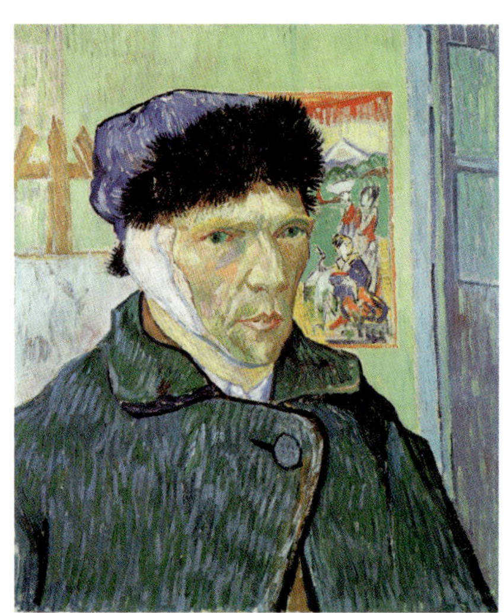

fig. 65

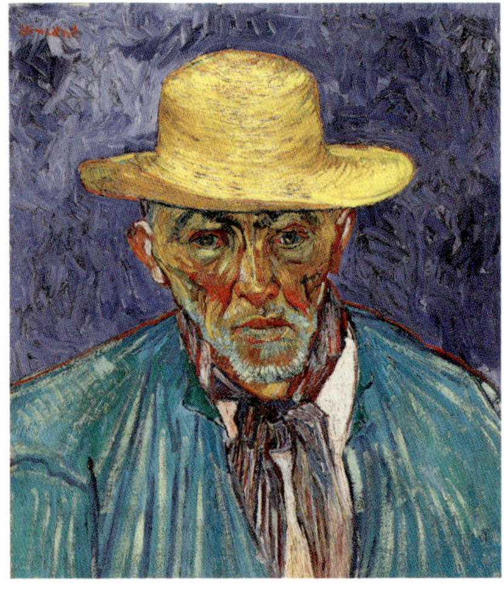

fig. 61

59 Vincent van Gogh,
Postman Joseph Roulin, July 1888
Oil on canvas, 81.3×65.4 cm
Museum of Fine Arts, Boston
Gift of Robert Treat Paine, 2nd

60 Vincent van Gogh, *La Berceuse (portrait of Madame Roulin)*,
c. March 1889
Oil on canvas, 92×72.5 cm
Kröller-Müller Museum, Otterlo

61 Vincent van Gogh, *Portrait of a Peasant (Patience Escalier)*, August 1888
Oil on canvas, 64.1×54.6 cm
Norton Simon Art Foundation

62 Vincent van Gogh, *L'Arlésienne: Marie Ginoux*, November 1888
Oil on canvas, 91×73 cm
Musée d'Orsay, Paris

63 Vincent van Gogh,
The Novel Reader, c. 16 November 1888
Oil on canvas, 73×92 cm
Private collection

64 Vincent van Gogh, *Self-Portrait Dedicated to Paul Gauguin*,
September 1888
Oil on canvas, 61.5×50.3 cm
Harvard Art Museum/Fogg Museum,
Bequest from the Collection of Maurice Wertheim

65 Vincent van Gogh, *Self-Portrait with Bandaged Ear*, January 1889
Oil on canvas, 60.5×50 cm
The Samuel Courtauld Trust,
The Courtauld Gallery, London

Another characteristic model was Marie Ginoux. She and her husband owned the Café de la Gare, where Van Gogh rented a room from the beginning of May until mid-September 1888. He painted her in early November as *L'Arlésienne* (fig. 62), and Gauguin, who had arrived in Arles on 23 October, made a drawing of her at that session. Van Gogh later made a replica of his painting (though he replaced the umbrella and gloves with an open and a closed book, thus representing her as a reader) and gave it to Madame Ginoux.

Under the influence of Gauguin, Van Gogh also began to paint from the imagination (see below). One result of this is a scene, produced in November, of a woman reading in a library, a painting made in a curious idiom that is rather unusual in Van Gogh's œuvre (fig. 63).

SELF-PORTRAITS

Two self-portraits that Van Gogh painted in 1888 in Arles were the result of an initiative he took to exchange paintings. We know from a letter written to Theo that Vincent had suggested to Émile Bernard and Gauguin, who were working in Brittany, that they paint each other and send him the resulting works.[54] He, in turn, would give them self-portraits. Bernard and Gauguin agreed to the plan. Instead of portraits, however, they painted self-portraits that included each other's likenesses: Gauguin's contains a small picture of Bernard, and Bernard's one of Gauguin. Charles Laval, who was also working in Brittany, took part in the project too.

Van Gogh gave Gauguin, in exchange, his self-portrait as a bonze (fig. 64). Bonze is the French term for a Buddhist monk: "I have a portrait of myself, all ash-coloured. The ashy colour that comes from mixing Veronese with orange lead, on a pale background of uniform Veronese, with a red-brown garment. But exaggerating my personality also, I looked more for the character of a bonze, a simple worshipper of the eternal Buddha" [695]. A slightly smaller self-portrait, now in a private collection, was intended for Laval.

The two self-portraits made in January 1889 are very personal documents, because they show Van Gogh with a bandage around his self-mutilated ear, the result of a violent row he had with Gauguin in late December 1888. The larger of the two shows him in his studio, having returned from the hospital (fig. 65). There is a Japanese print on the wall, and the canvas standing on the easel displays the vague design of what seems to be a flower still life. Considering that no fresh flowers were to be had in January, it is tempting to think that this is one of the three replicas of the sunflowers, on which he was working that month (see below). This self-portrait therefore presents a touching image: the wounded painter, disappointed by his collaboration with Gauguin, who nevertheless plucks up the courage to move on.[55]

STILL LIFES

The still lifes Van Gogh made in Arles include some very prestigious works, such as the famous series of sunflowers of August 1888.

His ability to compose a highly expressive picture from the simplest of household effects is evidenced by his *Still Life with Coffeepot* (fig. 66), "a variation of blues enlivened by a series of yellows ranging all the way to orange", as he described the palette to Bernard [612]. A short while later he wrote to Theo about the intense palette of *The Harvest* (fig. 55), and stated that it "absolutely kills all the rest; there's only a still life with coffee-pots and cups and plates in blue and yellow that can stand beside it" [624]. Another painting he was working on at this time was a study in shades of yellow, a basket of lemons against a yellow background.

Van Gogh, who had high hopes that Gauguin would soon join him in Arles, worked in August 1888, in expectation of his friend's arrival, on a series of sunflower still lifes. (That same month he also painted two still lifes with oleanders.) He planned to move into the Yellow House in September, and he wished to decorate it with paintings. The sunflowers (fig. 67) were intended for Gauguin, who had shown, in Paris, so much interest in the sunflower still lifes Van Gogh had made there. Van Gogh considered the sunflower to be his own personal flower, and in a certain sense he was competing with other flower painters whom he esteemed: "If Jeannin has the peony, Quost the hollyhock, I indeed, before others, have taken the sunflower," he wrote to Gauguin in January 1889, when the latter expressed his interest in buying one of the versions [739]. That month he worked on three replicas of three of the four sunflower still lifes that he had made five months earlier.

The importance Van Gogh attached to these still lifes is apparent not only from their number, but also from his intention to create a triptych by putting one on either side of *La Berceuse* (fig. 68), another highlight of his œuvre. The combination would exert a special effect on the portrait: "The yellow and orange tones of the head take on more brilliance through the proximity of the yellow shutters. And then you will understand what I was writing to you about it, that my idea had been to make a decoration like one for the far end of a cabin on a ship, for example" [776]. The last remark refers to an idea he got from reading Pierre Loti's *Pêcheur d'Islande* (1886): the presence of a painting of a mother figure in the cabin of a fishing boat could have a comforting effect on men who were far away from home.[56]

Van Gogh sometimes depicted a scene composed of objects, which, taken altogether, form a kind of self-portrait: his bedroom with his bed (fig. 69), his empty chair and its pendant, Gauguin's empty chair standing in for the absent sitter. *Still Life with a Plate of Onions*, of January 1889, also contains references to the artist himself (fig. 70). In late December 1888, after a violent confrontation with Gauguin, Van Gogh mutilated his own ear. After a fortnight in hospital, he returned to the Yellow House on 7 January 1889. Resuming work, he painted this touching personal still life, in which the letter undoubtedly refers to Theo, the pipe and tobacco to himself as an inveterate smoker, and the bottle of absinthe and the coffee to the simple pleasures he allowed himself. The book, a medical handbook, is a reference to his fragile health at that time, which he was apparently working actively to improve. It is a collection of simple objects that not only form a captivating whole, but also allow the painter almost literally to address the viewer.

Stemming from this same time is *Still Life with Potatoes* (cat. 22), which was long dated to February–March 1888, since it was presumed to have been made shortly after Van Gogh's arrival in Arles, when the snow had prevented him from working outdoors. Now, however, it is clear that this painting belongs in the proximity of a group of works that are known to have originated in January 1889.[57] It is plainly a modern version of the basket of potatoes that Van Gogh had depicted in Nuenen, and, in its ultimate simplicity, is strongly linked to the preceding still life with onions.

ONCE MORE, LANDSCAPES: AUTUMN EFFECTS, THE SPRING OF 1889

The summer of 1888 had provided Van Gogh with a wealth of subject matter, and he expected no less from the autumn, as he reported to Theo when he informed him in the first half of September that he could expect a large order of paint. Unfortunately, the beautiful autumn weather he was hoping for was rather unsettled at first. He nevertheless succeeded in finding a seasonal motif, a recently ploughed field (cat. 23),

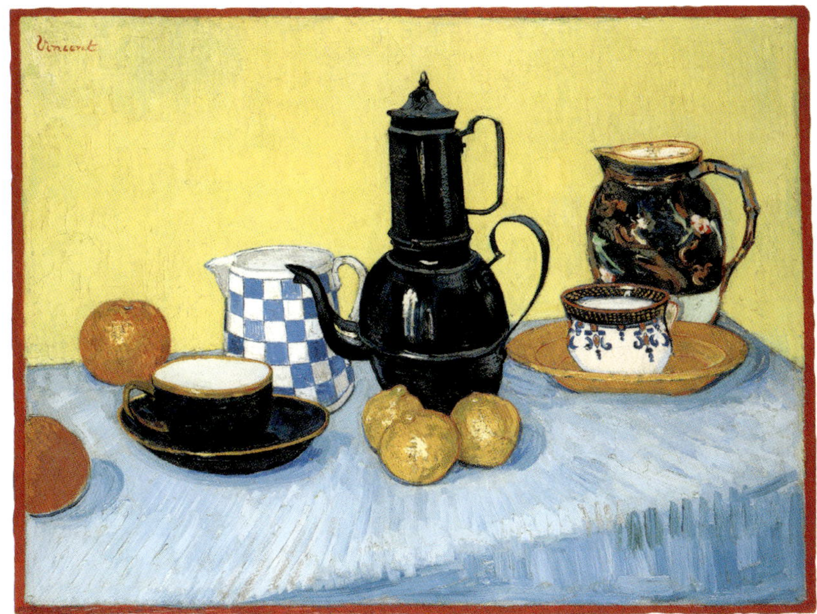

fig. 66

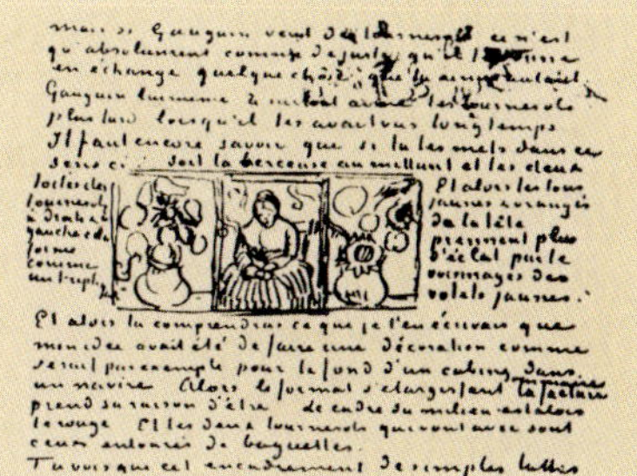

mais si Gauguin veut [illegible] ce n'est
qu'absolument comme de juste qu'il [illegible]
en échange quelque chose que tu aimes autant.
Gauguin lui-même a voulu avoir les tournesols
plus tard lorsqu'il les avait vus longtemps
Il faut encore savoir que si tu les mets dans ce
sens-ci soit la berceuse au milieu et les deux
toiles des tournesols à droite et à gauche cela forme comme un tripty-
Et alors les tons jaunes orangés de la tête prennent plus d'éclat par le voisinage des volets jaunes.
Et alors tu comprendras ce que je t'en écrivais que
mon idée avait été de faire une décoration comme
serait par exemple pour le fond d'un cabinet dans
un navire. Alors le format s'élargissant la facture
prend sa raison d'être. Le cadre du milieu est alors
le rouge. Et les deux tournesols qui vont avec sont
ceux entourés de baguettes.
Tu vois que cet encadrement de simples lattes

fig. 68

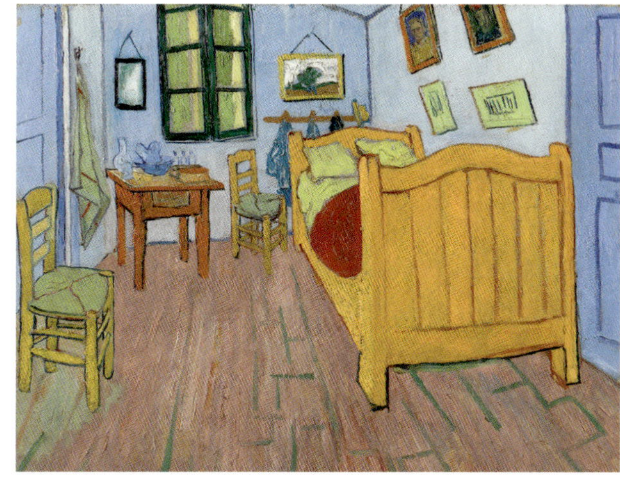

fig. 69

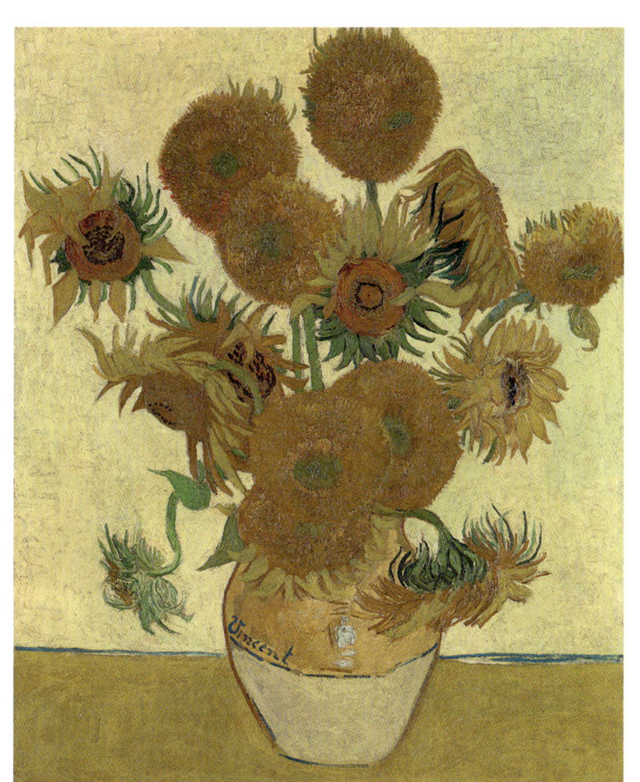

fig. 67

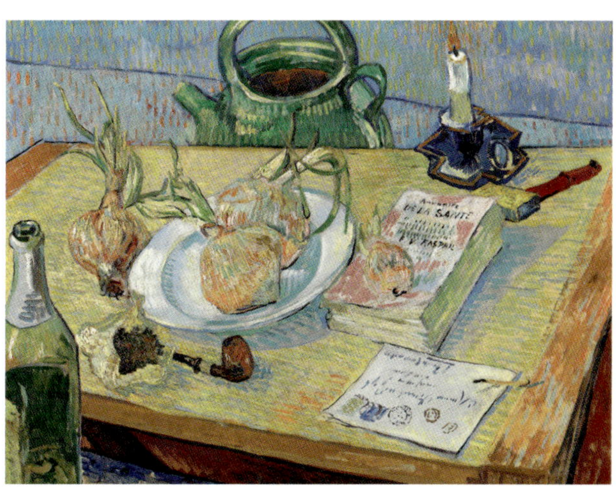

fig. 70

66 Vincent van Gogh, *Still Life with Coffeepot*, May 1888
Oil on canvas, 65 × 81 cm
Private collection

67 Vincent van Gogh, *Sunflowers*, August 1888
Oil on canvas, 92.1 × 73 cm
The National Gallery, London.
Bought, Courtauld Fund, 1924

68 Vincent van Gogh, sketch in letter 776, Saint-Rémy-de-Provence, 23 May 1889
Whereabouts of sheets unknown
Van Gogh Museum, Amsterdam

69 Vincent van Gogh, *The Bedroom*, October 1888
Oil on canvas, 72.4 × 91.3 cm
Van Gogh Museum, Amsterdam
(Vincent van Gogh Foundation)

70 Vincent van Gogh, *Still Life with a Plate of Onions*, January 1889
Oil on canvas, 49.6 × 64.4 cm
Kröller-Müller Museum, Otterlo

which marks the time when the wheat is brought in and the land made ready for the new crop. Van Gogh let the churned-up earth dominate the scene, while the ploughman and his team of horses remain distant details. Such fields, with or without figures, often played a major role in the work of the French realists: Millet, for example, was a master. Van Gogh knew Millet's *Winter: The Plain of Chailly* from prints, and made a large copy of it in Saint-Rémy (cat. 27, fig. 84). When visiting the Musée du Luxembourg in 1875, he had seen Rosa Bonheur's *Ploughing in the Nivernais* (fig. 71), which he listed among twenty of his favourite works.[58] He undoubtedly saw it again in 1886–88, and the grandiose painting certainly made an impression on him. Bonheur's almost palpable rendering of the clods of earth is deft, and, as evidenced by his own description, Van Gogh was striving to produce something similar, but with minimization of the ploughman: "A blue sky with white clouds. An immense field of an ashy lilac, furrows, innumerable clods of earth, the horizon of blue hills and green bushes and small farmsteads with orange-coloured roofs" [687]. As already apparent from works made in Nuenen, the earth—which underwent ploughing, planting and harvesting—had an important symbolic meaning for Van Gogh, and that is also the case here.

Landscape motifs could be found not only in the countryside around Arles, but also right in front of the Yellow House on the Place Lamartine, the site of a small public park where people could relax. Van Gogh depicted this park in a series of paintings (fig. 72). In earlier works, made in Nuenen and Paris, he had emphasized the comforting and poetic atmosphere of a garden where one could find peace (fig. 32, 48), and now he did this again in park scenes, some with strolling individuals and courting couples, others entirely without figures. He associated the public park with the Renaissance poets Boccaccio, Dante and Petrarch, and gave four of the paintings the title *The Poet's Garden*. It is obvious that he also depicted this park as an autumn effect.

In the first days of October, Van Gogh painted a completely different—but also seasonal—subject that was new to him: the grape harvest. The blossoming orchards and the wheat harvest were not specifically southern subjects, but now he depicted something he had not known in the north, a truly Provençal motif (cat. 24). "I have an extraordinary fever for work these days, at present I'm grappling with a landscape with blue sky above an immense green, purple, yellow vine with black and orange shoots. Little figures of ladies with red sunshades, little figures of grape-pickers with their cart further liven it up. Foreground of grey sand," he wrote to Gauguin [695]. As in *The Harvest* (fig. 55) and *'The Furrows'* (cat. 23), the charming figures are merely supporting actors.

On 23 October, Gauguin finally joined Van Gogh in Arles, and at the beginning of November both men painted a vineyard. In his letters, Van Gogh had been carrying on a discussion with Gauguin and Bernard about working from life, as he advocated, or from memory or the imagination, the method championed by his friends. During Gauguin's two-month stay in Arles, Van Gogh did in fact experiment with his friends' ideas, and his new vineyard—with working figures drenched in the red light of the setting sun—was therefore done from the imagination. It was given the name *The Red Vineyard* (fig. 73), and the previous painting, derived from reality, was called *The Green Vineyard*.

The two painters also set up their easels on the Alyscamps, the Roman necropolis of Arles with an avenue lined by poplars and sarcophagi. The trees were wearing their autumn colours and losing their leaves, and they both depicted this scene. In the four canvases Van Gogh painted, he dotted the avenue with strolling figures and couples (fig. 74), thus giving these compositions connotations similar to those pervading his versions of *The Poet's Garden*.

During the rest of Gauguin's stay, the men concentrated mainly on portraits and figure studies. Their work was sadly interrupted, however, by the violent clash that led

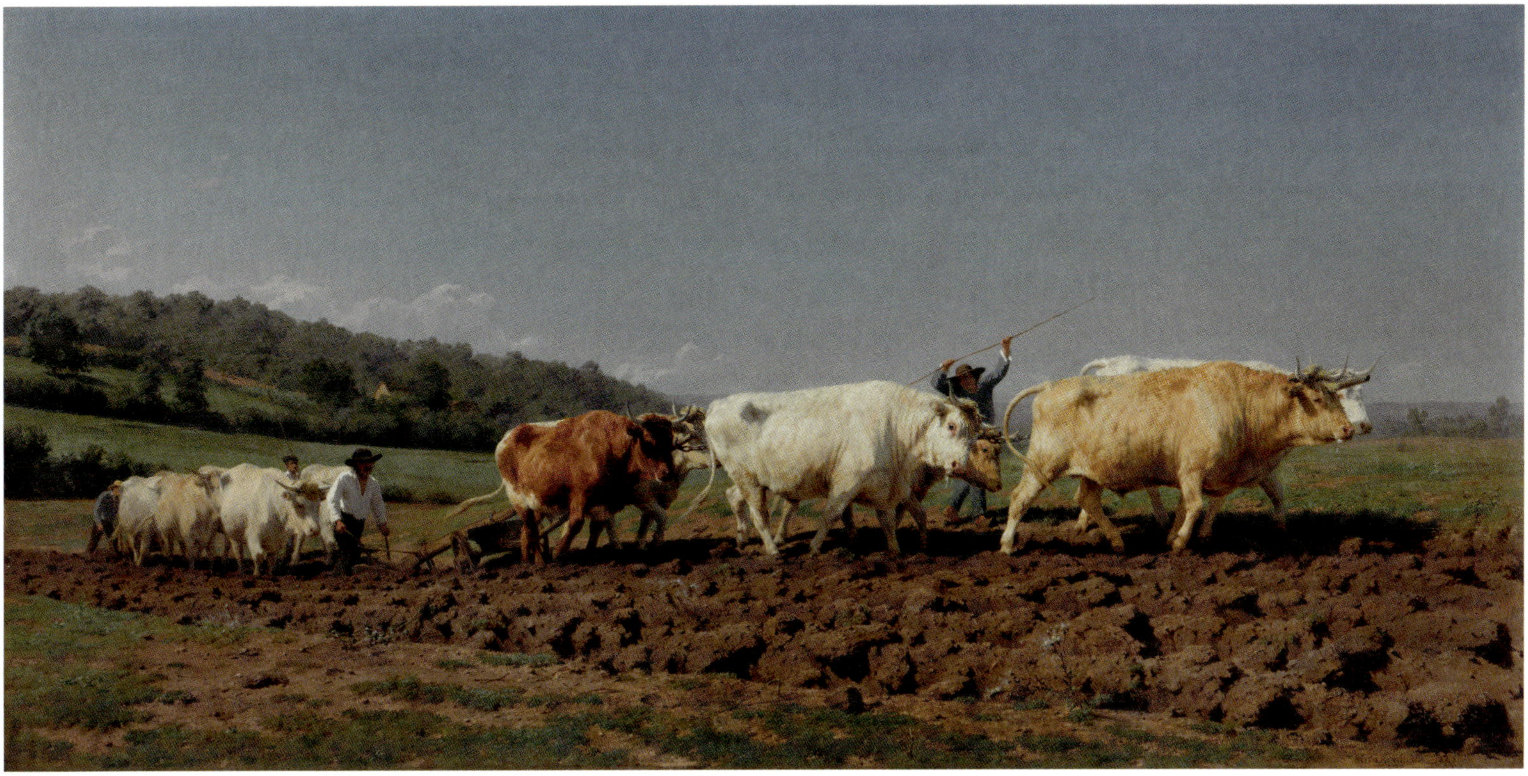

fig. 71

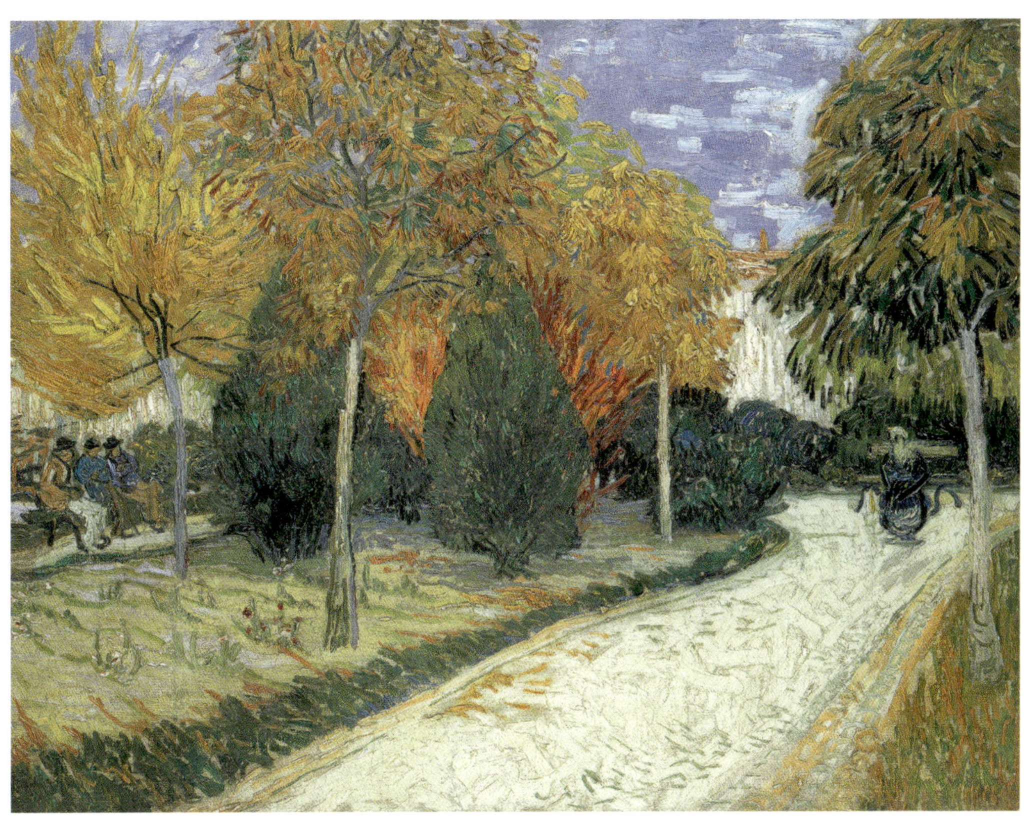

fig. 72

71 Rosa Bonheur,
Ploughing in the Nivernais, 1849
Oil on canvas, 133 × 260 cm
Musée d'Orsay, Paris

72 Vincent van Gogh,
The Public Park at Arles,
October 1888
Oil on canvas, 72 × 93 cm
Private collection

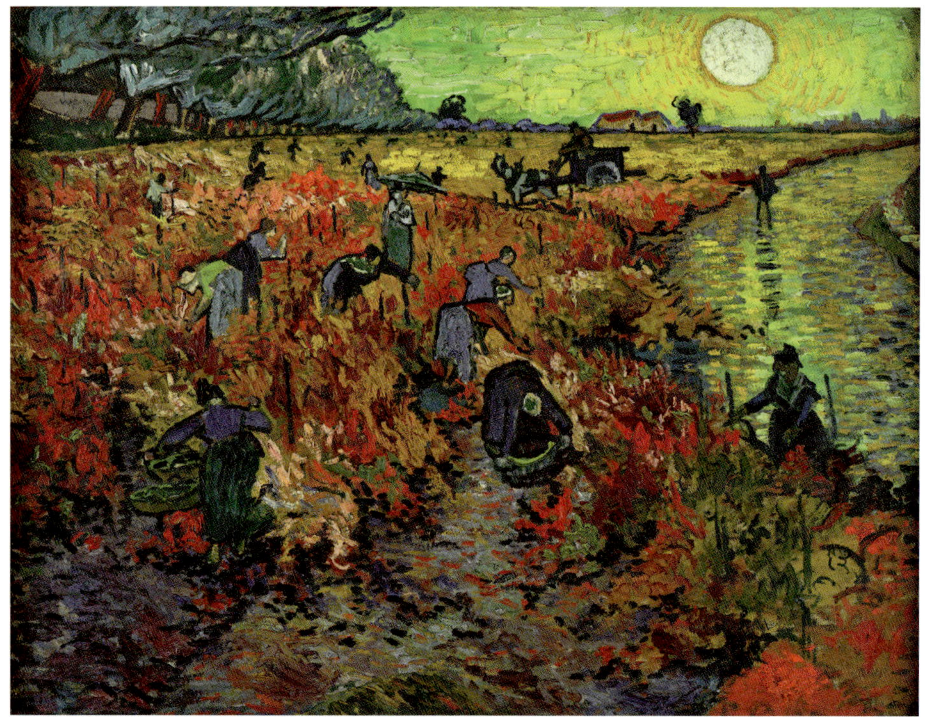

fig. 73

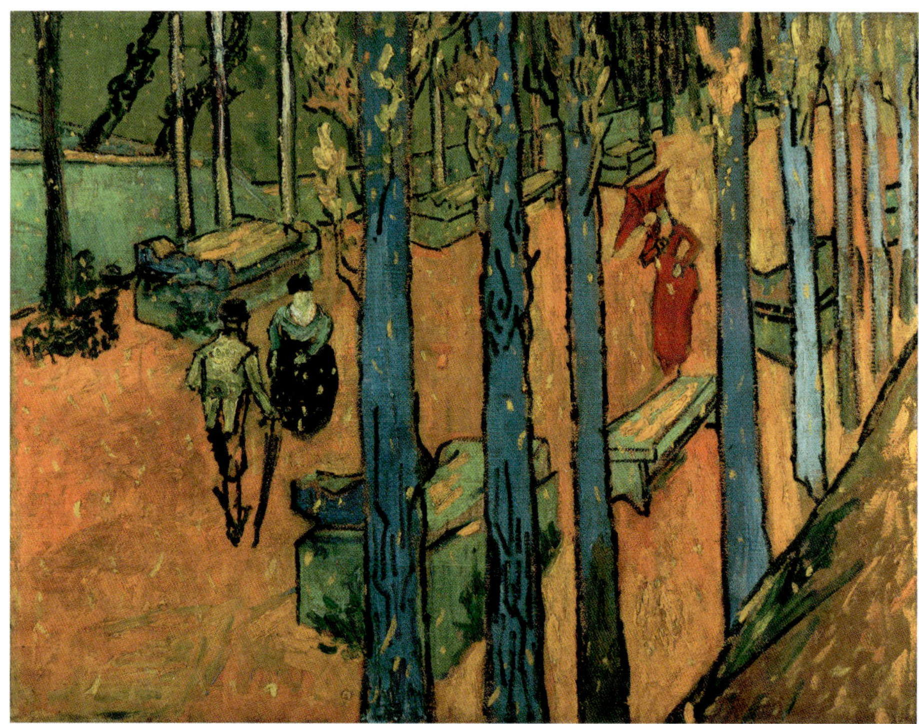

fig. 74

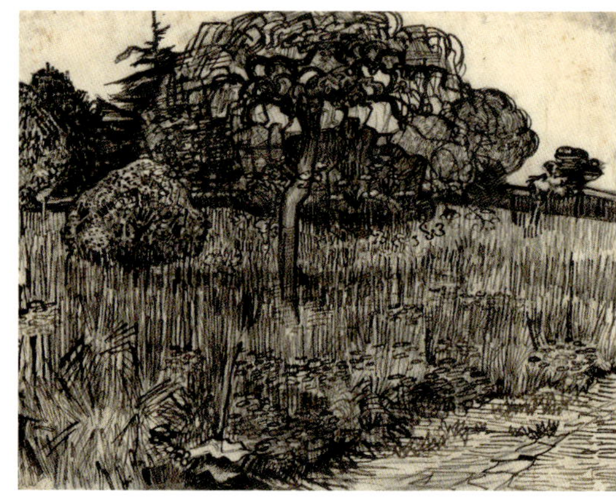

fig. 75

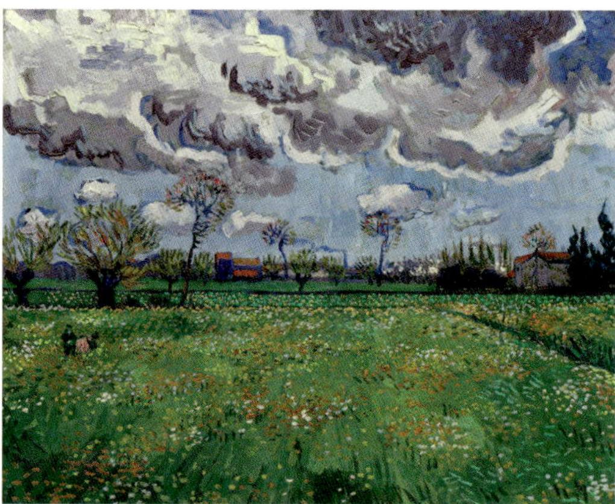

fig. 76

73 Vincent van Gogh,
The Red Vineyard, November 1888
Oil on canvas, 75×93 cm
Pushkin Museum, Moscow

74 Vincent van Gogh, *Falling Leaves (Les Alyscamps)*, November 1888
Oil on canvas, 72.8×91.9 cm
Kröller-Müller Museum, Otterlo

75 VVincent van Gogh,
Weeping Tree, May 1889
Reed pen and black-brown ink, with black chalk on wove paper, 49.8×61.3 cm
The Art Institute of Chicago, Gift of Tiffany and Margaret Day Blake

76 Vincent van Gogh,
Landscape under a Stormy Sky,
April 1889
Oil on canvas, 60.5×73.7 cm
Private collection

to Gauguin's sudden departure—which dashed Van Gogh's hopes for a community of artists working in Provence—and Van Gogh's two-week stay in hospital. In early January 1889, he found himself in a radically different situation. His illness, which had struck suddenly and without warning, had left him in a state of great uncertainty. He suffered several more attacks and required further hospitalization before finally leaving for Saint-Rémy in May. The neighbourhood residents had meanwhile turned against him and signed a petition demanding his admission to an asylum, which was subsequently approved by the mayor.

In spite of all these problems, Van Gogh continued to work whenever his health permitted. In April, the spring again offered enticing scenes of blossoming trees, but he could not find the energy or enthusiasm to tackle them, as he had done the previous year—the result was a mere four paintings. He also resumed making large pen drawings, but ended up producing only a few sheets.

Van Gogh's melancholy state seems to have seeped through into several works made in April and May. Writing about a scene in his beloved park on the Place Lamartine—to be sure, a rather grim-looking sheet (fig. 75)—he said: "Today I've made one of those drawings which became very dark and quite melancholic for springtime" [768]. A similar sentiment seems to be expressed in a painting that originated several weeks earlier (fig. 76). It is clearly a spring scene with a strolling couple—the woman is picking flowers—and everything is painted in bright colours with rapid brushstrokes, but above it is a mass of grey clouds, executed in heavy strokes. It is a very unusual combination in Van Gogh's work, and it is not unreasonable to interpret it as a reflection of his state of mind during his last months in Arles.

VAN GOGH IN SAINT-RÉMY

When Van Gogh had himself voluntarily admitted to the asylum of St-Paul-de-Mausole just outside Saint-Rémy on 8 May 1889, he immediately made several pleasant discoveries. After the commotion of his last five and a half months in Arles, the asylum offered him much-needed peace. In addition to people with serious mental illnesses, there were patients like himself, who, though ill, were still able to carry on a conversation and associate normally with others. He was given a room on the first floor, as well as one on the ground floor to use as a studio—an unexpected bonus. Moreover, the large old garden provided him with many landscape motifs, and in May there were flowers in bloom, so he could work without leaving the grounds of the asylum. He gratefully took advantage of this opportunity, working for weeks on end, giving in to his need for a trouble-free life.

For the most part, he was forced to suppress his desire to paint figures, because even the calmest of his fellow patients were unsuitable as models. Besides, posing was probably not allowed by the medical staff, who did not want to expose the patients to tension or anxiety. Van Gogh's love of portraiture had been rekindled during a visit he and Gauguin had paid on 18 December 1888 to the Musée Fabre in Montpellier, where they had seen portraits of Alfred Bruyas, including one by Delacroix. It would be months, however, before he had the opportunity to paint portraits. In Saint-Rémy, he complained repeatedly that he had no models, but in September 1889 he finally had the chance to paint several portraits and self-portraits. In that same month, he came up with an inventive and safe solution: he copied prints of figure pieces by his favourite masters, just as he had done at the beginning of his career.

Still lifes dating from his year in Saint-Rémy are also rare. No doubt the patients had a minimum of objects in their cells, and it is unlikely that Van Gogh even had a vase for flowers. A large drawing of his studio features, on the windowsill, two bottles,

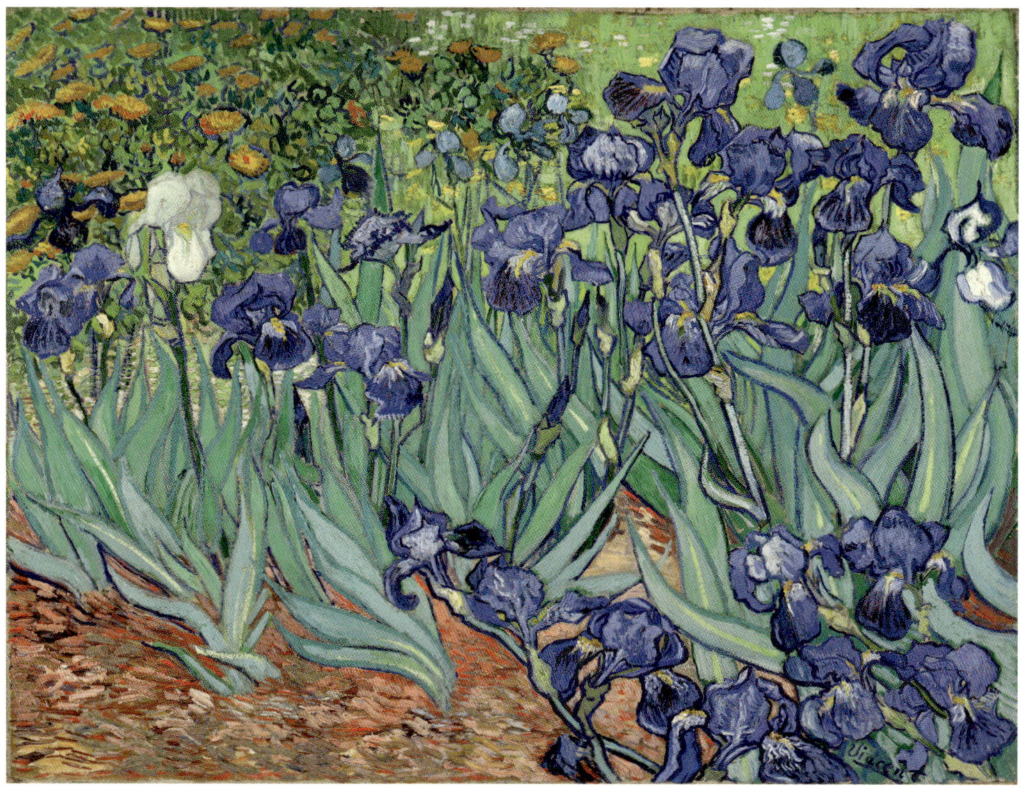

fig. 77

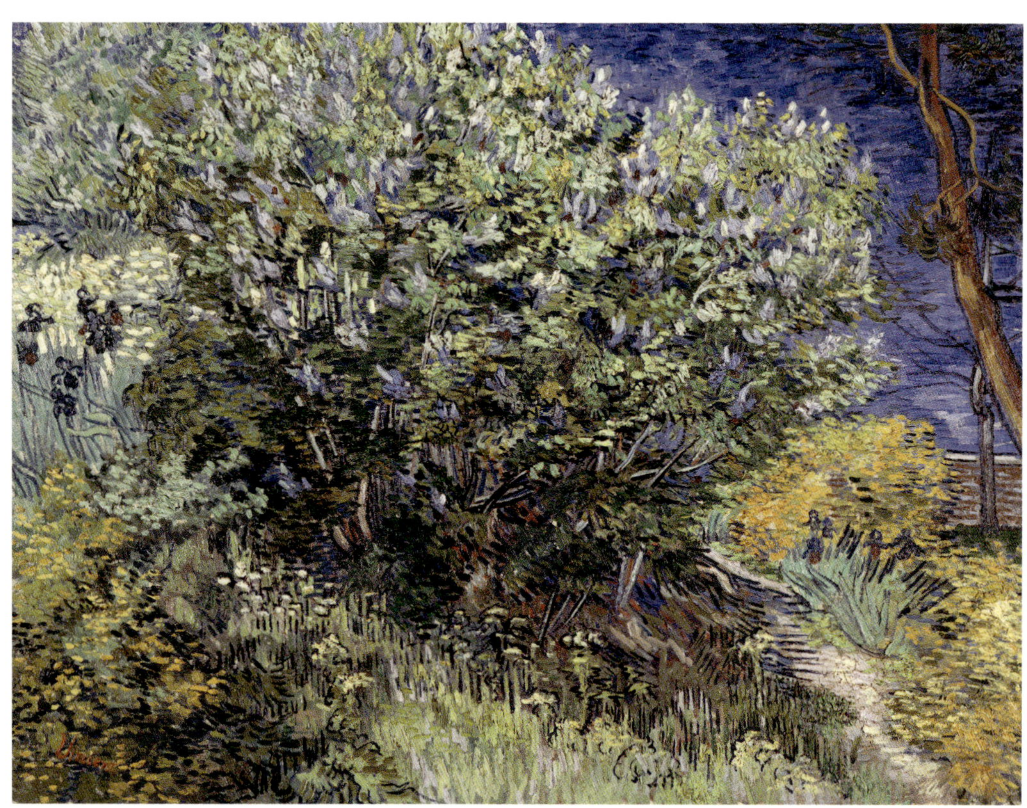

fig. 78

77 Vincent van Gogh, *Irises*, May 1889
Oil on canvas, 74.3 × 94.3 cm
The J. Paul Getty Museum, Los Angeles

78 Vincent van Gogh, *Lilacs*, May 1889
Oil on canvas, 72 × 92 cm
The State Hermitage Museum, St Petersburg

two glasses and a cylindrical container of some kind, while below them, on a table at the right, are a number of boxes that presumably contain artists' materials. He probably did not have much more than this to work with, and it is revealing that the only four still lifes from this period—two with vases of irises, two with roses—date from the last days of his stay in Saint-Rémy, when the rules governing the asylum's internal regime no longer applied to him, owing to his impending departure.

Not surprisingly, the landscape dominates Van Gogh's Saint-Rémy œuvre. The garden provided him with a wealth of subjects, and the walled wheatfield that he looked out on from his room became another leitmotiv of his work. It offered him an opportunity to follow the growth cycle of the wheat, which he documented in an impressive series of canvases.

THE GARDEN AND THE SURROUNDINGS OF THE ASYLUM

The garden obviously appealed to Van Gogh, for the day after his arrival he made paintings that are reckoned among the masterpieces of his œuvre, *Irises* and *Lilacs* (fig. 77, 78). There he also found small motifs, such as a moth that had alighted on a leaf.[59]

Vincent had painted various *sous-bois* in Paris (cat. 14), and he now took up this theme again, drawing and painting such scenes as early as May and again in the summer. In comparison with the work of his predecessors and his own Paris variants, he now went a step further, as one of the studies from that time shows (cat. 25): viewing the subject from a sharp downward angle, he depicted only the lowest part of the tree trunks and concentrated on the ground beneath and the undergrowth, making virtuosic use of green, yellow-green and blue hues and a wide range of varied brushstrokes.

In the autumn of 1889, Van Gogh painted the pine trees in the garden (cat. 26). The capricious idiom of the trees, as well as the earth colours used to evoke autumn, lend these paintings dramatic overtones that are perfectly in keeping with the season portrayed. The terms in which he spoke about pine trees show that he was still inclined to attribute them with anthropomorphic qualities.[60]

THE WHEATFIELD

In his depictions of the walled wheatfield, Van Gogh again paid tribute, above all, to the growth cycle of wheat. He first caught sight of the still-green crop from his room on the first floor, several metres above the field—later he stood in the field to paint it—and once again the scene made him think of another painter: "A square of wheat in an enclosure, a perspective in the manner of Van Goyen, above which in the morning I see the sun rise in its glory" [776]. At the end of June or beginning of July, the wheat was already ripe and he was able to paint the harvest (fig. 79). An attack of his illness prevented him from finishing this painting until September, at which time he described it to Theo: "A reaper, the study is all yellow, terribly thickly impasted, but the subject was beautiful and simple. I then saw in this reaper—a vague figure struggling like a devil in the full heat of the day to reach the end of his toil—I then saw the image of death in it, in this sense that humanity would be the wheat being reaped. So if you like it's the opposite of that Sower I tried before. But in this death nothing sad, it takes place in broad daylight with a sun that floods everything with a light of fine gold" [800]. Later on, he also depicted the clearing of the field, the ploughing, and the young wheat stalks shooting up again.

PROVENÇAL MOTIFS

In Saint-Rémy, more so than in Arles, Van Gogh was struck by characteristic aspects of the Provençal landscape, which he found while exploring the countryside around the asylum. In 1888 his view had been preconditioned by the Japanese character he had hoped to find in the south—a kind of self-fulfilling prophecy—and at first he had mostly seized upon familiar subjects, such as the wheat harvest. It took time to fathom his new surroundings in Provence: "To do nature here, as everywhere, one must really be here for a long time" [783]. Now, in Saint-Rémy, he began to realize that the southern landscape offered characteristic subjects other than wheatfields, and he resolved to capture these typically Provençal motifs: cypresses, whether or not growing in a wheatfield (fig. 80), and olive groves. Neither motif was simple to paint, certainly not in terms of colour. The dark green of the cypress had "such a distinguished quality. It's the *dark* patch in a sun-drenched landscape, but it's one of the most interesting dark notes, the most difficult to hit off exactly that I can imagine. Now they must be seen here against the blue, *in* the blue, rather". In Arles, Van Gogh had been searching mainly for vivid colour contrasts, but his palette in Saint-Rémy became more muted, which only increased his interest in hues such as that of the cypress. This was also true of the olive trees and their leaves, with their shimmering flux of colour: "Silver, sometimes more blue, sometimes greenish, bronzed, whitening on ground that is yellow, pink, purplish or orangeish to dull red ochre. But very difficult, very difficult. But that suits me and attracts me to work fully in gold or silver" [806] (fig. 81). He made no fewer than fifteen paintings of olive groves.

From Arles, Van Gogh had seen the low mountains of the Alpilles, another characteristic landmark, but only on the horizon. Now, in Saint-Rémy, they loomed large in the landscape, for the asylum lay almost at the foot of the mountain chain. Vincent searched for motifs during his walks in the Alpilles, but he also used their striking outlines to create impressive backgrounds (fig. 82). The work reproduced here is one of the paintings made in June, when Van Gogh—still a patient at the asylum—was again involved in a discussion with Gauguin and Bernard about the role of the imagination in the artistic process, and let himself be influenced to a large degree by their views. In the same period, he painted *The Starry Night* (fig. 83), according to the same procedure, and wrote about these canvases to Theo: "Although I haven't seen the latest canvases either by Gauguin or Bernard, I'm fairly sure that these two studies I speak of are comparable in sentiment. When you've seen these two studies for a while... I'll perhaps be able to give you, better than in words, an idea of the things Gauguin, Bernard and I sometimes chatted about and that preoccupied us" [782]. Both the starry night sky of the south that had captured his imagination in Arles (fig. 50) and the Provençal landscape with its enormous cypresses are compositional elements that he painted with great poetic licence from the imagination.

An unusual landscape that Van Gogh painted later that year is the exact opposite. *Snow-Covered Field with a Harrow (after Millet)* (cat. 27) was not observed from life, nor is it a product of the imagination; instead, it is a large copy after a modest black-and-white print (fig. 84). After a severe attack of his illness—which laid him low from mid-June until the end of August 1889—he was still not well enough in September to venture outdoors, though he did work in his studio. He made replicas of his own work, but also hit upon the idea to follow, once again, the example of the artists he revered, just as he had done at the beginning of his career: by copying prints after their work. He pursued this project, taking breaks when necessary, until the beginning of 1890. Not only did he translate the black-and-white images into colour, but this landscape of January 1890 after his hero Millet gave him another opportunity to depict the coarse

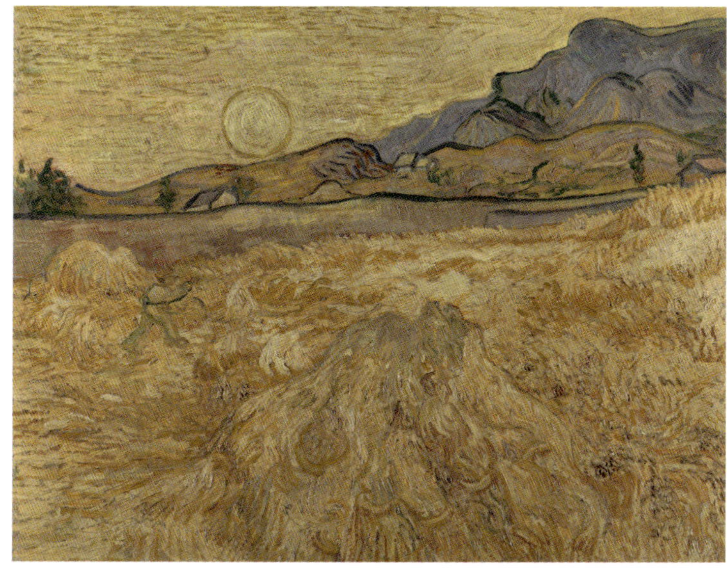

fig. 79

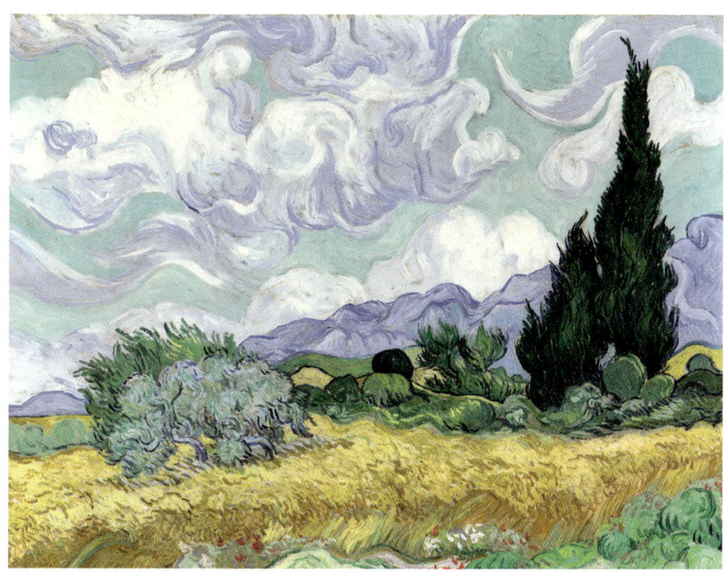

fig. 80

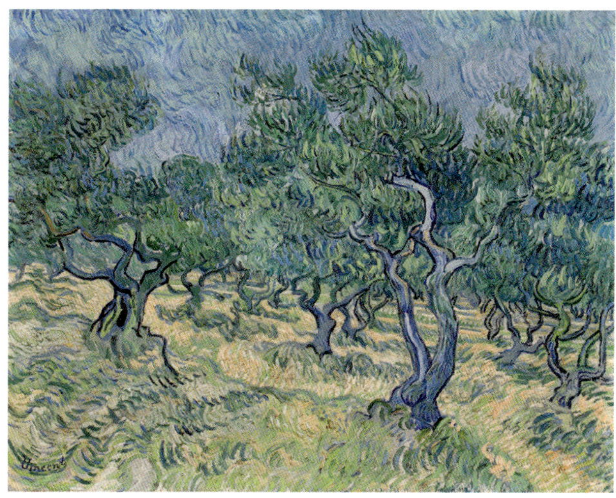

fig. 81

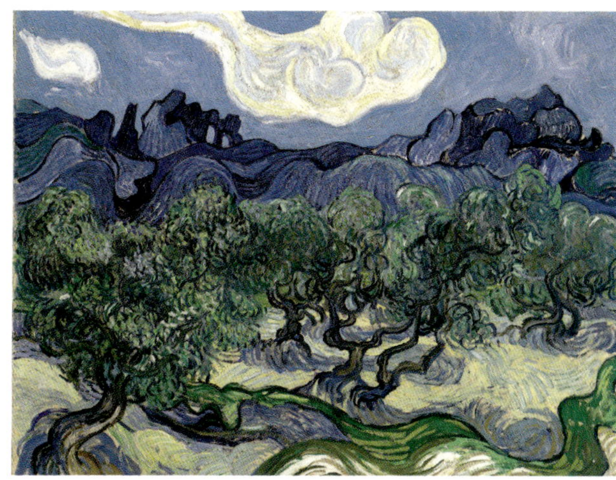

fig. 82

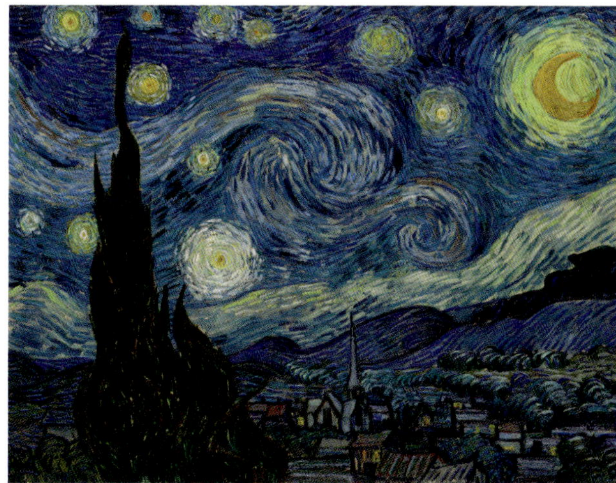

fig. 83

79 Vincent van Gogh, *Wheatfield with Reaper and Sun*, late June–early July 1889, completed September 1889
Oil on canvas, 73×92 cm
Kröller-Müller Museum, Otterlo

80 Vincent van Gogh, *A Wheatfield, with Cypresses*, September 1889
Oil on canvas, 73×91.8 cm
The National Gallery, London.
Bought, Courtauld Fund, 1923

81 Vincent van Gogh, *Olive Grove*, June 1889
Oil on canvas, 72.4×91.9 cm
Kröller-Müller Museum, Otterlo

82 Vincent van Gogh, *The Olive Trees*, June 1889
Oil on canvas, 72.6×91.4 cm
Museum of Modern Art, New York.
Mrs. John Hay Whitney Bequest

83 Vincent van Gogh, *The Starry Night*, June 1889
Oil on canvas, 73.7×92.1 cm
The Museum of Modern Art, New York.
Acquired through the Lillie P. Bliss Bequest

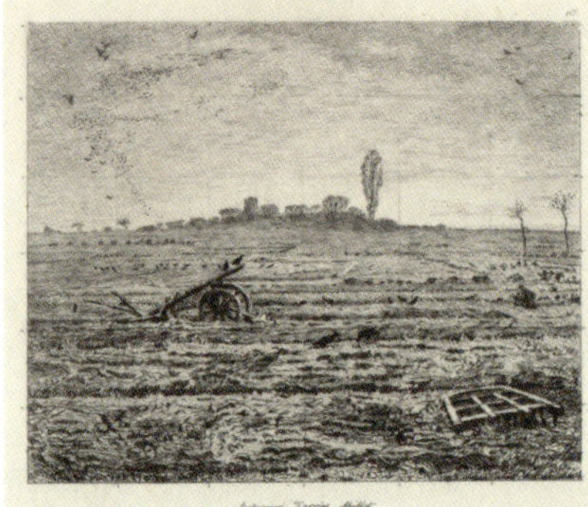

fig. 84

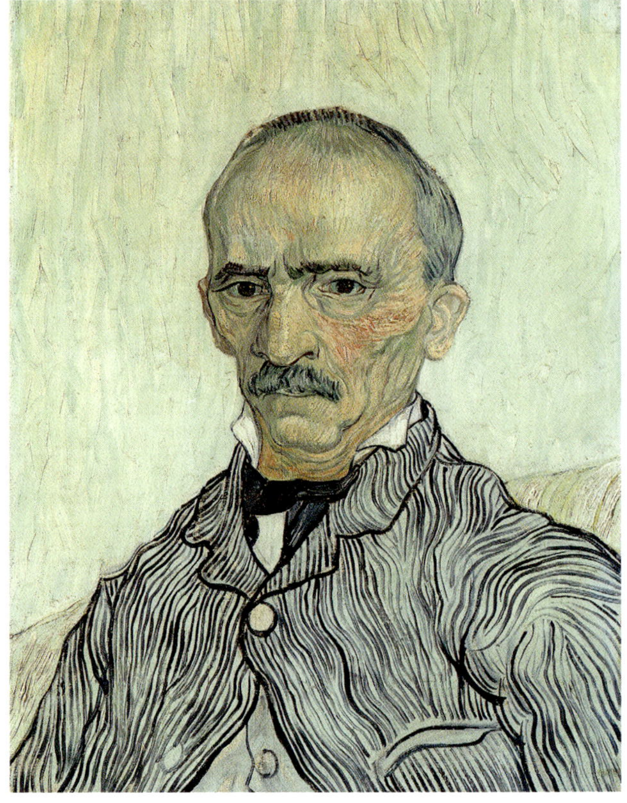

fig. 86

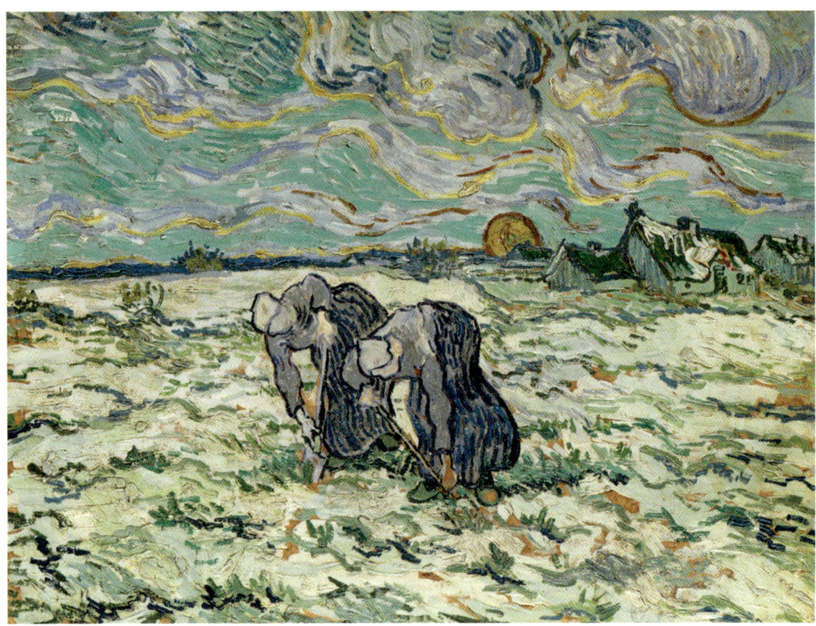

fig. 85

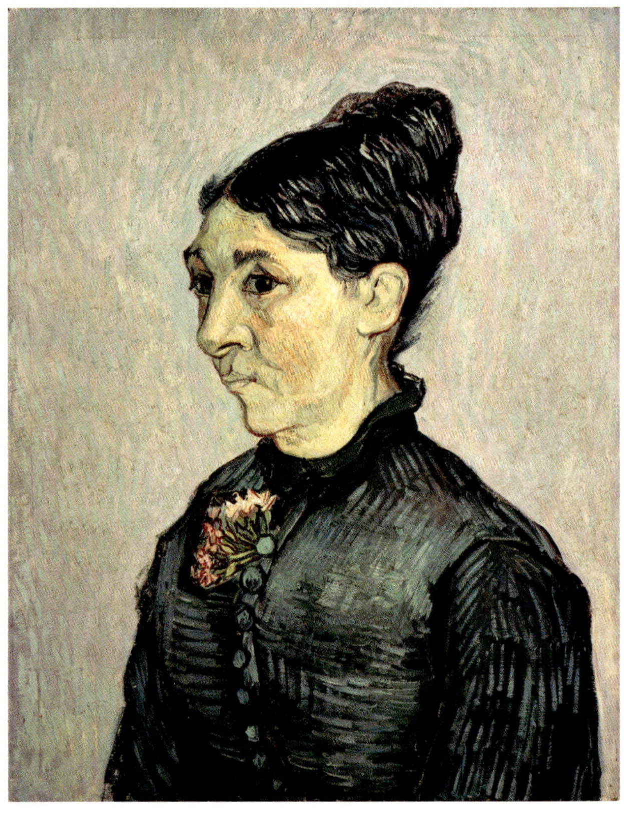

fig. 87

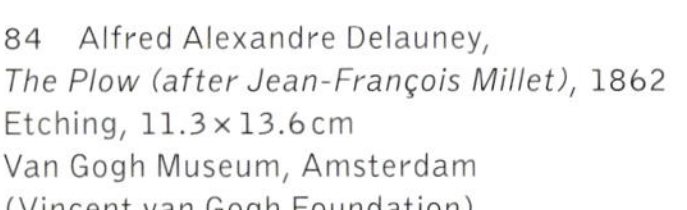

84 Alfred Alexandre Delauney, *The Plow (after Jean-François Millet)*, 1862
Etching, 11.3 × 13.6 cm
Van Gogh Museum, Amsterdam (Vincent van Gogh Foundation)

85 Vincent van Gogh, *The Weeders*, March–April 1890
Oil on paper on canvas, 49.3 × 64 cm
Foundation E.G. Bührle Collection, Zürich

86 Vincent van Gogh, *Portrait of Trabuc*, September 1889
Oil on canvas, 60 × 45 cm
Kunstmuseum Solothurn, Solothurn, Dübi-Müller Foundation, 1980

87 Vincent van Gogh, *Portrait of Madame Trabuc*, September 1889
Oil on canvas on panel, 63.7 × 48 cm
The State Hermitage Museum, St. Petersburg

clods of earth in a freshly ploughed field. The pale hues seen in this canvas are not actually those Van Gogh painted, because the organic pigments in the red paint he used have faded over time. The work originally had a more purple hue.

In February, when the almond trees began to blossom, Van Gogh enthusiastically set to work and made an impressive painting of blossoming branches against a blue sky, "perhaps the most patiently worked, best thing I had done, painted with calm and a greater sureness of touch" [857]. Sadly, his enthusiasm was snuffed out on 22 February by an attack of his illness that prevented him from working for many weeks. By the time he had recovered, the trees had finished flowering, so he was left with only one spring picture, which he decided to give to Theo and Jo for their recently born son.

Van Gogh's state of mind is evident in a number of wintry works conceived as reminiscences of the north, more specifically of Brabant, which he made in April 1890 during a period of deep melancholy (fig. 85). Various sketches from that time, which are closely related to this series, show people working or strolling, sometimes in the snow, against a background of one or more picturesque cottages with thatched roofs (which were not to be found in Provence). These works recollect both the Netherlands and rustic peasant life.

(SELF-)PORTRAITS

At the beginning of September 1889, Van Gogh was given the chance to paint two portraits: one of the asylum's chief orderly, Charles-Elzéard Trabuc, and another of his wife, Jeanne.[61] He made two versions of each, one for the sitter and another for Theo, but only one of each is now known (fig. 86, 87). He was not very happy with Mrs Trabuc's appearance, but her husband's care-worn face was exactly the kind of head he liked to portray: "A most interesting figure. There's a beautiful etching by Legros of an old Spanish nobleman, if you remember it that will give you an idea of the type. He was at the hospital in Marseille during 2 episodes of cholera, anyway he's a man who has seen an enormous number of people die and suffer, and there's an indefinable contemplation in his face, such that I can't help recalling the face of [the French writer François] Guizot—for there's something of that one in this head—but different. But he's a man of the people, and simpler. Anyway, you'll see it if I succeed in it and if I do a repetition of it" [800].

That month, Van Gogh portrayed himself in front of the mirror three times, and mentioned two of these self-portraits in the same letter: "People say—and I'm quite willing to believe it—that it's difficult to know oneself—but it's not easy to paint oneself either. Thus I'm working on two portraits of myself at the moment—for want of another model—because it's more than time that I did a bit of figure work. One I began the first day I got up, I was thin, pale as a devil. It's dark violet blue and the head whiteish with yellow hair, thus a colour effect. But since then I've started another one, three-quarter length on a light background."

In the former likeness, which is actually very evocative, he portrayed himself as a painter, with earnest features and a sharp gaze.[62] The second self-portrait, like the previous one, shows Van Gogh with a serious expression, but the eyes are more contemplative—"vague and veiled" in his own words [801] (fig. 88). He was rather satisfied with the portraits and self-portraits he made that month.[63] The contemplative self-portrait was apparently very dear to him, because he took it along when he travelled the following year to Auvers-sur-Oise.

There also exists a small self-portrait, showing a clean-shaven Van Gogh, painted slightly later for his mother and his sister Wil.[64]

THE HUMAN FIGURE IN COPIES

"I place the black-and-white by Delacroix or Millet or after them in front of me as a subject. And then I improvise colour on it but, being me, not completely of course, but seeking memories of *their* paintings—but the memory, the vague consonance of colours that are in the same sentiment, if not right—that's my own interpretation... So then my brush goes between my fingers as if it were a bow on the violin and absolutely for my pleasure" [805]. This is how Van Gogh described, around 20 September 1889, the project he had conceived, namely the copying of prints. He requested some from Theo. Just as he had done in 1880 in the Belgian Borinage, where he had embarked on his artistic career, he now passionately set to work interpreting the compositions of beloved masters. Although he made most of these copies between September and November 1889, he continued to produce them until the spring of 1890, painting a total of twenty-eight such interpretations. By Eugène Delacroix, he copied *The Good Samaritan* once and the *Pietà* twice. He made copies after two paintings by Rembrandt, *The Raising of Lazarus* (fig. 89) and *The Archangel Raphael* (now no longer attributed to Rembrandt). Works by Gustave Doré, Honoré Daumier and Virginie Demont-Breton also served as examples, but, just as he had done in 1880, he chiefly looked to his great hero Jean-François Millet, whose work inspired him to paint twenty canvases, including the ten scenes comprising the *Labours of the Fields* (*Travaux des Champs*) (to which *The Sheaf-Binder*, cat. 28, belongs), *The Sower* (twice) and *The Diggers*. With the exception of the previously mentioned winter landscape, all of these works are figure paintings. In this way Van Gogh again found support—and this time also solace—from his exemplary predecessors. Moreover, his friend Gauguin unknowingly offered him an opportunity to experiment, in this case with portraiture. When Van Gogh moved to Saint-Rémy, he took along the drawing Gauguin had made in Arles of Madame Ginoux, and in February 1890 he used it to paint four copies of L'Arlésienne (fig. 90, 91).

Remarkably, Van Gogh not only created colourful interpretations of others' prints, but in April and May 1890 he also revisited his own, older work. While painting and drawing his reminiscences of the north, he wrote to Theo: "Please send me what you can find of *figures* among my old drawings, I'm thinking of redoing the painting of the peasants eating supper, lamplight effect. That canvas must be completely dark now, perhaps I could redo it entirely from memory. You must above all send me the women gleaning and diggers, if there are any left. Then if you like I'll redo the old tower at Nuenen and the cottage. I think that if you still have them I could now make something better of them from memory" [863].

None of the works mentioned ever emerged in new versions. Van Gogh made scores of small sketches that can be considered studies for a new version of *The Potato Eaters* (fig. 92), but the canvas never materialized. In May, however, he did make a new version—this time a painting—of an important work from The Hague, the lithograph *At Eternity's Gate*, which Theo had evidently sent to him (cat. 29, fig. 10). At the time, it had been one of his most highly charged and ambitious figure pieces, deeply rooted in the work of the realists, who were foundational to his approach to art.

DEPARTURE FROM SAINT-RÉMY: FLOWER STILL LIFES

Van Gogh worked almost obsessively in the days before his departure from Saint-Rémy on 16 May 1890. On 11 May he wrote to Theo: "I'm working here with calm, unremitting ardour to give a last stroke of the brush. I'm working on a canvas of roses on bright green background and two canvases of large bouquets of violet Irises, one lot against a pink background in which the effect is harmonious and soft through the combination of greens, pinks, violets. On the contrary, the other violet bouquet (ranging up to

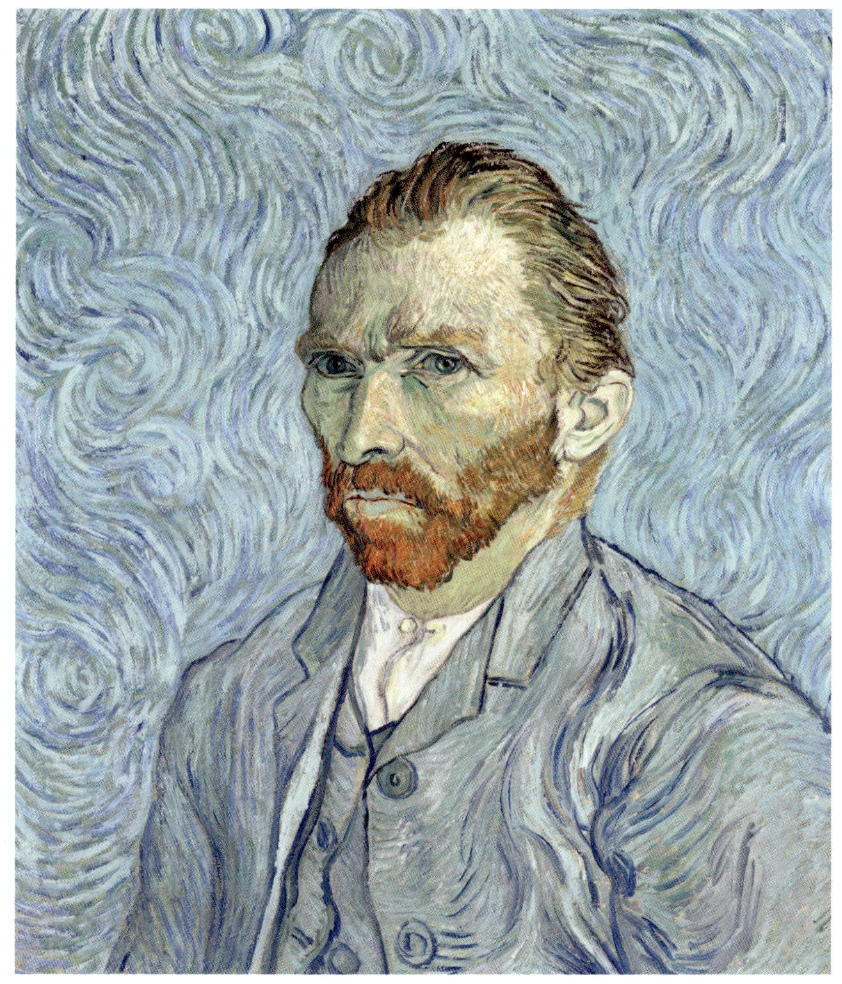

fig. 88

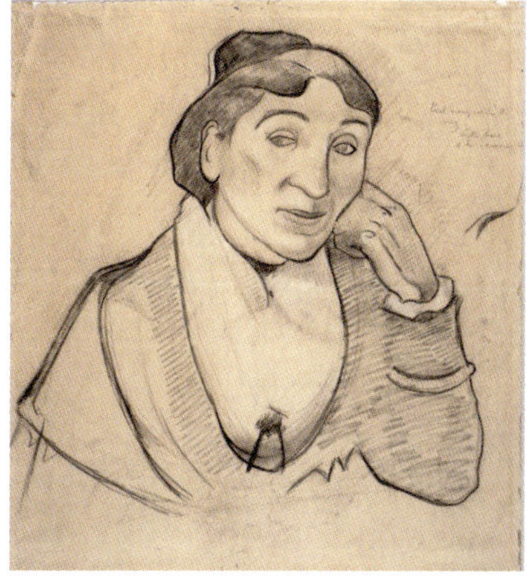

fig. 90

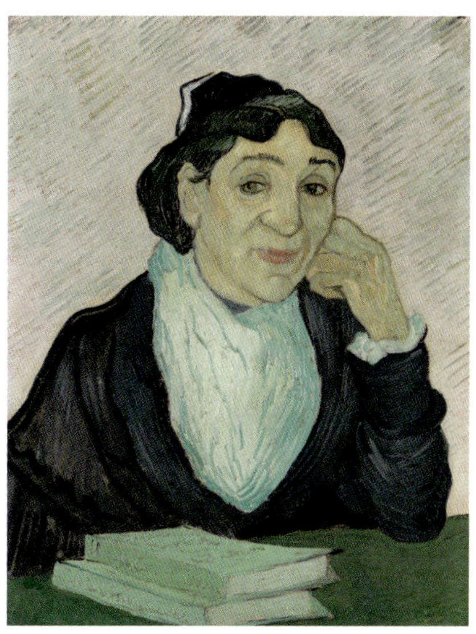

fig. 91

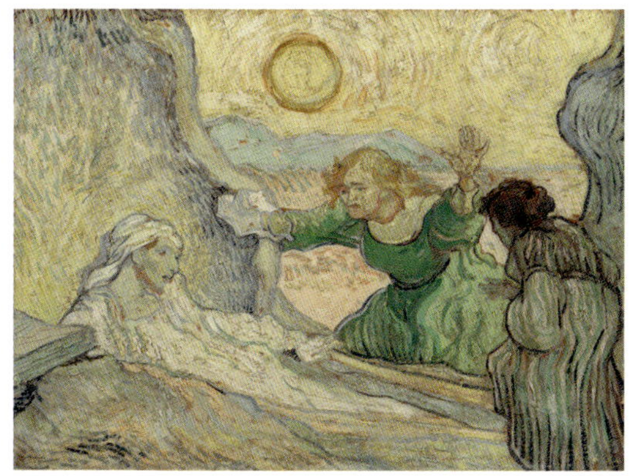

fig. 89

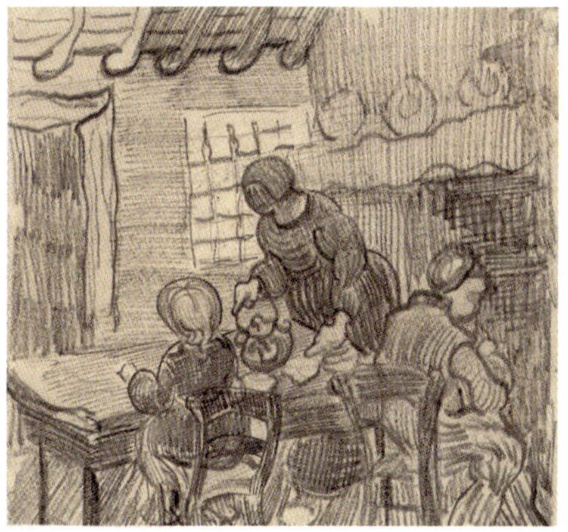

fig. 92

88 Vincent van Gogh, *Portrait of the Artist*, September 1889
Oil on canvas, 65×54.5 cm
Musée d'Orsay, Paris

89 Vincent van Gogh, *The Raising of Lazarus (after Rembrandt)*, May 1890
Oil on paper, 50×65.5 cm
Van Gogh Museum, Amsterdam
(Vincent van Gogh Foundation)

90 Paul Gauguin, *L'Arlésienne, Madame Ginoux*, November 1888
Beige chalk under charcoal with stumping, with salmon-colored pastel, heightened with white chalk on beige wove paper, 56.1×49.2 cm
The Fine Arts Museums of San Francisco, memorial gift from Dr. T. Edward and Tullah Hanley, Bradford, Pennsylvania

91 Vincent van Gogh, *L'Arlésienne (Portrait of Madame Ginoux)*, February 1890
Oil on canvas, 65.3×49 cm
Kröller-Müller Museum, Otterlo

92 Vincent van Gogh, *Interior with Three Figures at a Table*, March–April 1890
Pencil on paper, 25.3×24.4 cm
Van Gogh Museum, Amsterdam
(Vincent van Gogh Foundation)

pure carmine and Prussian blue) standing out against a striking lemon yellow background with other yellow tones in the vase and the base on which it rests is an effect of terribly disparate complementaries that reinforce each other by their opposition" [870] (fig. 93, 94).[65] Two days later he reported: "I've also just finished a canvas of pink roses against [a] yellow-green background in a green vase" [872].[66] All four canvases are in the largest format (c.92x72cm) used by Van Gogh in Arles and Saint-Rémy, and they may be seen as full-blown pendants to the masterly still lifes of sunflowers and oleanders painted in the summer of 1888.

PRODUCTIVE MONTHS IN AUVERS-SUR-OISE

Van Gogh travelled from Saint-Rémy to Paris, where he spent a few days with Theo and his wife, Jo, whom he now met for the first time, along with his nephew and namesake Vincent. On 20 May he travelled to Auvers-sur-Oise, where he rented a room in the Auberge Ravoux.

A number of famous artists had lived and worked in the village of Auvers. Daubigny had a house there, which was still inhabited by his widow. Van Gogh made three paintings of that house and its garden. Van Gogh's friend Camille Pissarro had lived in the neighbouring village of Pontoise and had painted, sometimes in the company of Paul Cézanne, in and around Auvers. Cézanne had in fact stayed with Dr Paul-Ferdinand Gachet, a collector and amateur artist whom Van Gogh met on his very first day in Auvers. Gachet was also a friend of Pissarro, who had been the one to tell Theo about him. The doctor agreed to keep an eye on Van Gogh's health during his stay in Auvers, and a warm friendship developed between the two men.

In the first letter he wrote from Auvers, Van Gogh told Theo that he liked the village: "Auvers is really beautiful—among other things many old thatched roofs, which are becoming rare" [873]. He realized at once that he would not be able to rest in such surroundings, and he reported this to Theo the following day: "Auvers is decidedly very beautiful. So much so that I think it'll be more advantageous to work than not to work" [874]. He was indeed immensely productive in Auvers, where he found old cottages and newer, charming houses that fascinated him (fig. 95). The rolling landscape, with cultivated fields where the crops had begun to ripen, provided fodder for new work. And once again he was eager to resume painting portraits.

RURAL SURROUNDINGS

An attack of his illness had caused Van Gogh to miss most of the blossoming trees in Saint-Rémy, but in Auvers-sur-Oise he encountered chestnut trees that were still in blossom. Not only did he paint these (cat. 30), but he also produced his most impressive still life of this period, composed of branches of blossoming chestnut (fig. 98).

Again, the fields of wheat assumed a major role in his depictions of the rural surroundings of Auvers (fig. 96). Clearly, he still had his revered peasant painters in mind when tackling such works. On 25 May he wrote a letter to the art critic Joseph Jacob Isaäcson, who had recently written an essay in which he drew attention to the progressive nature of Van Gogh's work.[67] Van Gogh pointed out other painters to him: "Let others better and more powerful than me express their symbolic language. Millet is the voice of the wheat, and Jules Breton also" (RM 21). His comment is odd, because Isaäcson was discussing the merits of the contemporary avant-garde, not the great artists of previous decades. Van Gogh, however, was obsessed once more with "the voice of the wheat". The landscape illustrated here bears witness to a

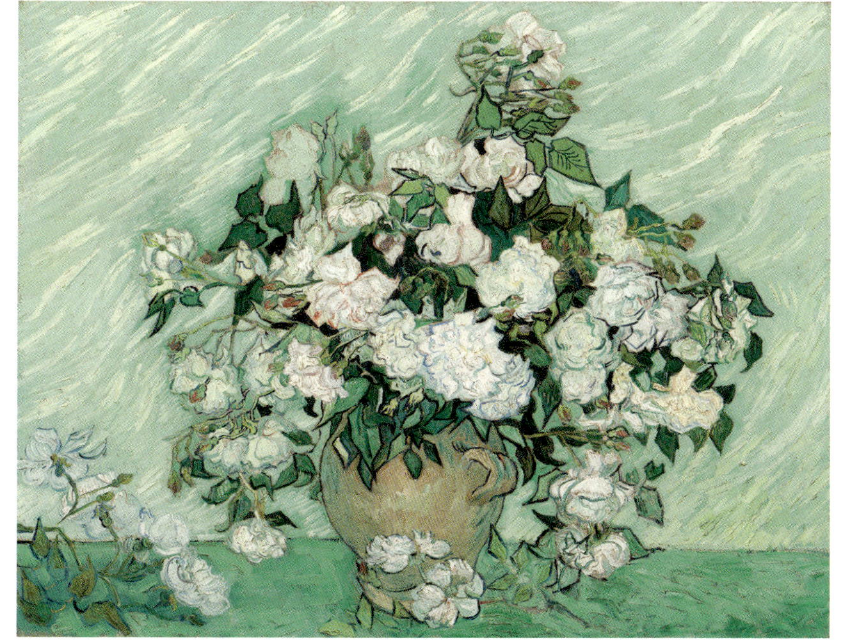

fig. 93

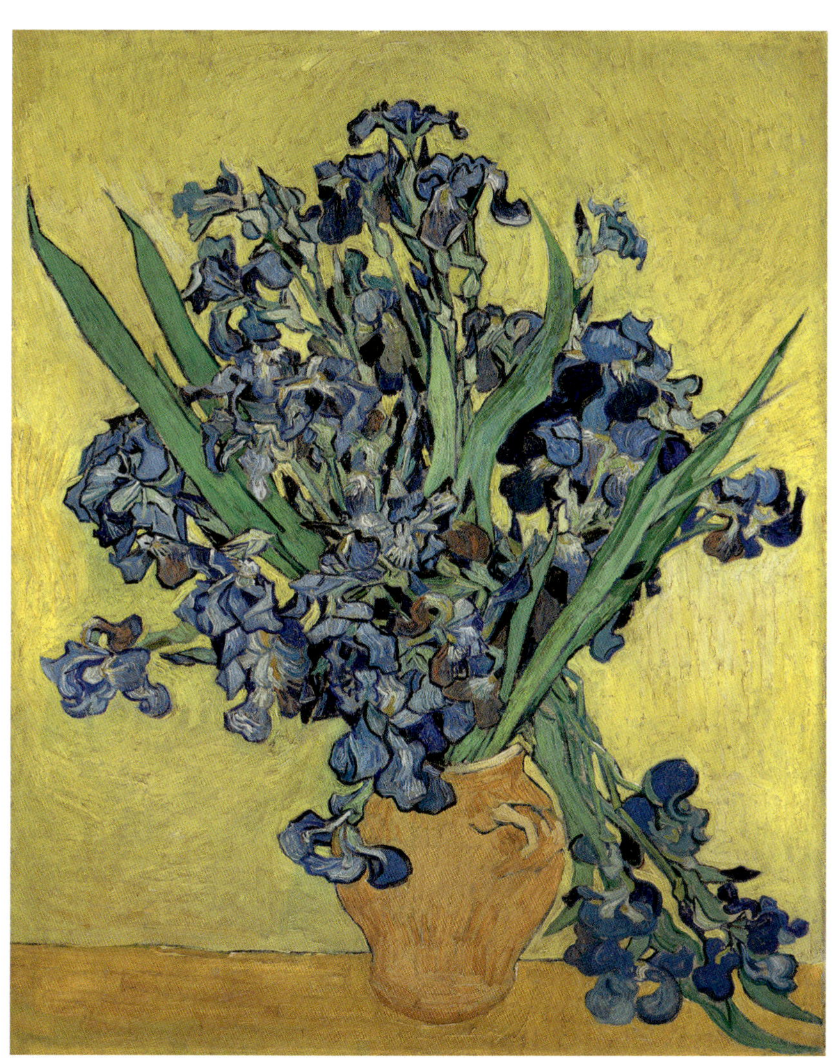

fig. 94

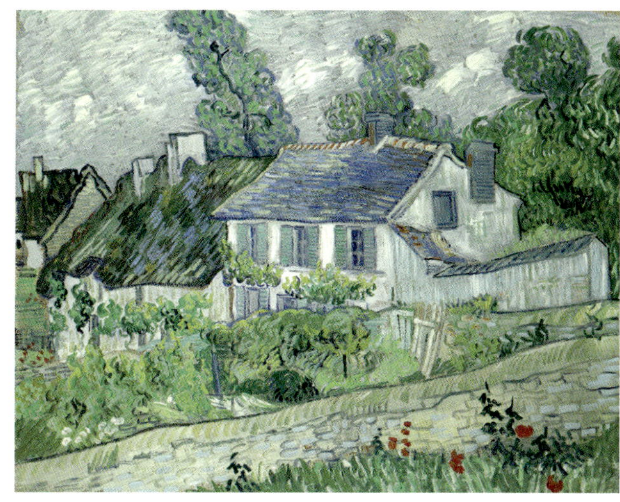

fig. 95

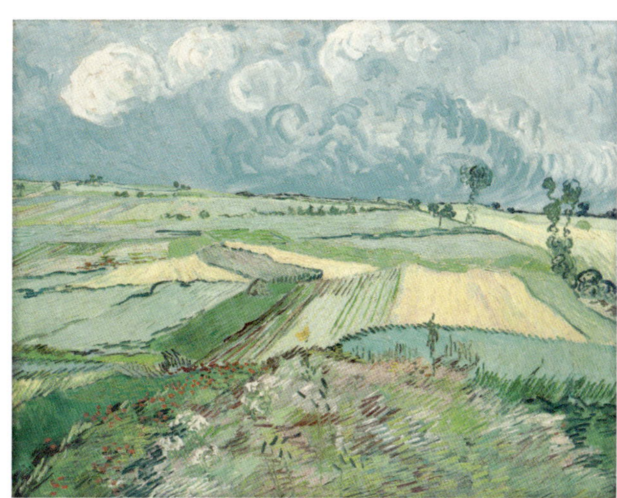

fig. 96

93
Vincent van Gogh, *Roses*,
May 1890
Oil on canvas, 71 × 90 cm
National Gallery of Art, Washington.
Gift of Pamela Harriman in memory
of W. Averell Harrimann

94 Vincent van Gogh, *Irises*,
May 1890
Oil on canvas, 92.7 × 73.9 cm
Van Gogh Museum, Amsterdam
(Vincent van Gogh Foundation)

95 Vincent van Gogh,
Houses at Auvers, June 1890
Oil on canvas, 60 × 73 cm
Toledo Museum of Art, Toledo.
Purchased with funds from the
Libbey Endowment, Gift of Edward
Drummond Libbey

96 Vincent van Gogh,
*Wheat Fields after the Rain
(The Plain of Auvers)*, 1890
Oil on canvas, 73.3 × 92.4 cm
Carnegie Museum of Art, Pittsburgh.
Acquired through the generosity
of the Sarah Mellon Scaife Family

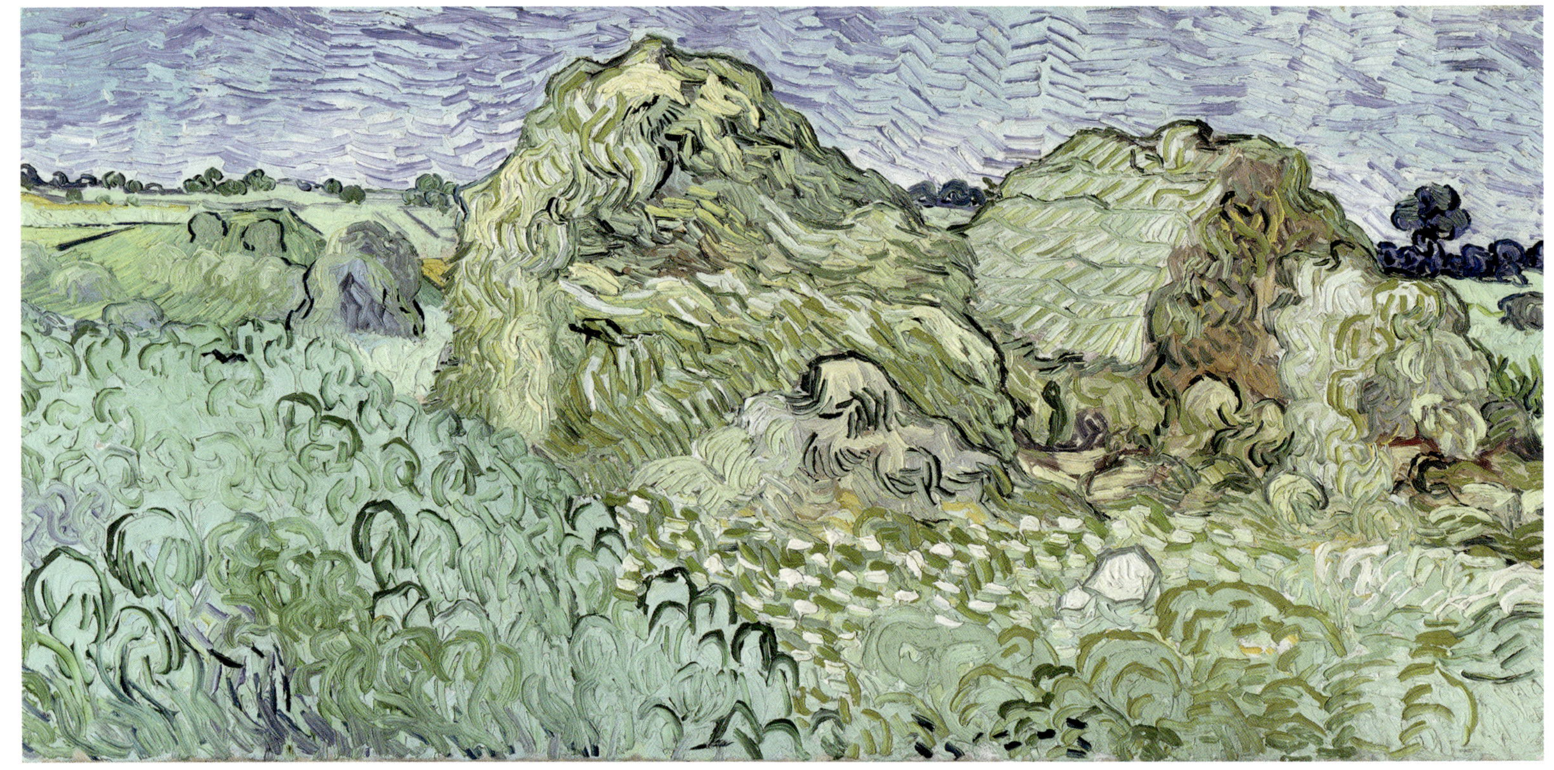

fig. 97

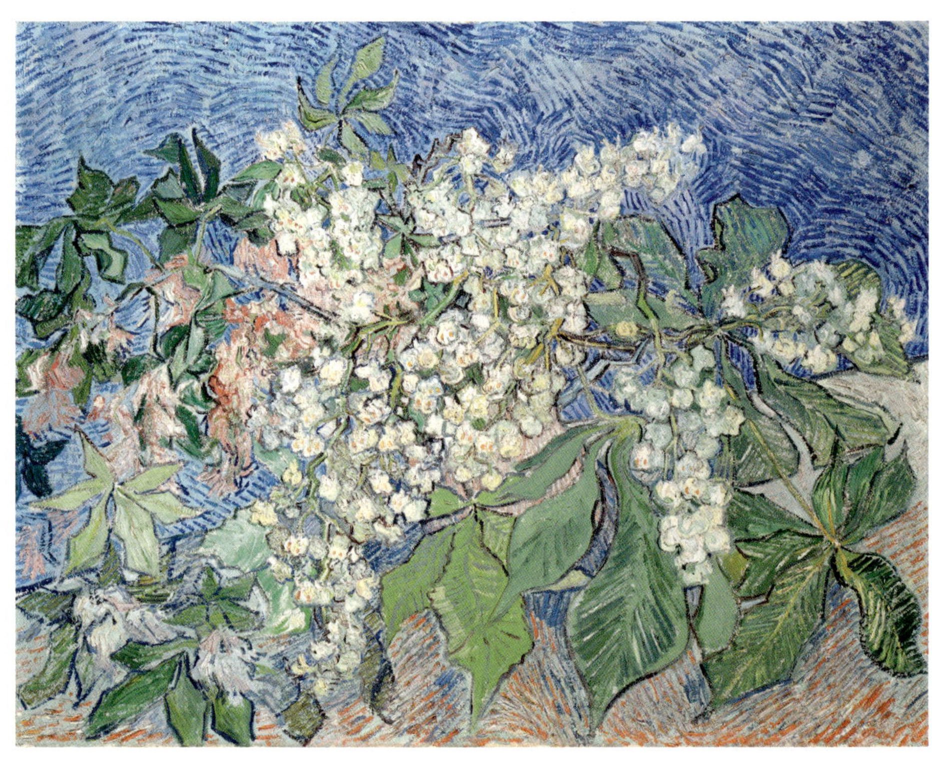

fig. 98

97 Vincent van Gogh,
Field with Wheat Stacks, July 1890
Oil on canvas, 50 × 100 cm
Beyeler Foundation, Riehen/Basel,
Beyeler Collection

98 Vincent van Gogh, *Blossoming Chestnut Branches*, May 1890
Oil on canvas, 73 × 92 cm
Foundation E.G. Bührle Collection, Zürich

phenomenon that had first manifested itself in Arles, developed further in Saint-Rémy, and matured fully in Auvers-sur-Oise: he now furnished his wheatfields and other harvest landscapes with a bare minimum of small figures, or even omitted them altogether (fig. 97). This is a rather curious development for an artist who felt so strongly about figures at work, yet it testifies, above all, to Van Gogh's realization that the crops in the fields actually possessed an eloquence of their own, and figures only detracted from it. The wheat is also the subject of a composition in which he zoomed in on the crop until the ears of wheat were the only thing to be seen (cat. 31).

In Auvers, Van Gogh used a striking format for a whole series of paintings, nearly all of them landscapes like the one mentioned above (fig. 97). This very elongated shape (50 × 100 cm) is fairly uncommon in his œuvre. In The Hague he had indeed made oblong works, and there is even a lost drawing of the same dimensions.[68] The designs he made for Antoon Hermans's dining room were also oblong. But now he used this format no fewer than thirteen times: for ten landscapes, two paintings of Daubigny's garden and a portrait. He knew of many artists who had produced work of comparable proportions, such as Breton (fig. 2), but it was probably the example of Daubigny, who had frequently utilized this characteristic landscape format (see fig. 51), that prompted Van Gogh once again to follow in the footsteps of the Barbizon masters—in the very place where one of them had lived.

STILL LIFES

The season now gave Van Gogh another opportunity to paint flowers, the only type of still life he made in Auvers. It is a small group of paintings, most of them in a relatively small format, and this time, too, they can be seen primarily as exercises in colour. One exception is the above-mentioned *Blossoming Chestnut Branches*, in which spring is almost palpable (fig. 98). He depicted it with pronounced colours and brushstrokes that almost make the painting tingle with life, which is highly appropriate for a scene of burgeoning springtime. The large format, identical to that of the irises and roses from Saint-Rémy and the bigger sunflowers done in Arles, indicates the importance he attached to this work.

THE MODERN PORTRAIT

Landscapes and village views dominate Van Gogh's Auvers production, but once he saw an opportunity to find models, he focused mainly on portraiture, which became increasingly central to his artistic considerations. On 5 June he wrote to his sister Wil: "What I'm most passionate about, much much more than all the rest in my profession—is the portrait, the modern portrait. I seek it by way of colour, and am certainly not alone in seeking it in this way. I would like, you see I'm far from saying that I can do all this, but anyway I'm aiming at it, I *would like* to do portraits which would look like apparitions to people a century later. So I don't try to do us by photographic resemblance but by our passionate expressions, using as a means of expression and intensification of the character our science and modern taste for colour" [879]. He had brought one of his Saint-Rémy self-portraits with him to Auvers-sur-Oise and had shown it to Gachet (fig. 88). Its highly expressive qualities were probably indicative of what he now had in mind. Gachet was enthusiastic about that canvas, so Van Gogh set to work on a portrait of the doctor (fig. 99): "Thus the portrait of Dr Gachet shows you a face the colour of an overheated and sun-scorched brick, with a reddish head of hair, a white cap, in surroundings of landscape, blue background of hills, his suit is ultramarine blue, this brings out the face and makes it paler, despite the fact that it's brick-coloured. The hands, hands of an obstetrician, are paler than the face. Before him on a red

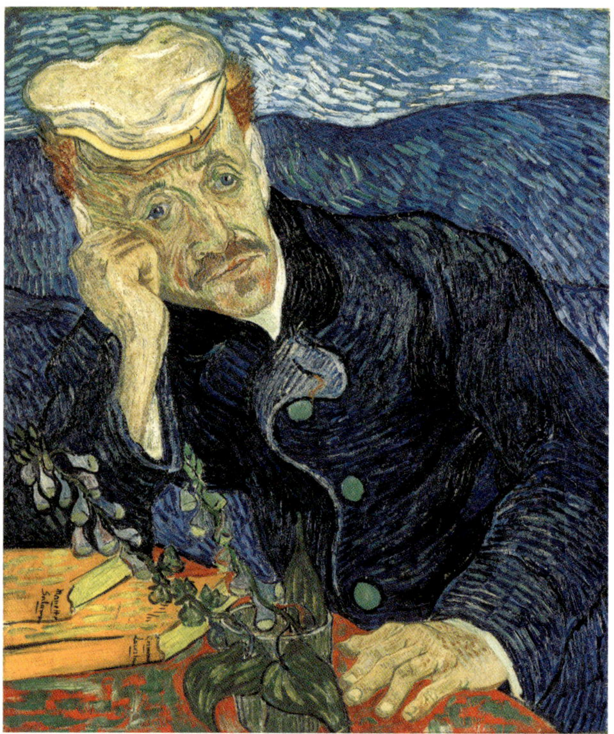

fig. 99

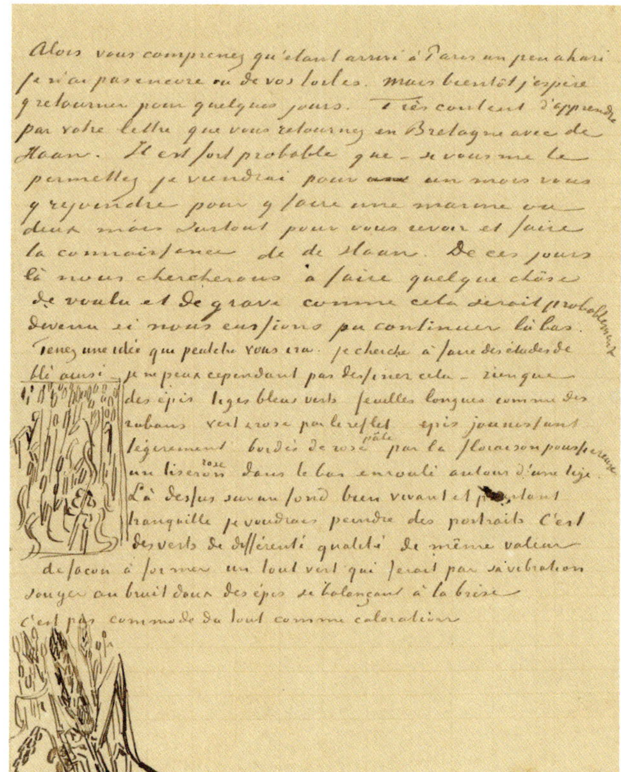

Alors vous comprenez qu'étant arrivé à Paris un peu ahuri
je n'ai pas encore vu de vos toiles. mais bientôt j'espère
y retourner pour quelques jours. Très content d'apprendre
par votre lettre que vous retournez en Bretagne avec de
Haan. Il est fort probable que — si vous me le
permettez je viendrai pour un mois vous
y rejoindre pour y faire une marine ou
deux mais surtout pour vous revoir et faire
la connaissance de de Haan. De ces jours
là nous chercherons à faire quelque chose
de voulu et de grave comme cela serait probablement
devenu si nous eussions pu continuer là bas.
Tenez une idée qui peutêtre vous ira. je cherche à faire des études de
blé ainsi je ne peux cependant pas dessiner cela — rien que
des épis tiges bleu vert feuilles longues comme des
rubans vert et rose par le reflet épis jaunissant
légèrement bordés de rose pâle par la floraison poussiéreuse
un liseron rose dans le bas enroulé autour d'une tige.
Là dessus sur un fond bien vivant et pourtant
tranquille je voudrais peindre des portraits C'est
des verts de différente qualité de même valeur
de façon à former un tout vert qui ferait par sa vibration
songer au bruit doux des épis se balançant à la brise
C'est pas commode du tout comme coloration

fig. 101

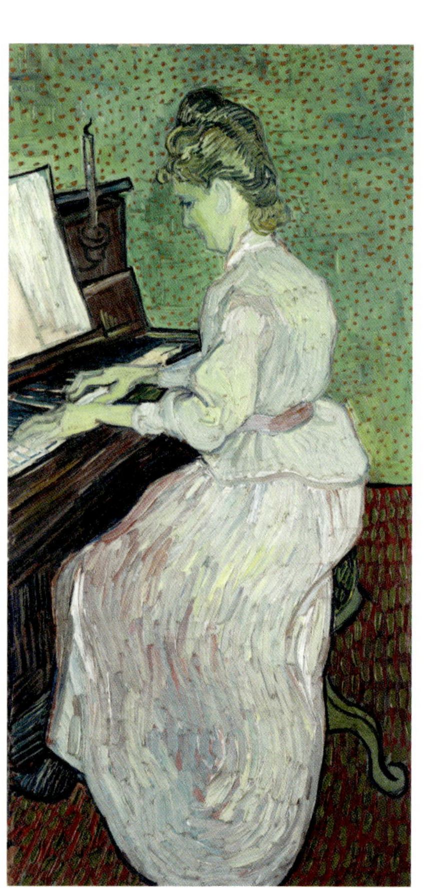

fig. 100

99 Vincent van Gogh, *Portrait of Dr Gachet*, June 1890
Oil on canvas, 66×57 cm
Private collection

100 Vincent van Gogh, *Marguerite Gachet at the Piano*, June 1890
Oil on canvas, 102.5×50 cm
Kunstmuseum Basel, Basel,
Martin P. Bühler

101 Vincent van Gogh, sketch in letter RM 23, c. 17 June 1890
Pen and ink on paper, 21.8×34 cm
Van Gogh Museum, Amsterdam
(Vincent van Gogh Foundation)

102 Vincent van Gogh, *Portrait of a Peasant Girl in a Straw Hat Sitting in the Wheat*, late June 1890
Oil on canvas, 92×73 cm
Private collection

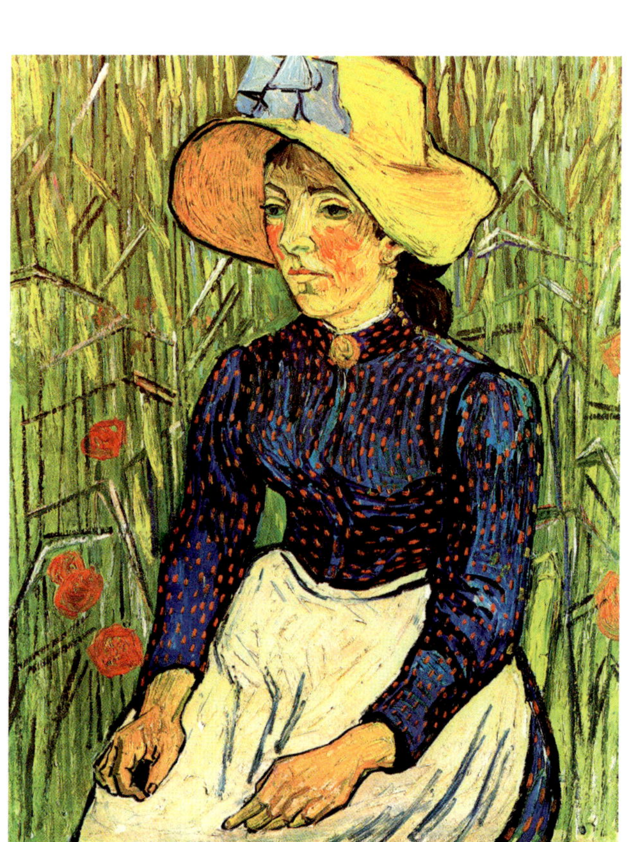

fig. 102

garden table yellow novels and a dark purple foxglove flower. My portrait of myself is almost like this too, but the blue is a fine southern blue and the suit is light lilac" [879].

Van Gogh painted a second portrait of the doctor and also immortalized him in an etching. He portrayed Gachet's daughter, Marguerite, as a full-length figure sitting at the piano in one of the oblong canvases, which he used vertically (fig. 100). He also made compelling portraits of several children of the village. Adeline Ravoux, the daughter of the hotel keeper, posed for three canvases.

Reflecting on the modern portrait even while fully occupied with the wheat motif, Van Gogh suddenly had a brilliant idea. In an unfinished (and never sent) letter to Paul Gauguin of around 17 June, he wrote about the painting that was nothing but ears of wheat (cat. 31), and accompanied its description with a sketch (fig. 101): "Look, an idea which will perhaps suit you. I'm trying to do studies of wheat like this, however I can't draw it—nothing but ears, blue-green stems, long leaves like ribbons, green and pink by reflection, yellowing ears lightly bordered with pale pink due to the dusty flowering. A pink bindweed at the bottom wound around a stem. On it, on a very alive and yet tranquil background, I would like to paint portraits. It is greens of different quality, of the same value, in such a way as to form a green whole which would by its vibration make one think of the soft sound of the ears swaying in the breeze. It's not at all easy as a colour scheme" [RM 23]. On 2 July he appeared to have carried out that plan, and he reported to Jo and Theo that he had made a portrait, "a figure of a peasant woman, big yellow hat with a knot of sky-blue ribbons, very red face. Coarse blue blouse with orange spots, background of ears of wheat" [896] (fig. 102). He painted another canvas with the same young woman seen against a similar background,[69] but that second painting lacks the power of the first. With the figure of the young, rosy-faced peasant woman seen before a backdrop of wheat, symbolic of the peasant life and the never-ending cycle of existence, Van Gogh imposed an extremely modern and highly personal interpretation on existing traditions of landscape and figure painting. In doing so, he brought together, at the end of his life, concerns that had dominated his art for a decade.

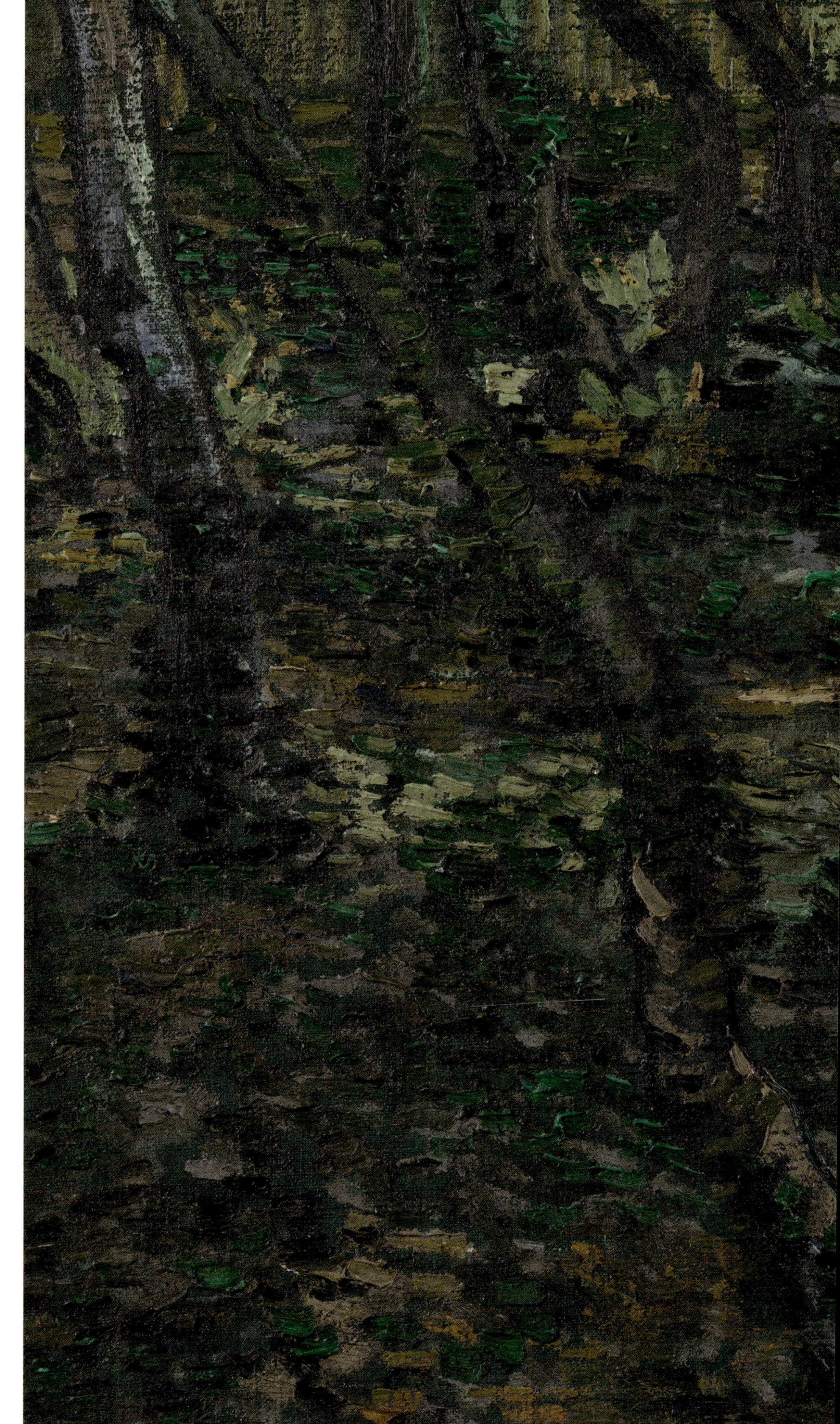

Cat. 25
Vincent van Gogh, *Undergrowth,*
Saint-Rémy-de-Provence, July 1889
Oil on canvas, 49.0×64.3 cm

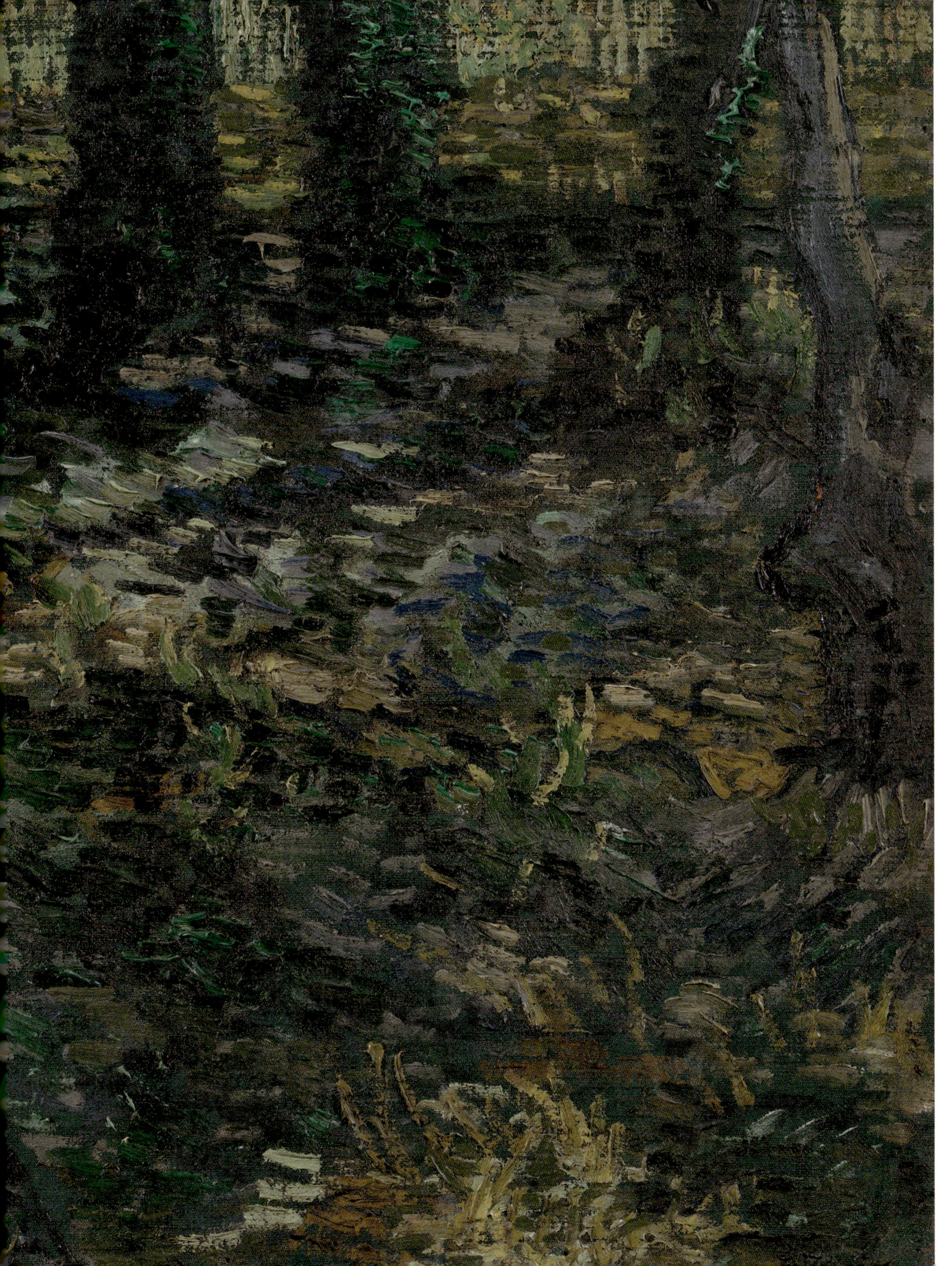

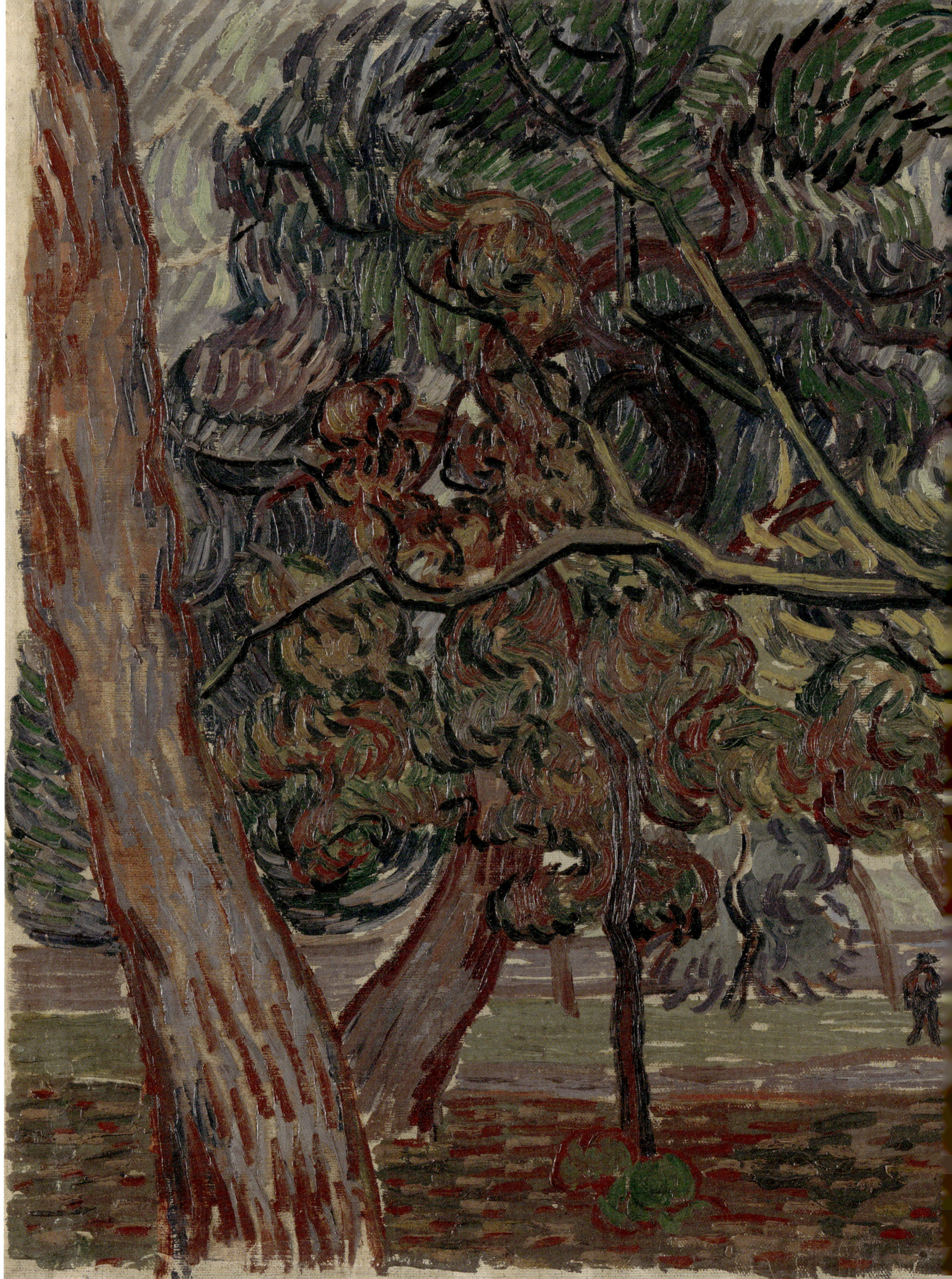

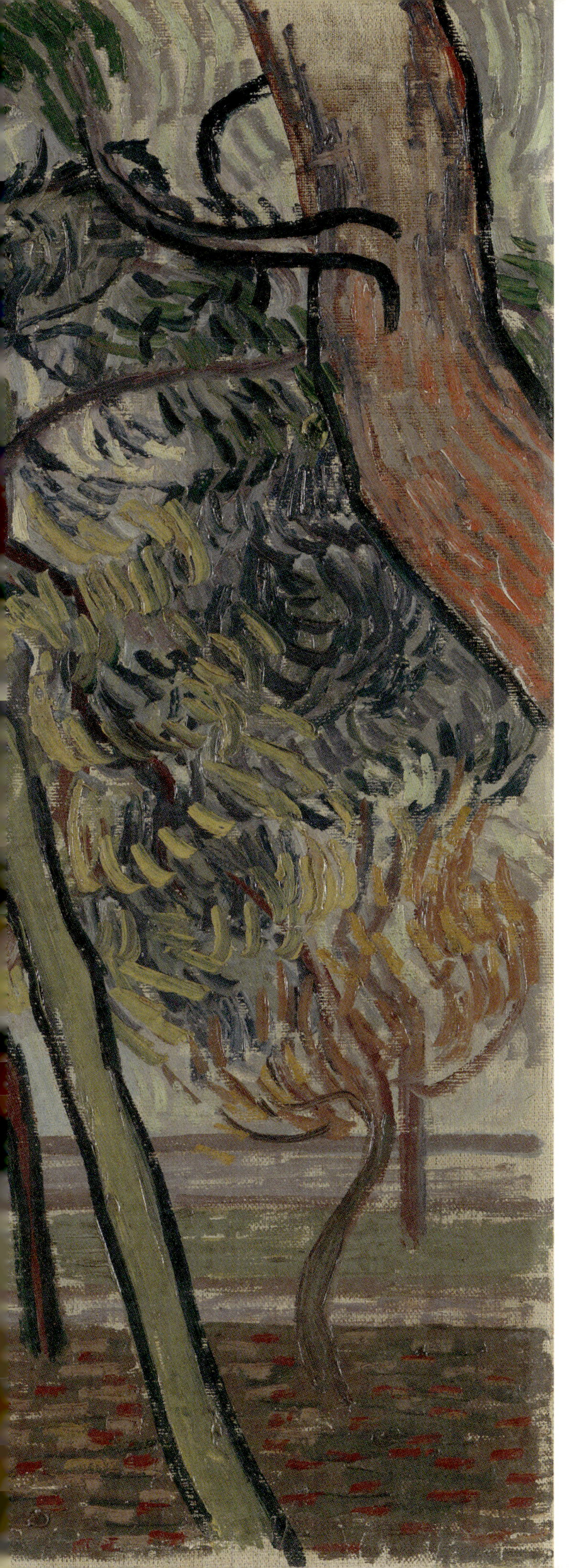

Cat. 26
Vincent van Gogh, *Pine Trees in the Garden of the Asylum,* Saint-Rémy-de-Provence, November 1889
Oil on canvas, 46×51 cm

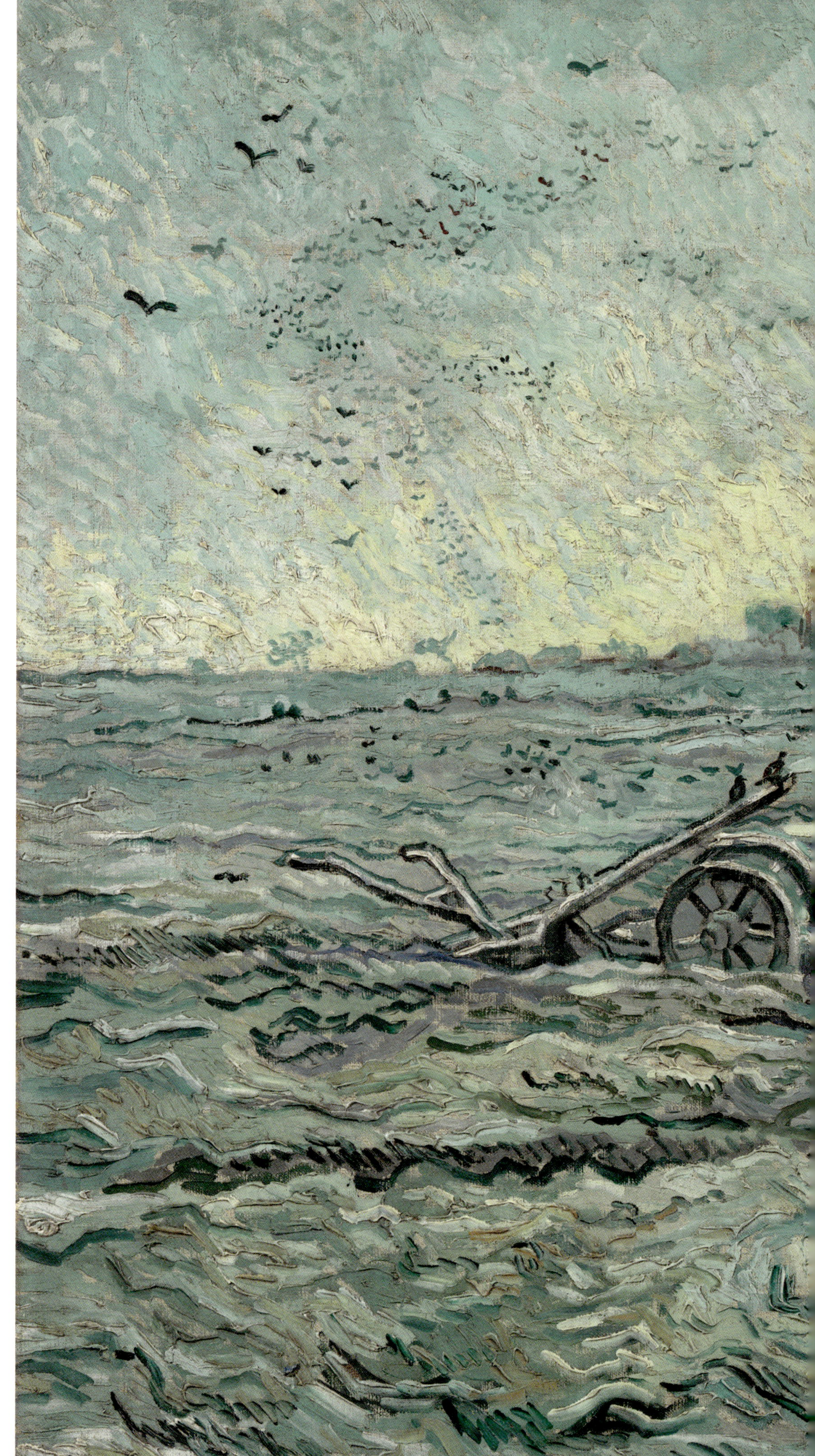

Cat. 27
Vincent van Gogh, *Snow-Covered Field with a Harrow (after Millet)*,
Saint-Rémy-de-Provence, January 1890
Oil on canvas, 72.1×92.0 cm

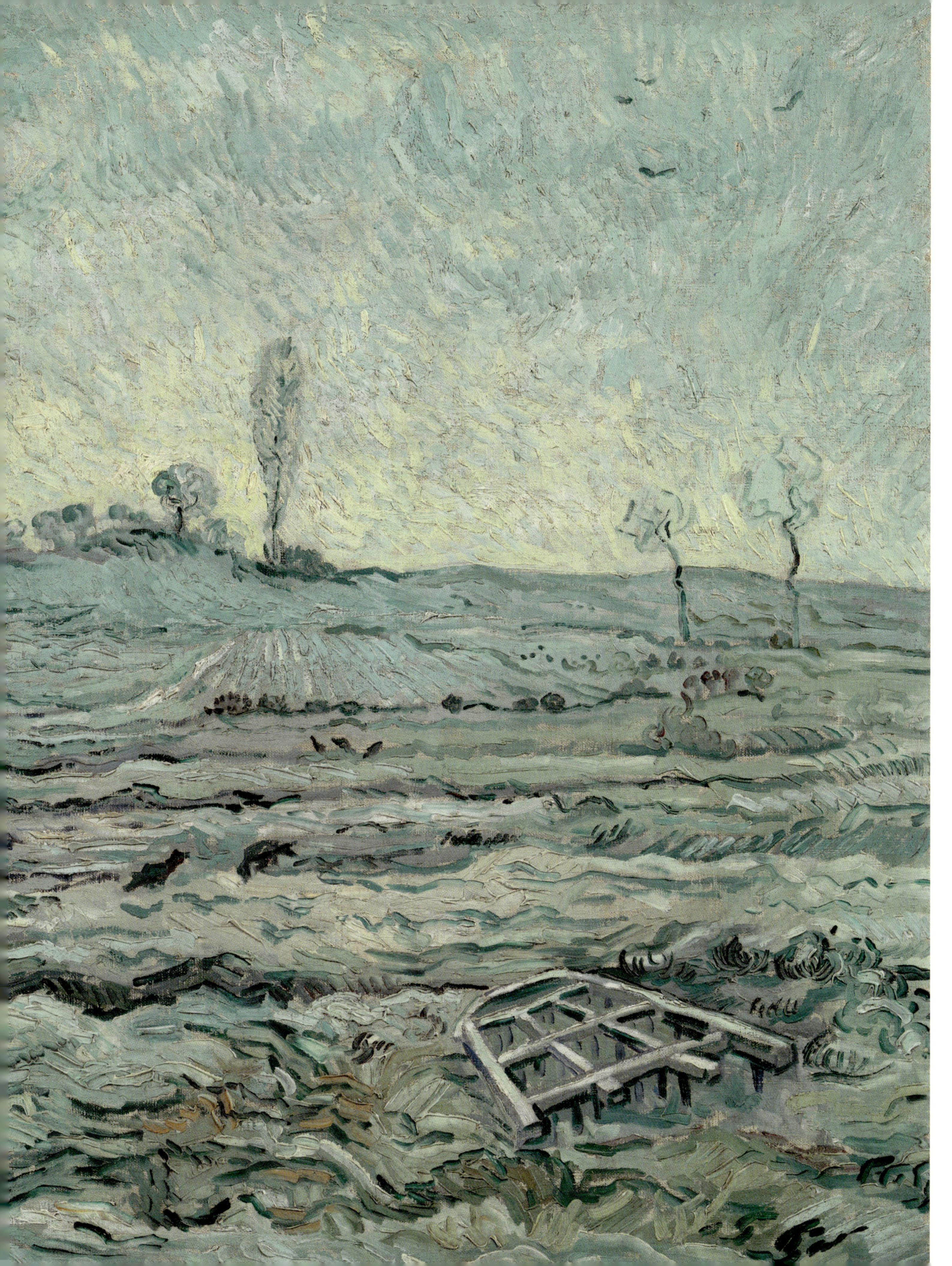

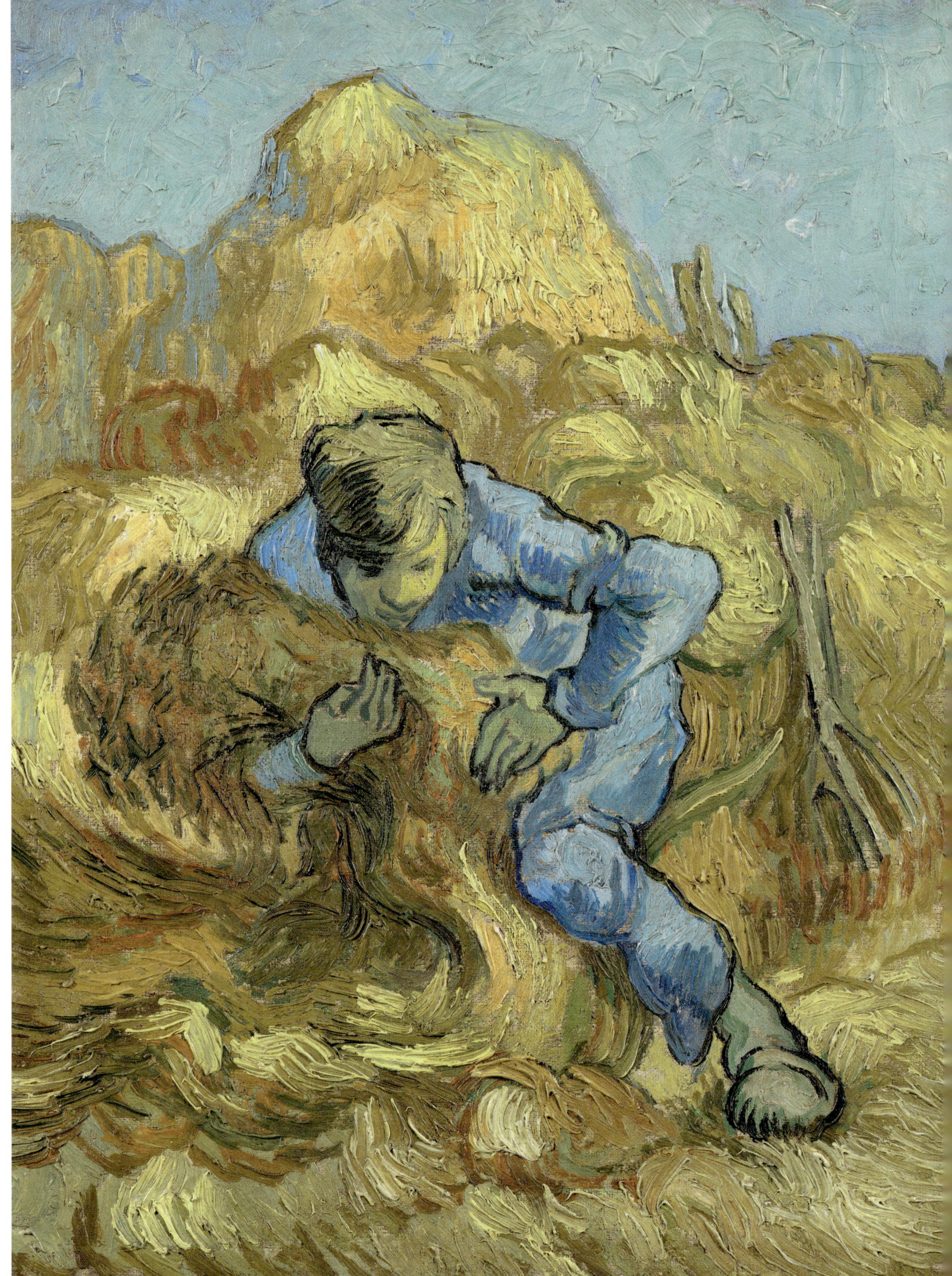

Cat. 28
Vincent van Gogh, *The Sheaf-Binder (after Millet),* Saint-Rémy-de-Provence, September 1889
Oil on canvas, 44.5 cm × 33.1 cm

Cat. 29
Vincent van Gogh, *Sorrowful Old Man ('At Eternity's Gate')*,
Saint-Rémy-de-Provence, May 1890
Oil on canvas, 81.8 × 65.5 cm

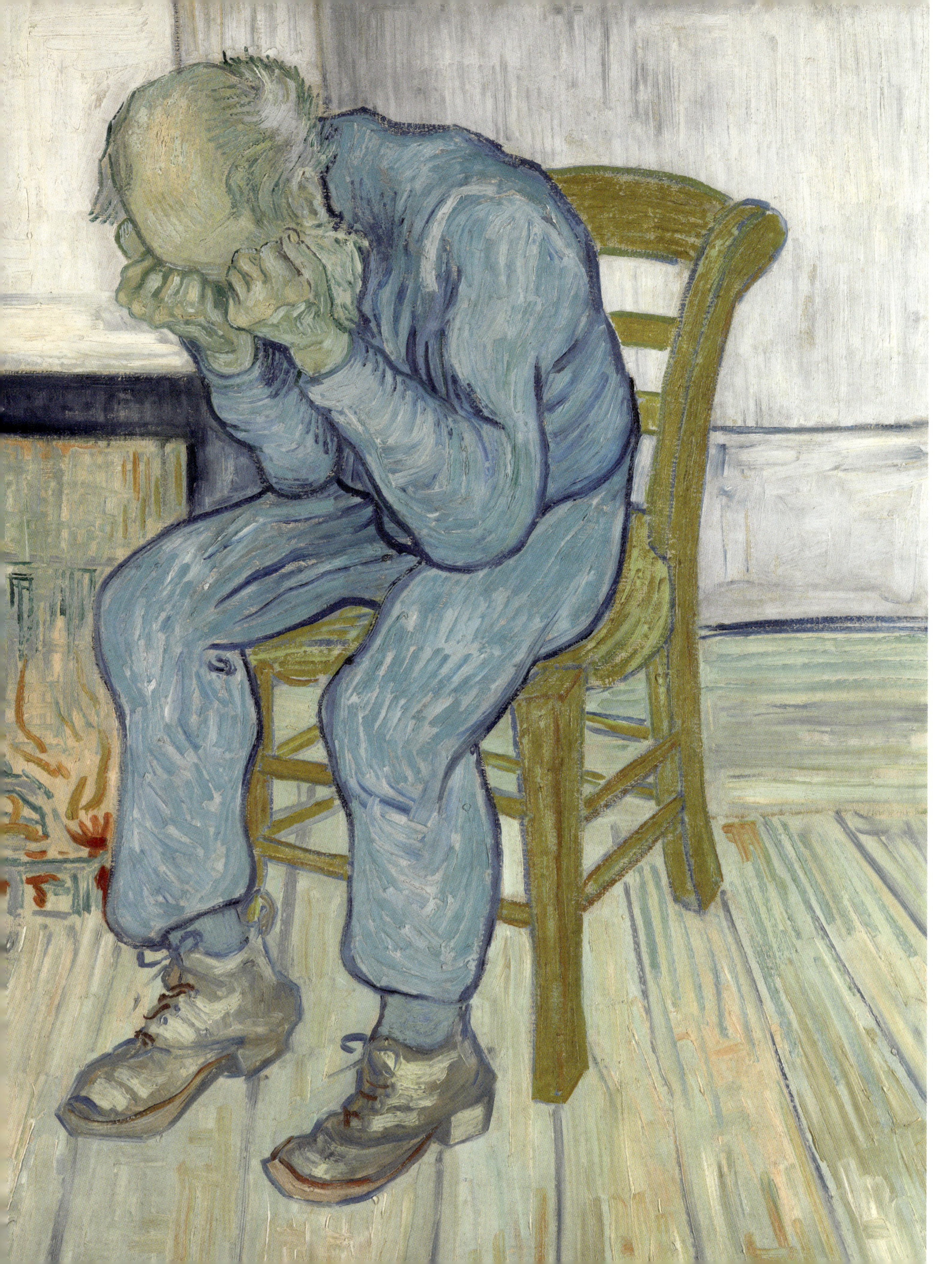

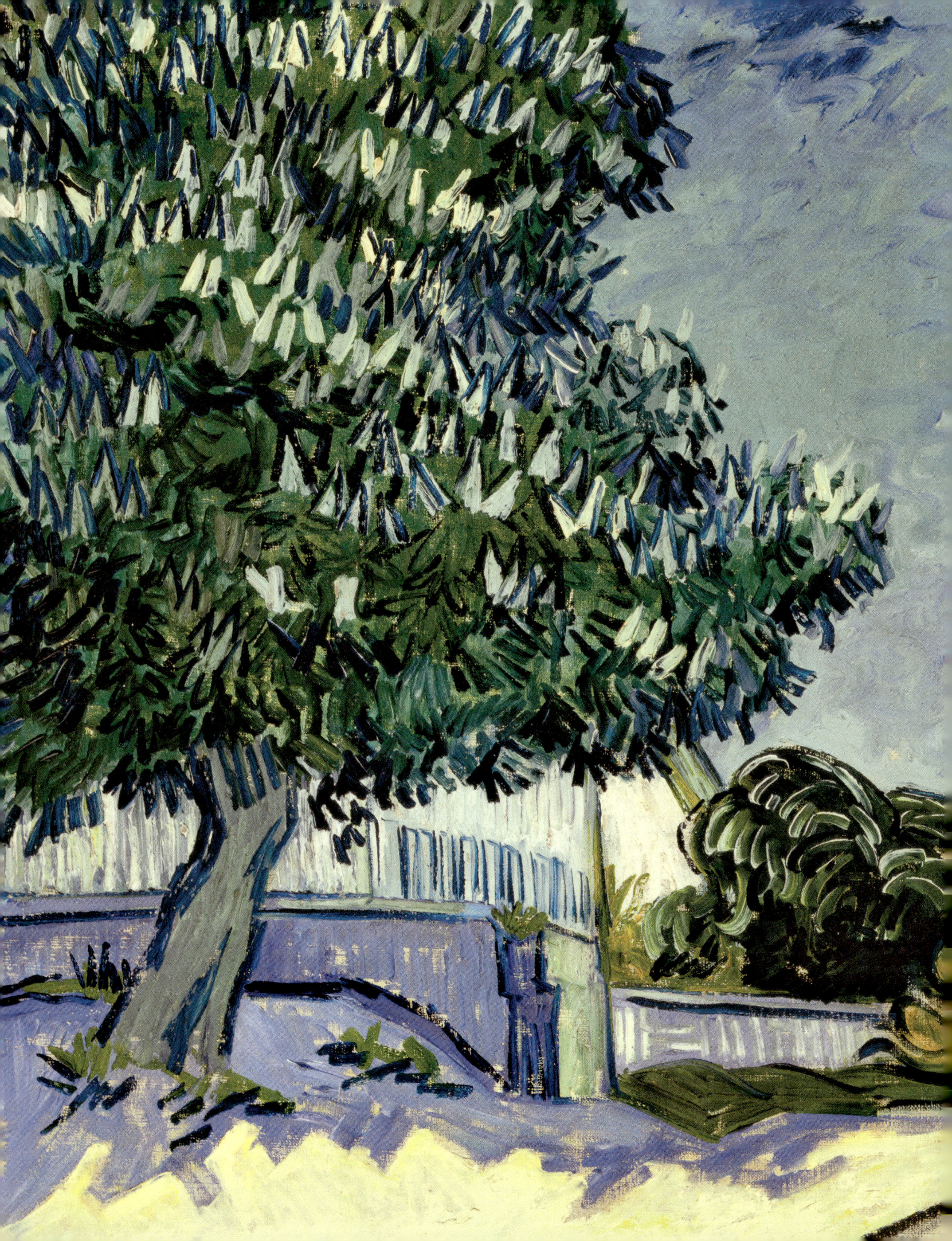

Cat. 30
Vincent van Gogh, *Blossoming Chestnut Trees,* Auvers-sur-Oise, 22–23 May 1890
Oil on canvas, 63.3 × 49.8 cm

Cat. 31
Vincent van Gogh, *Ears of Wheat,*
Auvers-sur-Oise, June 1890
Oil on canvas, 64 × 48 cm

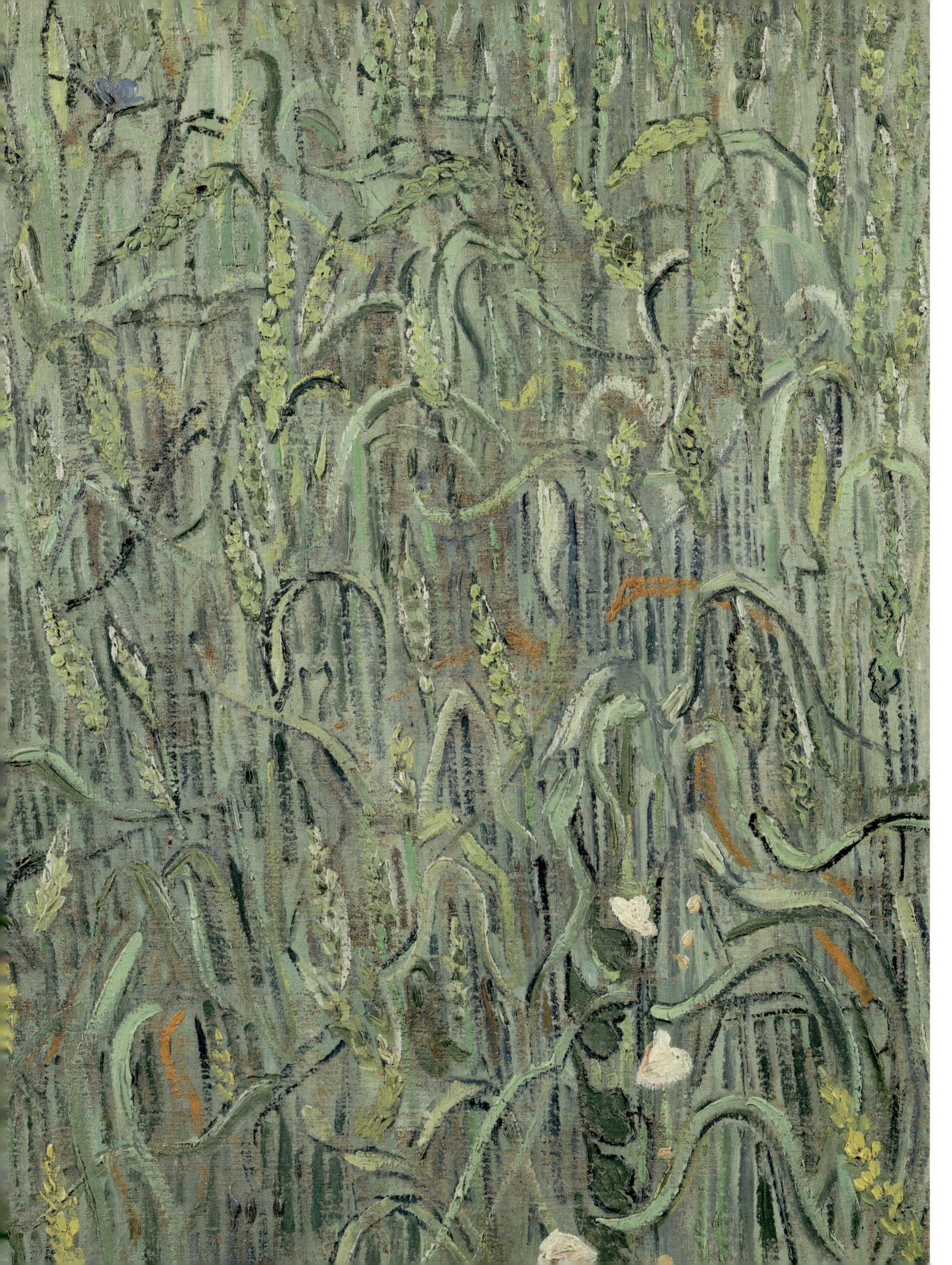

NOTES

1—See note 5 to letter 771.
2—These artists and Van Gogh's collection of prints are treated in detail in cat. Arles 2015.
3—Van Heugten and Pabst 1995, p. 41.
4—Here Van Gogh quotes Émile Zola rather freely: "Une œuvre d'art est un coin de la création vu à travers un tempérament" ("A work of art is a corner of creation seen through a temperament"). From *Mes Haines*, p. 38, vol. 10 in Émile Zola, *Œuvres complètes*. Ed. sous la direction de Henri Mitterand. 15 vols. Paris 1966–1970.
5—See letter 386, in which Van Gogh refers to such a work by Dupré.
6—Both remarks are from letter 387.
7—Letters 393 and 402.
8—Letters 396, 397 and 400.
9—Cat. Arles 2014.
10—Bruno Vouters, 'The Long March to Courrières or the Hope of a "Promised Land"', *in*: Sjraar van Heugten *et al.*, exh. cat. *Van Gogh in the Borinage: the Birth of an Artist*, Mons (Mons Fine Arts Museum) 201511—Letter 261.
12—This composition is hidden beneath *Winter (The Vicarage Garden under Snow)*, Norton Simon Museum, Pasadena, F 194 JH 603.
13—As seen (with difficulty) in an X-radiograph of a still life with baskets of potatoes in the Van Gogh Museum, F 107 JH 933. On that canvas Van Gogh portrayed yet another scene, a shepherd with his flock, before finally using it for the still life. See Van Heugten 1995, no. 5.
14—Van Gogh Museum, F 83 JH 777. For the other paintings of shepherds with their flocks, see note 13 and Van Heugten 1995, no. 6.
15—See note 16 to letter 454.
16—For this painting, see Van Tilborgh and Vellekoop 1999.
17—Cat. Arles 2014 is completely devoted to Van Gogh's use of colour and colour theories.
18—With regard to this, see cat. Arles 2014.
19—F 99 JH 930 in the Van Gogh Museum.
20—Van Heugten 1995, no. 4 and letter 466, note 4.
21—Letters 467, 468, 470 and 479.
22—Gordina de Groot, the young woman wearing a white cap in *The Potato Eaters* (fig. 22), is also recognizable in various studies.
23—Benno J. Stokvis, "Nieuwe nasporingen omtrent Vincent van Gogh in Brabant", *Opgang* 1927, pp. 11–14, Wakker's statement is on p. 12.
24—Letter 276.
25—See note 17 to letter 211.
26—F 77r JH 686, Van Gogh Museum and F 78 JH 734, Kröller-Müller Museum.
27—Cat. Arles 2015.
28—Alfred Sensier, *La Vie et l'Œuvre de Jean-François Millet*. Manuscrit publié par Paul Mantz, Paris 1881.
29—Cat. Arles 2015, pp. 37–39 and 53–33.
30—Anton Kerssemakers, "Herinneringen aan Vincent van Gogh I", *de Amsterdammer*, April 1912, no. 1816, p. 6; and E.H. Du Quesne-Van Gogh, Vincent van Gogh. *Persoonlijke herinneringen aangaande een kunstenaar*, Baarn 1910, pp. 66–67, respectively.
31—Jules Michelet, *L'Oiseau*, Paris 1856, pp. 207–15.
32—Van Tilborgh and Vellekoop 1999, p. 201.
33—F 124 JH 995.
34—Cat. Arles 2015, pp. 55 and 69.
35—Han van Crimpen, Leo Jansen and Jan Robert, *Brief Happiness: The Correspondence of Theo Van Gogh and Jo Bonger*, Amsterdam and Zwolle, pp. 160–61.
36—The self-portraits in question are F 180 JH 1194 (here cat. 7), F 208a JH 1089 and F 263a JH 199 and *In the Café: Agostina Segatori in Le Tambourin*, F 370 JH 1208. See Van Heugten 1995, nos. 10, 16, 17 and 18 and Hendriks/Van Tilborgh 2011, nos. 74, 75, 77 and 84.
37—There he painted in the autumn of 1888 a sketch-like brothel scene in the modest format of 33 × 41 cm (F 478 JH 1599).
38—It had been hanging there since 1881. In 1986 it was transferred to the Musée d'Orsay.
39—Letter 620.
40—Letter 628.
41—The painting was previously dated to the autumn of 1888, but the earlier dating is convincingly defended in Ten Berge *et al.* 2003.
42—Van Gogh destroyed two paintings of *Christ in the Garden of Gethsemane*, on which he had worked in July and August 1888.
43—Letter 292. In this letter Van Gogh refers to "orphan men", meaning old men.
44—Letter 55.
45—F 554 JH 1388 in a private collection; see note 3 to letter 596.
46—The original version of *Pink Peach Trees* became a special gift: Anton Mauve had recently died, to Van Gogh's great sorrow, so he supplied this painting with a dedication to Mauve and presented it to his widow, Jet Mauve-Carbentus, a cousin of Van Gogh.

47—The work was supposed to be flanked on the right by *The White Orchard* (F 403 JH 1378) and on the left by *The Pink Orchard* (F 555 JH 1380). The works are permanently displayed like this in the Van Gogh Museum.
48—F 551 JH 1396.
49—Cat. Arles 2015 and the accompanying exhibition were devoted to Van Gogh's drawings. On the Arles drawings, see pp. 104–21.
50—Strictly speaking, the area north of Arles is not the plain of La Crau—which actually lies south east of the city—but the plain of Trebon. In Van Gogh's letters and in the Van Gogh literature, however, reference is almost always made to the plain of La Crau, and this essay adheres to that convention.
51—On this subject, see letter 628 to Bernard.
52—F 575a JH 1596 and F 494 JH 1617.
53—In letter 687 Vincent tells Theo that he would like to use Milliet as a model for a painting of a courting couple. He did not actually give Milliet's portrait the subtitle *The Lover*, but his descriptions of Milliet make it clear that he saw him as such, with the result that the portrait has been given this title.
54—Letter 680.
55—The canvas is usually described as blank, but a stalk and leaves are discernible at the upper centre, and there seems to be a preliminary drawing of a flower somewhat lower down, at the left. The whole is too vague to link it convincingly to a specific canvas.
56—Letter 739, see note 5: Loti wrote about the custom among fishermen to hang the icon of a saint in the ship.
57—This is one of the results of extensive research into the weave of the canvas on which Van Gogh painted: Louis van Tilborgh *et al.*, "Weave Matching and Dating of Van Gogh's Paintings: An Interdisciplinary Approach", *The Burlington Magazine*, no. CLIV, February 2012, pp. 112–22, esp. p. 112.
58—Letter 55.
59—F 610 JH 1702.
60—See, for instance, letter 822: "This dark giant—like a proud man brought low—contrasts, when seen as the character of a living being, with the pale smile of the last rose on the bush, which is fading in front of him."
61—The portrait of a young bearded man in a hat, with the garden of the asylum in the background, F 531 JH 1779, is also usually dated to this month. It is not mentioned in the letters, but the likelihood that it was painted outdoors suggests that the dating should be reconsidered, given that Van Gogh worked indoors in September.
62—F 626 JH 1770.
63—As emerges from letter 803.
64—F 525 JH 1656.
65—The version of *Irises in a Vase* not reproduced here is F 680 JH 1978.
66—F 682 JH 1979.
67—J.J. Isaäcson, "De revolutionaire schildersgroep in Frankrijk" ("The revolutionary group of painters in France"), *De Portefeuille. Kunst- en Letterbode* of 10 May 1890, pp. 75–76 and of 17 May 1890, pp. 88–89. See letter RM 21, note 1, and the additional remark found on≈the website (vangoghletters.org). This letter remained in the possession of Theo and is now in the Van Gogh Museum. It is unclear whether it is a rough draft and Isaäcson received a clean copy, or whether the letter was never sent.
68—F 1031 JH 363, known only from a photograph.
69—F 788 JH 2055.

LIST OF WORKS EXHIBITED

Cat. 1
Vincent van Gogh, *Farm with Stacks of Peat,* Nieuw-Amsterdam, October 1883
Oil on canvas, 37.5 × 55.0 cm
Van Gogh Museum, Amsterdam (Vincent van Gogh Foundation)

Cat. 2
Vincent van Gogh, *Loom and Weaver,* Nuenen, April-May 1884
Oil on canvas, 68.3 × 84.2 cm
Kröller-Müller Museum, Otterlo

Cat. 3
Vincent van Gogh, *Avenue of Poplars in Autumn,* Nuenen, October 1884
Oil on canvas on panel, 99 × 65.7 cm
Van Gogh Museum, Amsterdam (purchased with support from the Vincent van Gogh Foundation and the Rembrandt Association)

Cat. 4
Vincent van Gogh, *Head of a Woman,* Nuenen, March 1885
Oil on canvas on triplex, 42.2 × 34.8 cm
Van Gogh Museum, Amsterdam (Vincent van Gogh Foundation)

Cat. 5
Vincent van Gogh, *Woman Winding Yarn,* Nuenen, March 1885
Oil on canvas, 40.5 × 31.7 cm
Van Gogh Museum, Amsterdam (Vincent van Gogh Foundation)

Cat. 6
Vincent van Gogh, *Man at a Table,* Nuenen, March-April 1885
Oil on canvas, 44.3 × 32.5 cm
Kröller-Müller Museum, Otterlo

Cat. 7
Vincent van Gogh, *Still Life with Apples and Pumpkins,* Nuenen, September 1885
Oil on canvas, 59 × 84.5 cm
Kröller-Müller Museum, Otterlo

Cat. 8
Vincent van Gogh, *Self-Portrait with Pipe,* Paris, September-November 1886
Oil on canvas, 46 × 38 cm
Van Gogh Museum, Amsterdam (Vincent van Gogh Foundation)

Cat. 9
Vincent van Gogh, *Self-Portrait with Grey Felt Hat,* Paris, September-October 1887
Oil on canvas, 44.5 × 37.2 cm
Van Gogh Museum, Amsterdam (Vincent van Gogh Foundation)

Cat. 10
Vincent van Gogh, *Roses and Peonies,* Paris, June 1886
Oil on canvas, 59.8 × 72.5 cm
Kröller-Müller Museum, Otterlo

Cat. 11
Vincent van Gogh, *Flowers in a Blue Vase,* Paris, June 1887
Oil on canvas, 61.5 × 38.5 cm
Kröller-Müller Museum, Otterlo

Cat. 12
Vincent van Gogh, *Kneeling Ecorché,* Paris, June 1886
Oil on cardboard, 35.2 × 26.8 cm
Van Gogh Museum, Amsterdam (Vincent van Gogh Foundation)

Cat. 13
Vincent van Gogh, *Café Table with Absinthe,* Paris, February-March 1887
Oil on canvas, 46.3 × 33.2 cm
Van Gogh Museum, Amsterdam (Vincent van Gogh Foundation)

Cat. 14
Vincent van Gogh, *Trees and Undergrowth,* Paris, July 1887
Oil on canvas, 46.2 × 55.2 cm
Van Gogh Museum, Amsterdam (Vincent van Gogh Foundation)

Cat. 15
Vincent van Gogh, *Montmartre: Behind the Moulin de la Galette,* Paris, July 1887
Oil on canvas, 81 × 100 cm
Van Gogh Museum, Amsterdam (Vincent van Gogh Foundation)

Cat. 16
Vincent van Gogh, *Patch of Grass,* Paris, April-June 1887
Oil on canvas, 30.8 × 39.7 cm
Kröller-Müller Museum, Otterlo

Cat. 17
Vincent van Gogh, *Pollard Willows at Sunset,* Arles, March 1888
Oil on canvas mounted on cardboard, 31.6 × 34.3 cm
Kröller-Müller Museum, Otterlo

Cat. 18
Vincent van Gogh, *Orchard Bordered by Cypresses,* Arles, April 1888
Oil on canvas, 64.9 × 81.2 cm
Kröller-Müller Museum, Otterlo

Cat. 19
Vincent van Gogh, *Field with Irises near Arles,* Arles, May 1888
Oil on canvas, 54 × 65 cm
Van Gogh Museum, Amsterdam (Vincent van Gogh Foundation)

Cat. 20
Vincent van Gogh, *Fishing Boats on the Beach at Les Saintes-Maries-de-la-Mer,* Arles, June 1888
Oil on canvas, 65 × 81.5 cm
Van Gogh Museum, Amsterdam (Vincent van Gogh Foundation)

Cat. 21
Vincent van Gogh, *An Old Woman of Arles,* Arles, February 1888
Oil on canvas, 58 × 42 cm
Van Gogh Museum, Amsterdam (Vincent van Gogh Foundation)

Cat. 22
Vincent van Gogh, *Still Life with Potatoes,* Arles, mid-January 1889
Oil on canvas, 39.5 × 47.5 cm
Kröller-Müller Museum, Otterlo

Cat. 23
Vincent van Gogh, *Ploughed Fields ('The Furrows'),* Arles, September 1888
Oil on canvas, 72.5 × 92.5 cm
Van Gogh Museum, Amsterdam (Vincent van Gogh Foundation)

Cat. 24
Vincent van Gogh, *The Green Vineyard,* Arles, 3 October 1888
Oil on canvas, 73.5 × 92.5 cm
Kröller-Müller Museum, Otterlo

Cat. 25
Vincent van Gogh, *Undergrowth,* Saint-Rémy-de-Provence, July 1889
Oil on canvas, 49.0 × 64.3 cm
Van Gogh Museum, Amsterdam (Vincent van Gogh Foundation)

Cat. 26
Vincent van Gogh, *Pine Trees in the Garden of the Asylum,* Saint-Rémy-de-Provence, November 1889
Oil on canvas, 46 × 51 cm
Kröller-Müller Museum, Otterlo

Cat. 27
Vincent van Gogh, *Snow-Covered Field with a Harrow (after Millet),* Saint-Rémy-de-Provence, January 1890
Oil on canvas, 72.1 × 92.0 cm
Van Gogh Museum, Amsterdam (Vincent van Gogh Foundation)

Cat. 28
Vincent van Gogh, *The Sheaf-Binder (after Millet),* Saint-Rémy-de-Provence, September 1889
Oil on canvas, 44.5 cm × 33.1 cm
Van Gogh Museum, Amsterdam (Vincent van Gogh Foundation)

Cat. 29
Vincent van Gogh, *Sorrowful Old Man ('At Eternity's Gate'),* Saint-Rémy-de-Provence, May 1890
Oil on canvas, 81.8 × 65.5 cm
Kröller-Müller Museum, Otterlo

Cat. 30
Vincent van Gogh, *Blossoming Chestnut Trees,* Auvers-sur-Oise, 22–23 May 1890
Oil on canvas, 63.3 × 49.8 cm
Kröller-Müller Museum, Otterlo

Cat. 31
Vincent van Gogh, *Ears of Wheat,* Auvers-sur-Oise, June 1890
Oil on canvas, 64 × 48 cm
Van Gogh Museum, Amsterdam (Vincent van Gogh Foundation)

BIBLIOGRAPHY

Cat. Arles 2014
Sjraar van Heugten, exh. cat. *Van Gogh: Colours of the North, Colours of the South*, Arles (Fondation Vincent van Gogh Arles), 2014

Cat. Arles 2015
Sjraar van Heugten, exh. cat. *Van Gogh Drawings: Influences and Innovations*, Arles (Fondation Vincent van Gogh Arles), 2015

Ten Berge *et al.* 2003
Jos ten Berge *et al.*, *The Paintings of Vincent van Gogh in the Collection of the Kröller-Müller Museum*, Otterlo 2003

Hendricks and Van Tilborgh 2011
Ella Hendriks and Louis van Tilborgh, *Vincent van Gogh Paintings: Antwerp & Paris 1885–1888*, Amsterdam and Zwolle 2011

Van Heugten and Pabst 1995
Sjraar van Heugten and Fieke Pabst, *The Graphic Work of Vincent van Gogh*, Amsterdam and Zwolle 1995

Van Heugten 1995
Sjraar van Heugten, `Radiographic Images of Vincent van Gogh's Paintings in the Collection of the Van Gogh Museum', *Van Gogh Museum Journal 1995*, 65–85, Amsterdam 1995

Van Tilborgh and Vellekoop 1999
Louis van Tilborgh and Marije Vellekoop, *Vincent van Gogh Paintings: Dutch period 1881–1885*, Amsterdam and London 1996

BIOGRAPHY

Sjraar van Heugten (1957) studied History of Art at Utrecht University. From 1988 until 2010 he worked at the Van Gogh Museum, including as Head of Collections for the last 11 years of his time there. In 2010 he became an independent art historian.

Van Heugten has published numerous books and articles, primarily about Van Gogh and his contemporaries. Among other things, he wrote three volumes (the third as co-author) of the catalogue of Van Gogh's drawings in the Van Gogh Museum collection. He has been responsible for exhibitions in Europe, Japan and the USA. In 2012 he published a book about the collection of the Triton Collection Foundation.

He was curator of the opening exhibition at the Fondation Vincent van Gogh Arles in 2014, *Van Gogh: Colours of the North, Colours of the South*, as well as its successor in 2015, *Van Gogh Drawings: Influences & Innovations*. In 2015 he also he curated the exhibition *Van Gogh in The Borinage. The Birth of an Artist*, which opened in Mons, Belgium, in January, and was co-curator for *Van Gogh and Nature* at The Clark, Williamstown, USA. He is currently working on the preparation of various future exhibitions.

THE FONDATION VINCENT VAN GOGH ARLES: FULFILLING VINCENT'S WISH

"And I hope that later on, other artists will emerge in this beautiful part of the country."
Letter from Vincent to his brother Theo (Arles, Monday 7 May 1888)

In 1983 an association was founded by Yolande Clergue with the aim of inviting contemporary artists to present a work in homage to Van Gogh. Thanks to patron Luc Hoffmann, in 2010 the association became a public utility foundation. The City of Arles placed at its disposal a prestigious building which, renovated and transformed, was inaugurated in April 2014 by Maja Hoffmann, the current president of the Fondation.

The design concept by the architectural agency FLUOR embraces the rich history of the site, while treating the 1000 m² of exposition space in a resolutely contemporary manner. It thereby incorporates two permanent artworks—by Raphael Hefti and Bertrand Lavier—which link the interior and exterior spaces and which respectively allow Van Gogh's iridescent colours and his "Vincent" signature to shine forth.

Thanks to partnerships established with public and private collections, including the Van Gogh Museum in Amsterdam and the Kröller-Müller Museum in Otterlo in the Netherlands, the Fondation plays continuous host to one or more original canvases by Vincent van Gogh.

It assumes an innovative role in encouraging the public to rediscover the art and thinking of Van Gogh in constant interaction with contemporary artistic production. Conscious of the historical dimension of art and of its reception by society, the artistic director of the Fondation, Bice Curiger, seeks to generate a creative energy by provoking productive confrontations.

Thus the Fondation fulfils the wish, cherished by the world's most famous painter, to create in Arles a place of reflection and of free and abundant creation; a place where, much like the wind and river that pass through the city, ideas and exchanges can flow.

Van Gogh in Provence: Modernizing Tradition, our third major Van Gogh retrospective, focuses on a theme emblematic of the Fondation: that of artistic heritage and its transformation.

"Then, as you well know, I love Arles so much, *[...]"*
Letter from Vincent to Theo (18 February 1889)

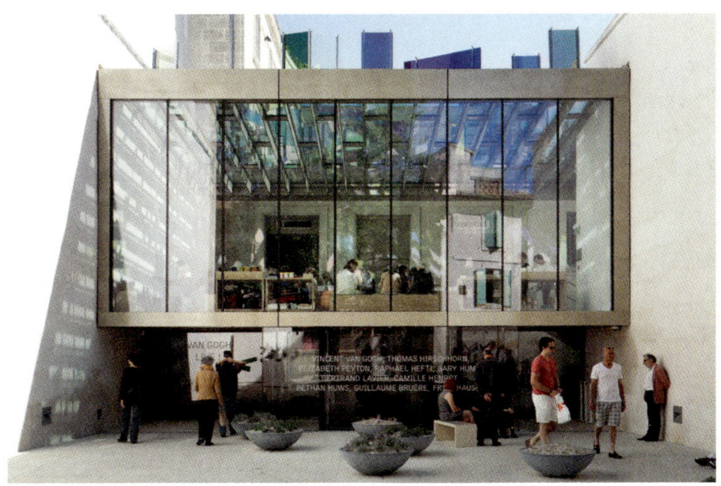

View of the courtyard of the Fondation.
Building designed by architects
of the Fluor Agency.
Installation on the glass roof
by Raphael Hefti,
The Violet Blue Green Yellow Orange Red House, 2014

This catalogue was published on the occasion of the exhibition *Van Gogh in Provence: Modernizing Tradition* at the Fondation Vincent van Gogh Arles, held from 14 May to 11 September 2016.

EXHIBITION

Curator
Sjraar van Heugten

Organisation and coordination
Fondation Vincent van Gogh Arles:
Bice Curiger, artistic director
Christine Taris, administrative director, Julia Marchand, assistant curator

Van Gogh Museum, Amsterdam:
Axel Rüger, Nienke Bakker, Karlijn Berends, Marije Vellekoop, Maria Patijn

Kröller-Müller Museum, Otterlo:
Rinus Vonhof, Lisette Pelsers, Liz Kreijn, André Straatman, Roel van As

Registrars
Éric L'Hospitalier
Émilie Choffel-Claire

Conservator
Benoît Dagron

Technical management
Daniel Gimenez-Frontin

Exhibition design (concept)
Ulrich Zickler

Exhibition design (path)
L'agence privée,
Geoffroy Rigoulot

Installation
Giroa-Veolia

Lighting
Éric Rolland Bellagamba

Visitors department
Anne-Sophie Foron

Educational programmes
Sophie Viguier

Partnership development
Laurent Éginard

Press relations
Pierre Collet

Signage
Bureau Vue, Claudia Wildermuth

CATALOGUE

Translations
Sjraar van Heugten's essay:
Diane Webb
Preface: Karen Williams

Proofreading
Ian Massey (for the English text),
Marleen Blokhuis (for the Dutch text)

Graphic Design
Studio Marie Lusa

Editorial coordination
Delphine Ménage

Production
Laurence Gibert

Photoengraving
Terre Neuve, Arles

ACKNOWLEDGEMENTS

Vincent van Gogh Foundation
Jantine van Gogh
Willem van Gogh
Machteld van Laer-Cramer

Van Gogh Museum
Albertien Lykles-Livius
Maria Patijn
Lisa Smit

Kröller-Müller Museum
Margaret Nab

PHOTO CREDITS

Pages 10–11, 16, 19, 28, 30, 36, 39, 42, 44, 47, 52, 53, 54–55, 56–57, 60, 63, 66, 68, 71, 72, 75, 81, 86–87, 88–89, 90, 94–95, 98, 103, 112, 115, 117, 120, 122–123, 126–127, 128, 135: © Van Gogh Museum, Amsterdam (Vincent van Gogh Foundation)
Pages 12–13, 21, 22–23, 28, 33, 35, 41, 48–49, 50, 58–59, 65, 72, 82–83, 84–85, 92–93, 96-97, 100, 103, 106, 111, 115 124–125, 131, 132: © Kröller-Müller Museum, Otterlo
Page 15: Van Gogh Museum, Amsterdam (purchased with support from the Vincent van Gogh Foundation and the Rembrandt Association)
Pages 60, 103: © Van Gogh Museum, Amsterdam
Page 24: © Museum of Fine Arts, Boston. Gift of Quincy Adams Shaw through Quincy Adams Shaw, Jr., and Mrs. Marian Shaw Haughton
Pages 24, 105: © Musée d'Orsay, Paris. Photo credit: RMN-Grand Palais (musée d'Orsay) / Michel Urtado
Pages 72, 75, 77: © Musée d'Orsay, Paris. Photo credit: RMN-Grand Palais (musée d'Orsay) / Hervé Lewandowski
Page 27: © Rijksmuseum, Amsterdam
Page 28: © Uehara Museum of Modern Art, Shimoda, Japan
Pages 30, 75: © The Mesdag Collection, The Hague
Page 30: © Collection P. & N. de Boer Fondation
Pages 39, 100: © Norton Simon Art Foundation

ISBN 978-2-330-06302-3
www.actes-sud.fr

Printed in April 2016 at Geers, in Gent (Belgium) for Actes Sud, Le Méjan, Place Nina-Berberova, 13200 Arles

Fondation Vincent van Gogh Arles
35 ter, rue du Docteur Fanton
13200 Arles, France
www.fondation-vincentvangogh-arles.org

Legal deposit: May 2016
Printed in Belgium